DYNAMIC PLANNING

DYNAMIC PLANNING

THE ART OF MANAGING BEYOND TOMORROW

BEVERLY GOLDBERG AND JOHN G. SIFONIS

NEW YORK   OXFORD

OXFORD UNIVERSITY PRESS

1994

Oxford University Press

Oxford New York Toronto
Delhi Bombay Calcutta Madras Karachi
Kuala Lumpur Singapore Hong Kong Tokyo
Nairobi Dar es Salaam Cape Town
Melbourne Auckland Madrid

and associated companies in

Berlin Ibadan

Published by Oxford University Press, Inc.
200 Madison Avenue, New York New York 10016

Oxford is a registered trademark of Oxford University Press

Library of Congress Cataloging-in-Publication

Goldberg, Beverly.
    Dynamic planning: the art of managing beyond tomorrow / by Beverly Goldberg
and John G. Sifonis.
        p.   cm.
    Includes bibliographical references and index.
    ISBN: 0-19-508308-3 (alk. paper)
    1. Strategic planning.   I. Sifonis, John G.   II. Title.
HD30.G63   1994   93-35402
658.4'012--dc20   CIP

Printing: (last digit): 9 8 7 6 5 4 3 2 1

Printed in the United States of America
on acid-free paper

*T*o our moms, Bessie Goldberg and Jean Sifonis, who can now stop asking when the book will be finished, and to our children Cindy Sifonis, Mark Sifonis, Meg Janifer, and Seth Janifer, who probably have no idea how important they were to us in writing this book. And to Damian, the next generation.

PREFACE

This book, which is aimed at providing a framework for thinking about business, is the result of almost five years that have included a number of shared consulting assignments and much intense discussion between two colleagues with very different backgrounds—think tank and corporate America. It grew out of mutual dismay at the shortsightedness each of us saw around us, which convinced us both that our leaders at every level—from federal and state governments and bureaucracies to schools, nonprofit institutions, and, most specifically here, to businesses—must stop looking for miracles, for quick fixes to the problems they face. They must instead change the way they think.

Because we believe that the strength of the American economy is a reflection of the strength of American business, this book is aimed at helping corporations compete in an increasingly turbulent environment. Continual globalization, rapidly changing technologies, and time compression have not only changed the corporate context but ensure that it will keep changing. Our approach encourages the kind of dynamic thinking and planning needed to cope with those changes; it provides a framework that encourages corporate managers and others to continuously study and evaluate both their organizations and the world in which they have to compete. The Dynamic Planning Framework^{SM} we propose also brings technology into the organizational mainstream, increasing understanding between business and information technology (IT) executives so that business and IT strategy will be integrated—a critical component for success today and tomorrow.

In fact, those managers (both business and IT) who are trying to find ways to bridge the gap between business strategy and information technology strategy have made enormous strides. Unfortunately, it is still not enough. Managers must work together to see to it that business and IT integrate, not interface. Those who set a company's business strategy can no longer decide on a path and then go to the IT managers and say, "What can IT do to make this path easier?" They must instead say to the IT managers,

"We want to achieve a certain goal and think there are four possible paths. Which do you think makes the most sense?" The answer might be one of the paths the business manager would have been less likely to choose. Or it might be a fifth path.

The intelligent use of the right technology in the right amounts will make a significant difference, but technology will not solve every problem. The most important point about the Dynamic Planning Framework is that it recognizes that no single process, innovation, theory, or technology will dramatically improve competitiveness. Everything around us—from those ideals we seem to have abandoned (such as trust, ethics, loyalty, and hard work) to the discoveries over the horizon (the new medicine, science, technology)—must be considered and may make a difference. The Framework opens us to many and varied approaches to dealing with what can be.

The pages that follow are meant to help businesses look beyond tomorrow. Along with the Framework comes a warning: the steps involved in it are useful only as part of comprehensive holistic thinking. We are concerned that they not become the latest buzzwords or five-minute cures. They are not. They are part of an approach to dealing with a complex world, the business world, leading to a strategy for carefully and thoughtfully institutionalizing the concept of continuous change.

Once management has learned to look outside and inside holistically, it must change the rest of the organization—its culture and the mindset of all those who work for it—to allow for ongoing growth, change, and innovation. Then managers must put in place monitoring and evaluation programs, because such programs *are* the road to flexibility and anticipatory capability.

Our goal, in other words, is to awaken corporations and their leaders to an awareness that all aspects of life affect and are affected by everything that goes on—not only in the business sector, or the industrial sector, but in the world beyond. That is dynamic thinking.

New York   B.G.
October 1993   J.G.S.

ACKNOWLEDGMENTS

S ince this book draws on our experiences over the past two decades, we have many people to thank.

John Henderson and N. Venkatraman brought Strategic Alignment Modeling into being. They have always been available to answer questions, discuss new ideas, offer encouragement, add intellectual insights. Their advice and relevant anecdotes have enriched us immeasurably. We also owe a debt of gratitude to their wives—Marti and Meera.

Carol Kahn Strauss polished this manuscript, challenging our thinking and clarifying our writing time and time again. The subtlety of her editing is remarkable: she improves everything she touches, enhancing but never intruding, a skill every writer seeks in an editor, but few find. Carol's shining intelligence and impeccable logic inspired many a redraft.

Frank Sonnenberg is the person responsible for this book; we met when he put us together on a project at Ernst & Young. Frank's name should appear on any number of the lists below, as co-author with Beverly Goldberg on numerous articles, as a colleague, as a virtual partner in Siberg, as a dear and good friend to us both, and as a model of what we would like everyone to be—loyal, honest, and just plain nice.

Danny Halperin, a champion of change, whose skills at bringing information technology into the center of organizations—and involving us in the process—gave us the opportunity to work through many of the ideas that inform this book. His encouragement and incisiveness often helped us to reach our goals.

Siberg Associates, Inc.: Starting a new enterprise is always a risky—and exciting—adventure. The experience has been enlivened by John Stone and Wendy Mercer. The members of our Advisory Board have enhanced our work and our thinking about issues in ways we never expected: Chris Bullen, Joshua Hammond, Benn Konsynski, Luis Rubio, and Robert F. Wagner, Jr., as well as John Henderson and N. Venkatraman who are mentioned above.

Ernst & Young (Arthur Young): For years of learning together in the midst of assignments in every part of the globe, for companionship and friendship, thanks are owed to everyone, but special mention is owed Douglas Aldrich, John Bowrage, James Cross, Michael Davidson, Lawrence Dodge, Joseph Fiore, James Harrison, Vince Hussian, Robert McDowell, Philip Osborn, David Owen, Joe Richardson, Gabriel Rozman, Thomas Samson, Clinton Shrout, Gregory Stratis, Robert Suh, Norihiko Takebayashi, David Tierno, Richard Welsh, Steve Yearout.

The Twentieth Century Fund: Richard C. Leone, president of the Fund, is the perfect example of the manager who allows his employees the freedom to learn; without his encouragement and understanding, finding the time to write this book would have been impossible. We are also most grateful to the Fund authors over the past twenty years whose books have provided a broad and vast education, and to the Fund's Board of Trustees, who are justly renowned for the provocative ideas they generate. In addition, during the two and half years we have spent writing this book, the entire staff of the Fund has helped in one way or another: to them, and especially to Nancy Romano and Jason Renker, we say thank you for favors, patience, and good cheer when it was needed most.

The MIT "Management in the 1990s" project: To all the participants over the five years of the project and especially to the faculty and staff of MIT, who made all the participants welcome and taught us all so much.

Fellow consultants, clients, those interviewed, those who provided reality checks, those who read and commented on parts of the book: Phyllis Berte, Charles Bingham, James Cash, Brian Clark, Karl Coke, Paul Dudiak, Neil Duffy, Michael Eichenberg, Hermann Evert, John Glaser, Clifford Hall, David Hancock, John Higgins, Benny Huff, Abigail Janifer, Pamela Innes, Michael Intille, Darlene Jacobs, Marie L'Hereaux, Elliott McNeill, Kevin McShea, Thomas Main, Richard O. Mason, Kathy Means, Jonathan Miller, Larry Mills, John Morganto, Kris Paper, Leo Petkoon, James Porter, Mark Sandberg, Don Saulic, John Rockart, Arthur Sharff, Michael Sloan, Carl Steiner, Anthony Urso, William Wade, James Wagner, Les Ward, Murray Weidenbaum, Don Young, Pieter Zaanen.

For articles published in their magazines, shaped by conversations with them, that found their way into the book: Tracy Benson at *Industry Week*, Martha Peak at *Management Review*; Ken Shelton at *Executive Excellence*.

Herb Addison, our editor at Oxford who told two people who had never written a book that he wanted the book they were thinking about writing, and then helped make it happen. He is responsible for turning an idea into a reality. Neither of us can think of anyone else we'd rather do a book with.

Those who helped produce the book: Carol Starmack, who is responsible for the way the book, especially the artwork, looks; Brenda Melissaratos, for copyediting the manuscript—and especially the bibliographic materials;

Trina King, for research (sometimes more than we wanted, but always exactly what we needed) and for indexing the book. And to those at Oxford who helped so much, expecially Ellen Fuchs, Amy Roberts, and Susan Rotermund.

We have probably forgotten to list many people. To all those, our thanks. And, of course, we alone are responsible for the words that follow.

CONTENTS

PREFACE   vii

ACKNOWLEDGMENTS   ix

CHAPTER 1   Introduction   3

CHAPTER 2   The Tool for Competing in the World of Tomorrow:
             The Dynamic Planning Framework ^{SM}   13

APPENDIX TO
CHAPTER 2   User's Guide to This Book   26

PART I   IDENTIFYING THE PROBLEM   33

CHAPTER 3   Organizing Your Resources   35

CHAPTER 4   The External Analysis   48

CHAPTER 5   The Internal Analysis   65

PART II   SEARCHING FOR SOLUTIONS   87

CHAPTER 6   Developing the Position Paper   89

CHAPTER 7   Generating Options   105

PART III   ANALYZING THE SOLUTIONS   119

CHAPTER 8   Strategic Alignment Modeling   121

CHAPTER 9   The Four Questions   142

CHAPTER 10   SAM: A Three-Dimensional Approach   158

PART IV   PUTTING THE SOLUTIONS IN PLACE   171

CHAPTER 11   The Grand Strategy   173

CHAPTER 12   Dynamic Planning in Action   197

CHAPTER 13   Managing the Change to a Dynamic Organization   219

CHAPTER 14   Formalizing the Monitoring and Evaluation Process   236

CHAPTER 15   Looking Beyond Tomorrow   248

NOTES   257

SELECT BIBLIOGRAPHY   266

INDEX   276

LIST OF FIGURES

1.1	The New Enterprise	9
2.1	Conceptual Planning Model	15
2.2	Dynamic Planning Framework: With Conceptual Planning Model Overlaid	16
2.3	Dynamic Planning Framework	21
2.4	Environmental Analysis	22
2A.1	Areas of Concentration	28
2A.2	When You Need Assistance	30
4.1	Interactive Forces Model	53
5.1	Critical Assumption Set Evaluation Matrix	84
7.1	Option/Criteria Matrix	113
8.1	Strategic Alignment Model: Aligning Business and IT Strategy	122
8.2	Strategic Alignment Model: Strategy Execution	139
8.3	Strategic Alignment Model: Technology Transformation	140
8.4	Strategic Alignment Model: Business Transformation	140
8.5	Strategic Alignment Model: Level of Service	141
10.1	Maintaining Alignment over Time	160
10.2	Current Channel Member Relationships	162
10.3	Enhanced Channel Member Relationships	163
10.4	Strategic Direction of the Enterprise	164
11.1	Mission Statement: Gerber	177
11.2	Mission Statement: Texaco	178
11.3	Mission Statement: Johnson & Johnson	179
11.4	Hierarchy of Enterprise Plan Elements	182
11.5	Fit & Hearty Enterprise Plan Elements	191
12.1	Dynamic Planning Framework: A Phased Approach	204
12.2	Analyzing Options: Empowerment	215
13.1	Change Management Framework	223
13.2	Cascading Change into the Organization	231
14.1	Dynamic Planning Framework: Feedback Loop	237
15.1	Dynamic Planning Principles	249
15.2	Looking Beyond Tomorrow	250

Dynamic Planning

CHAPTER 1

INTRODUCTION

"Would you tell me, please, which way I ought to go from here?" asked Alice. "That depends a good deal on where you want to get to," said the Cat.

Lewis Carroll,
Alice's Adventures in Wonderland

Today, the only certainty is uncertainty. The rate of change is continuing on a steep curve upward, information is growing in volume constantly, and the complexity of the marketplace is increasing exponentially. To survive, businesses must be run in such a way that their leaders have anticipatory capability, a quality that, when combined with flexibility and adaptability, can make the critical difference when it becomes necessary to adjust to the next major changes that occur in the marketplace or the world.

Disaster is preceded by various actions: the failure to anticipate and accommodate developments in the world outside, especially changes in technology as well as those created by technology; the drive to ensure a strong bottom line no matter what the long-term cost; the insistence on maintaining a corporate culture untouched, frozen in time; and the use of quick fixes applied without a sense of what they will do to the organization as a whole. Some companies watch the world change without accepting the fact that they must take those changes into account, no matter how successful they are at the moment; some manage to avoid seeing that the world is changing. Both face the same fate that befell the dinosaurs.

Indeed, such long-established companies as IBM, GM, and Sears are now facing major problems that if not remedied could lead to their extinction. *Fortune* magazine recently noted that "what swept over these companies was profound change in their markets, to which they were required

3

to adapt. None did, neither fast enough nor fully enough, in part because the erosion of their positions was so gradual as to leave them unaware that they were descending into a state of crisis. They could have profitably brooded over an opinion stated recently by Andrew S. Grove, chairman of Intel: 'There is at least one point in the history of any company when you have to change dramatically to rise to the next performance level. Miss the moment, and you start to decline.'"[1]

The problem at companies such as IBM, according to an article in *Business Week*, is that "too often, leaders are slow to recognize the need for change. Industry dynamics slowly outmode companies' products or services, eroding their ability to compete. But many executives, lulled by continuing profits or dulled by long experience with the same employer, don't see the problem until it's too late."[2] Unfortunately, the collapse of such large organizations is likely to continue; indeed, *The Economist* says that "the humbling of big firms has only just begun."[3]

Cases like these can be found in smaller firms as well. A recent assignment highlights the problem. After being contracted to help the senior leadership of a mining company in the Mid- and Southwest develop a new governance structure, we asked about the origin and duration of the previous structure. We were told that they'd restructured and downsized a "few" times over the past five years. Since they were still in trouble, they wanted to try yet another way to organize themselves. We were in the midst of a series of meetings in which we were explaining the need to attack the problems more holistically—that redoing their governance in isolation was like applying a Band-Aid—when the company was acquired.

The simple truth is that organizations do not benefit from the quick-fix approach. Such attempts merely slow the slide downhill. Turning these companies around to ensure that they do not become dinosaurs takes enormous energy, constant analysis, innovative thinking—Dynamic Planning.

Dynamic Planning is different from the buzzwords that seem to take over the business universe for six months at a time: quality, strategic planning, business process reengineering, empowerment, activity-based accounting, computer-aided software engineering (CASE) technology, benchmarking, outsourcing, the flattened organization. These solutions fail to bring the major improvements they promise because each is used to address specific problems in specific areas of the organization. They don't look at the impact that the changes they bring will have on the rest of the organization, nor do they include processes for implementation and methods for overcoming the resistance of employees to change. They also run into trouble because they are put in place without determining whether or not they duplicate or conflict with other initiatives under way in the organization. The result, when added to the uncertainty caused by constant change in the world outside the organization, is turbulence.

If, however, we consider turbulence another challenge that we can overcome if we do the right thing, there is room for a great deal of optimism. Americans have a tradition of overcoming obstacles. We have always been an innovative, resourceful nation, at our best when facing challenges. These characteristics still describe America, and American business.

After all, American creativity and industrial development brought the world into the Information Age. We spread the benefits of scientific and technological advances around the planet, providing many other nations with the tools and techniques with which to grow and compete. The problem is that what we brought the world has made us just one of a number of leading nations. We still have a key role in the world economy, but no longer control it.[4] This slide from total hegemony, along with a growing trade deficit and lagging sales in a number of major sectors, has led to countless analyses. We keep wondering what happened.

The answer is that business today is suffering from a focus on the short-term combined with an inability to accept the need to adapt to the rapid changes in technology, markets, and consumer demands that have permanently altered the global business environment. We remain wedded to the ways we did things in the past because they worked. Today, no matter how overwhelming the evidence that the old ways of doing things no longer work, we ignore it because our culture has led us to believe that we can find the magic bullet to cure the problem.

DYNAMIC THINKING:
A PERMANENT SOLUTION, NOT A QUICK FIX

We believe that the Dynamic Planning Framework^{SM}—applied in the context of a broader world that is in constant flux economically, politically, socially, and technologically—can help organizations overcome many of their current problems. It was developed as a means of maintaining long-term competitiveness in the midst of turbulence.

If you learn to think dynamically, you will not have to go back to square one when the next set of changes occurs because you will have been making incremental adjustments all along. By having everything in place, you can climb the next rung of the ladder faster than your competitors can. The Framework starts from the understanding that everything is affected by and affects everything else; in other words, it posits that you cannot examine anything in isolation. In business, as in the natural world, every change you make in one area impacts another. That is why individual theories that become the buzzwords of the moment never bring the momentous changes they promise. The fact that everything is interrelated means it is necessary to think holistically.

A decade ago, political scientist and public executive Harlan Cleveland and scientist Alexander King wrote that "the adjectives 'holistic' and 'integrative'. . . mean, quite literally, that the problems of a nation, of a city, of a village are to be seen as interconnected and therefore to be tackled simultaneously and as a complex, not separately or sequentially. The community's future comprises economic, social, cultural and political as well as technical facets; these cannot be dealt with by the politician alone, or by the economist, the engineer, or the scientist in isolation."[5] Five years later, Cleveland wrote, "I cannot find a single individual who is against integrative thinking. Everyone seems to know that in the real world, all the problems are interdisciplinary and all the solutions interdepartmental, interprofessional, interdependent, and international."[6]

The problems facing business today demand a turn to integrated, holistic thinking. And that is what we are proposing, a new way of looking at your organization internally and in the context of the world in which it competes. Moreover, the Dynamic Planning Framework will help you think about the possible benefits and costs to your organization of changes in the world, new technologies, and new processes. It will also help you decide how to use those changes to your advantage and how to adapt the technologies and processes to make them work for you.

The Dynamic Planning Framework is a structure for thinking that deals with the four key issues facing business today: the lack of long-term planning; the failure to think holistically; the new relevance of technology to corporate profitability; and the inability to keep pace with change.

THE CRITICAL FORCES OF CHANGE

What do you and your business have to do to begin to think differently? To start, there are trends in a number of areas that have obvious, enormous impacts on business: the economy and politics, social and technological change. Each of these encompasses a vast amount of complex material, more than most people are able or willing to deal with. But there are certain general trends in these areas that are important to keep in mind.

THE ECONOMY

No longer, we have been told, can we think locally; we have to think globally. Walter Wriston, former chief executive officer (CEO) of Citicorp, summed it up by saying that "national economies can no longer be understood—or operated within—unless you understand them in connection with all other economies. There are no islands anymore."[7] Indeed, the interrelatedness of national economies has created a push for the international coordination of national economic policies—and those have a direct impact on every business.

POLITICS

There have been—and there still are—dramatic changes taking place in the world order: the end of the communist bloc and the new European union, along with the development of new trading blocs, most notably of the east Asian nations and the nations of North and South America. In addition, the strength of environmentalism as a political force is likely to impact American business in the short and long term. Today, regulations protecting areas from excessive growth and industrial pollution, rules protecting endangered species, clean air and water acts, action against dumping of wastes, and related clean-up requirements are often the subject of legal wrangling. Businesses fight interference that they believe threatens their survival and concerned citizens demand the preservation of those things they believe make life richer, fuller, and in some cases, possible.

SOCIETY

Our educational system, once considered a great leveler and a path to success for all citizens, no longer serves our needs. It is failing to provide employers with the technologically skilled and empowered workforce needed today. Instead, we are faced with an overabundance of middle managers with few specific skills at a time when middle management is being constantly downsized, as well as with a large body of unskilled, poorly educated workers who are finding fewer and fewer jobs that will allow them to participate in the workforce. We are also finally beginning to face the issue of diversity in the workplace as women, minorities, and the disabled are making their voices heard. All of these changes impact business.

TECHNOLOGY

Technological changes have had an unprecedented effect on business; technology—from mainframes to personal computers to laptops to telecommunications—is not only helping organizations do what they do, but is beginning to change the very nature of organizations. Moreover, while technology has changed the way we do business and the business we do, perhaps even more disquieting, technology itself has been changing and is likely to continue to change constantly. In fact, the speed with which these technologies are developed and brought to market creates adjustment problems that are compounded by their pervasiveness.

THE ROLE OF TECHNOLOGY IN TODAY'S BUSINESS

All of these trends will have an impact on your organization, but today, the greatest impact will come from new information technologies. The importance of technology today presents a problem for organizations because the conventional planning techniques used by most organizations tend to relegate technology, particularly information technology (IT), to the role of adjunct to the various functional areas of the business. It should be treated as a partner in determining strategic possibilities; in fact, we will not be able to realize all the competitive advantages technological advances can bring until information technology is treated as one of the cornerstones of the business.

The Dynamic Planning Framework assumes that technology is a major player in the organization and incorporates it into the heart of the planning process. To ensure that technology is used wisely, adding to the core competencies of the organization and not needlessly draining its resources, Strategic Alignment Modeling (SAM) has been incorporated into the Dynamic Planning Framework. SAM, a concept developed in the course of work done on a multiyear research program conducted at MIT, "The Management in the 1990s Project," ensures that strategic business options generated by more conventional planning techniques are augmented by IT-initiated options that not only support but can transform the business.

Business today needs to plan in this way because technology has become an integral part of business. IT does more than enable; it enhances and even promotes creativity and innovation. Over and over, when you look at organizations, you see that the difference between yesterday and today is speed, scale, and scope—all of which are made possible by IT.

The best way to understand the changes in the organization brought about by technology is to visualize the current structure of major businesses as towers consisting of four blocks, each with a quarter of a circle missing at one edge, surrounding a tube (Figure 1.1). The business strategy and IT strategy are two of the four blocks; the other two blocks represent the two major operational areas of the business—the business structure (that is, the business operation) and the IT structure (that is, the operation of the IT function). The functional areas of the business—manufacturing, financial, marketing, sales, legal, R&D, and so on—fit into the tube.

THE PLAN OF THE BOOK

The Dynamic Planning Framework can prevent your organization from becoming a dinosaur. It forces you to examine what is happening in the world outside and examine its probable impacts on your operation. It teaches you not to make hasty decisions, but allows you to be imaginative

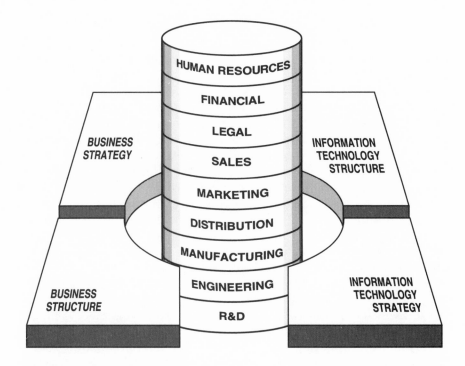

Figure 1.1. The New Enterprise
© 1993 B. Goldberg and J. G. Sifonis

and innovative. There is, after all, an enormous difference between intuition based on information and snap judgments. The Framework also makes certain that new ideas are discussed, tested, and explored across the organization before they are brought into it, providing employees with a sense of the excitement that new developments can bring while preventing the kind of secrecy that makes people fearful and resistant to change. Thus, Dynamic Planning serves as a change agent, affecting the way people think and opening them to new ideas.

The Framework is composed of nine activities carried out in four steps. In the chapters that follow, we will explain all of the activities—why they need to be done, how to do them, and the benefits that will accrue. Although many of the activities are done concurrently, the chapters present them in a linear fashion. In this chapter, we have tried to explain the need for a new way of dealing with the turbulence in the business environment.

Chapter 2 will introduce the Dynamic Planning Framework, our process for handling turbulence, including the conceptual framework it fits within. The Appendix to Chapter 2 is a user's guide to the book.

Part I of the book (Chapters 3, 4, and 5) helps you identify the problems you are facing. It shows how the Dynamic Planning Framework helps you do an internal analysis as well as an analysis of your organization in the context of the world in which it operates. Although this part of the book employs some familiar techniques, it uses the information generated in a new way.

Since one of the goals of the book is to help the business and information technology sides integrate, it is critical to overcome the language barriers between them (and the differences in techniques and focus they have that result in that barrier). As a result, some of the material in this section will be a refresher course for the business side. In the same way, some material in Part II will be a refresher course for the information technology side.

Chapter 3 spells out in detail how to organize the resources you need in order to go through the Dynamic Planning Framework, a process that requires time and commitment on the part of senior management. It explains who should be involved and the advantages of their involvement.

Chapter 4, the external analysis, explains the why and how of analyzing the external environment. It helps organizations think about their place in the broader political, social, technological, and economic scheme of things and lets them discover where the world in which they must compete is likely to go, providing a needed edge by allowing them to plan to get there first.

Chapter 5, the internal analysis, provides the information needed to diagnose your company's current condition; it helps you pull together information that, when folded together with and tested against the information collected in the external analysis chapter, allows you to determine your organization's competitive position now and in the future.

Part II of the book (Chapters 6 and 7) covers the search for solutions, explaining the processes used to analyze what you discover in the first part. It shows how the information you collected can help you determine what your organization may be able to do in the future.

Chapter 6 explains how to develop a position paper, a summary of the current state of your organization and what is happening around it that is likely to impact it. The sessions in which this analysis is performed are a major part of the process aimed at helping those in your organization understand where you are now and what you can become.

Chapter 7 teaches techniques for generating strategic options, the process by which you delve into the information presented in the position paper and, through discussion and intense analysis in a group setting, come up with new ways to do things, develop new products or services, or possibly design new ways of running your organization. Option generation makes all those involved in planning look at the possibilities of the organization, opening them to change and encouraging innovative thinking.

Part III of the book (Chapters 8, 9, and 10) is an analysis of the options that you have generated in Part II. It teaches you how to determine their effects on your organization's basic structure and the strategies you have in place. Different options will affect different parts of the organization, from its governance, scope of business, and competencies to the skill sets needed by employees, the processes in place, and the technology platforms you use. The tool for this examination is the Strategic Alignment Model (SAM), an elegant theoretical construct that has been proven an effective analytical tool.

Chapter 8 describes Strategic Alignment Modeling, the process for ensuring that any change you bring to your organization fits into its basic structure; if the option selected does not seem to fit, this chapter helps determine what you have to do to make it fit, taking into account changes in governance, technology, organization structure, skill sets, and more. Performing this analysis of the effects of a change on the basic structure of the organization means that you will not invest millions in unneeded technology, and it means that you will buy the technology you do need and will properly train your employees to use it to its fullest. It means that you will not decide to downsize one department and expand another without noticing that you can save a lot of money and improve morale by retraining some of those you would otherwise layoff. It teaches you to examine and reexamine your options with care—and with an eye to the future.

Chapters 9 and 10 examine the kinds of changes that can be made using the Strategic Alignment Model through examples, showing what SAM can teach you and the advantages it can bring in a series of case studies. (The identities of the companies used are not disclosed because of the confidentiality of the client-consultant relationship; only industry sector and general geographic location, with an indication of the size of the organization, are given in order to allow for comparisons.)[8]

Part IV of the book (Chapters 11, 12, 13, and 14) shows you how to put the solutions in place. It discusses the derivation of a company's Grand Strategy, its formal plan for moving into the future. It also explores the need to help the organization adapt to the changes the Grand Strategy will bring. It then examines ways to monitor, measure, and evaluate what is happening in the new organization to ensure that the Grand Strategy helps the organization achieve a competitive advantage.

Chapter 11 describes the creation of the organization's Grand Strategy, the point at which you begin to fit the chosen option into your company in a very public and open and dynamic way. It guides you in drawing on all the information uncovered in the previous steps to draft the public communication of the direction you plan to take—your mission statement. It also helps you design an enterprise plan to guide you in your assault on the future. In order to simplify the complex voyage taken to date, the chapter closes with an example of Dynamic Planning in action in a small, start-up enterprise.

Chapter 12 is another case history; this time Dynamic Planning takes place within a huge organization. This case shows the flexibility of the

Framework, which had to be altered somewhat to accommodate the nature of the company and the processes for planning it already had in place. The ease with which it was adapted highlights its nature as a framework, not a methodology, and shows how Dynamic Planning actually serves as a change agent.

Chapter 13 discusses the formal processes for managing specific changes required by new options as well as presents ways to institutionalize the idea that change is now a constant. The goal is to help open the culture of the organization, creating a dynamic learning environment that will make implementing changes far easier.

Chapter 14 explains the need for measurement. It shows that continual monitoring of the organization's progress—and the world around it—is necessary. It explains the importance of monitoring and evaluating as ongoing disciplines, for they are the tools that let you know when something on the horizon calls for you to enter the Framework again—and at which point to reenter.

Chapter 15 explores the effects of using the Dynamic Planning Framework on the way you think about business.

CONCLUSION

You can no longer run your business the way you always have and assume that you will continue to succeed. To remain competitive, you must be able to envision tomorrow and reach for it. The tool for enabling you to do this—to find out "where you want to get to"—is the practical set of processes, the Dynamic Planning Framework, described in this book.

CHAPTER 2

The Tool for Competing in the World of Tomorrow: The Dynamic Planning Framework ^{SM}

Executives should rethink their planning process. Too often the planning process reflects what organizations know how to do rather than what they should do.

John C. Henderson and N. Venkatraman[1]

Executives facing the changes that are the norm today must manage their businesses not only to ensure that they survive in the short term, but they must do so while planning and building for the future. That is a task that requires a new kind of thinking, a holistic approach that does not seize on a quick cure for a specific problem and then assume that the emergency repair has solved the underlying structural problems that caused the emergency. Unless the foundation and all the layers built upon it are sound, problems that crop up will keep demanding time and money that a business involved in an increasingly competitive global environment cannot afford.

We believe that Dynamic Planning, a new holistic approach to business management, is the answer. It is not a Band-Aid approach; indeed, as will be seen in case studies, it is a careful process that takes time to carry out and that by its very nature changes the way management thinks and acts. Those who are involved in Dynamic Planning learn to see the world and their businesses in very different ways as a result of the things they do in the course of carrying out the Dynamic Planning process.

Since the Dynamic Planning Framework must be adapted to each organization, it should not be treated as if it were, in any sense, a methodology—a formal and rigid set of procedures that have specific associated tasks that are always carried out at the same stage of the process and in the same way. As the name implies, it is dynamic—changing and active. The size, scope, scale, and objectives of those entering into it will determine its application in each company. A rigid approach is the opposite of the goal of the entire process—open, innovative thinking. For example, in very large organizations Dynamic Planning works well when applied to functional areas, such as marketing, or individual business units. It also can be used as a way of evaluating any organization that plans to see where new procedures may be added to the current planning process to make it more holistic. Of course, applying it to the whole organization will provide the greatest benefits.

How Dynamic Planning Works

Dynamic Planning is a generic, comprehensive, concurrent, and iterative process. It is built on a concept that is carried out in four steps. These steps serve to identify the problems a business is facing, to help management search for possible solutions and then analyze the likely effects of each of the possible solutions on the business, and last, but far from least, to put the solutions in place. Each step, in turn, consists of a series of activities. The specific methods used in connection with each of the activities differ according to the nature of the business involved, but the activities remain the same. They include constant monitoring and changing of the business, strategically and operationally; Strategic Alignment Modeling (SAM), which requires managing necessary changes in such a way that each new level of change can be easily accommodated by both the business and information technology (IT) side; and seeing to it that the decisions made in the planning process are properly implemented.

When done correctly, Dynamic Planning makes the business receptive to change and instills in the corporate culture the flexibility to anticipate and rapidly adapt to new conditions. To do this, Dynamic Planning starts by challenging the existing business and forcing management to ask difficult questions: What business are we in? Why do we do what we do? How well are we performing compared to our competitors? Are there events on the horizon that could impact us, perhaps providing new options that would offer strategic advantage? What role can IT play in helping us do better? Can IT provide new opportunities? Do we need to change our mission statement and enterprise plan to prepare for the future?[2] How do we ensure that our plans are implemented? And how do we adjust to the rapid changes in the competitive arena?

Although Dynamic Planning can help you find the answers to these questions, keep in mind that Dynamic Planning is a journey, not a destination that is visited and then forgotten when the trip is over. It is not something that is done when problems emerge as though doing it were by itself a solution. Dynamic Planning is a pragmatic approach that forces implementation; it pushes the journey.

The Dynamic Planning Framework is based upon a Conceptual Planning Model that incorporates both proven planning techniques and innovative models that generate an integrated business and information technology strategy for the business. It ensures that the process is inherently ongoing, reflecting the real-world effects of constant change and business turbulence. The Conceptual Planning Model, which is illustrated in Figure 2.1, is a series of four steps, each of which encompasses a number of activities. These activities make up the Dynamic Planning Framework, which is illustrated in Figure 2.2 in combination with the Conceptual Planning Model so that the activities that comprise each of the steps of the Conceptual Model are easier to understand.

The first step of the Conceptual Model is to identify the problem or problems the business is facing. The first activity necessary to complete this step is to set up a group or committee to oversee the process; that is, to organize the resources you will need to do Dynamic Planning. Identifying the problem also requires two complex analyses—external and internal—that must be done concurrently.

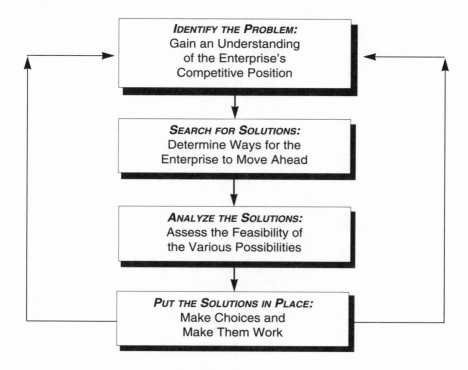

Figure 2.1. Conceptual Planning Model
© 1993 B. Goldberg and J. G. Sifonis

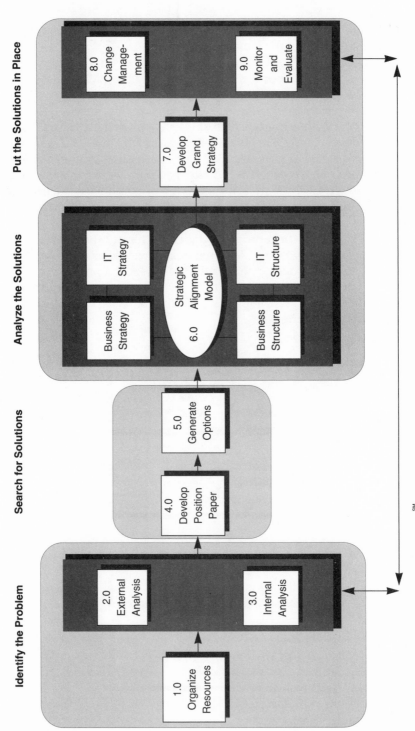

Identify the Problem

1.0 Organize Resources

2.0 External Analysis

3.0 Internal Analysis

Search for Solutions

4.0 Develop Position Paper

5.0 Generate Options

Analyze the Solutions

Business Strategy

IT Strategy

Strategic Alignment Model 6.0

Business Structure

IT Structure

Put the Solutions in Place

7.0 Develop Grand Strategy

8.0 Change Management

9.0 Monitor and Evaluate

Figure 2.2. Dynamic Planning Framework^SM**: With Conceptual Planning Model Overlaid**

© 1993 B. Goldberg and J. G. Sifonis

Before a business decides to move forward, it must gain a thorough understanding of its own strategy and structure by conducting an internal analysis to address the questions that were raised above. The organization must get a handle on the "what, why, and how" of its business by realistically assessing its strengths and weaknesses. However, to really be of benefit, the internal analysis must be done in the context of how well the company is functioning in relation to its competitors. Performing the internal analysis in a vacuum—that is, by looking only at one's own performance—tends only to highlight areas of common concern or reaffirm the beliefs the business has always held. The value of the internal analysis is in the evaluation and interpretation of the performance of the business with respect to its competition.

This procedure requires another activity, namely, an analysis of the external environment; that is, analyzing a selected set of direct competitors and the competition within the sector in which the business and its direct competitors compete (baseball teams compete with other baseball teams directly, and baseball as a sport competes against sports such as gymnastics). In addition, the social, political, economic, and technological factors that are most likely to impact the general environment must be assessed. The information gathered in this external analysis, in conjunction with the internal analysis, provides a sound basis for evaluating where a business stands against its competitors.

The evaluation and interpretation of the results of the internal and external analyses provide the foundation that allows the business to move on to the second step in the Conceptual Planning Model, the search for solutions. Having completed the first step, the organization has the information it needs to generate and evaluate viable strategic options—rational choices the company can make to alter the business in which it competes, how it competes, where it competes, and against whom it competes. The first activity required to complete this step is developing a position paper that analyzes the gaps between how good the business perceives itself to be as compared to how good it really is in terms of its competition. The information in the position paper must then be analyzed in the most objective, creative, and imaginative way possible to generate options for future directions.

It would be ideal, of course, if all strategic options were viable and rational. Since they are not, establishing evaluation criteria is a necessary condition for ensuring that the options generated by the external and internal analyses are within the organization's means—in terms of dollars, skill sets, and time. Establishing an evaluation criteria that allows you to complete the third step in the Conceptual Planning Model, analyzing the solutions, places realistic boundaries on the choices the organization can make.

Up to this point, our proposed Conceptual Planning Model would appear to be no different from a number of other, time-tested planning models. Conceptually, we evaluate the company and the environment in which the company must compete, perform a gap analysis, and develop an evaluation criteria on which to assess strategic options to move the firm forward. In most planning models, the strategic options would be directed toward the traditional views of enhancing the scope of business, augmenting the distinctive competencies of the organization, and redesigning its structure to support a new set of strategies.

In most instances, the role of information technology and systems in this process is, at best, an afterthought, and at worst, ignored. Dynamic Planning adds a new dimension to strategy formulation—the explicit recognition and incorporation of a process for integrating information technology and systems with the elements of traditional business strategy formulation. Given the importance and role of IT today, a failure to accept IT as an integral part of strategy formulation may prevent an organization from generating and evaluating those possibly critical strategic options provided by IT.

The activity called for in this third step of the Conceptual Model is Strategic Alignment Modeling—a method that considers IT strategy and structure as an equal partner with business strategy and structure. We use SAM to address the criticality, and necessity, of IT in the formulation of an organization's business strategy. Although SAM will be discussed in far greater detail in subsequent chapters, the underlying concept is the recognition of the need to align the components of IT (namely, IT strategy and IT structure) with the traditional view of the components of the organization (namely, business strategy and structure). The implications of this perspective are that the changes the organization makes to its business strategy impact not only the business structure, but also have an explicit impact on the organization's IT strategy and IT structure. Conversely, changes in the IT strategy have an explicit impact on the organization's business strategy and structure.

Given the impact of IT, and the substantial investments companies have made in IT, the relationship between business and IT strategy can no longer be ignored—changes in one strategy have a significant impact on the other. Consequently, the two strategies, and ultimately, the structure of both the business and IT side, must be viewed concurrently when developing and evaluating strategic options to determine their impact on the organization. Many of the IT problems that companies are faced with today are due to the misalignment of the business and IT strategies; this misalignment often results in the formulation of a business strategy that is not integrated with the IT strategy, which is one of the reasons existing investments made in IT are often not leveraged fully.

Once the strategic options have been evaluated and one or perhaps a set of options has proven viable, the fourth and last step of the Conceptual Planning Model, putting the solutions in place, begins. It is composed of three activities, the first of which is formulating an integrated business and IT strategy—a Grand Strategy. This strategy may entail modifying the existing, or perhaps creating a new, mission statement for the organization. Or it may entail merely revising the existing enterprise plan to incorporate action steps to implement the new options that were generated. In either case, the results will reflect the inclusion of IT in the generation and evaluation of options—a notion that is normally not considered in strategy formulation.

The next two activities in the Framework, taken together, can be called strategy implementation. This is a combination of putting in place programs aimed at changing the corporate culture to be sure it can accommodate the new directions the firm will be moving in and putting in place evaluation procedures to ensure that the changes being made are working and that the business is ready for future changes.

As is clear in both the Conceptual Planning Model and the Dynamic Planning Framework, this final pair of activities in this last step are linked back to our original starting point, the internal and external analysis. The rationale for this linkage is the concept of creating an organization that is able to anticipate and deal with change through continuous monitoring and evaluation—both internally and externally—of activities or events that could impact the implementation of the organization's strategy. We are using the processes and techniques from the internal and external analysis (1) to identify and assess, for example, the changes in the external environment that will have an impact on the implementation of the organization's strategy and (2) to determine what course corrections must be made to adjust to such changes. In addition, we are monitoring and evaluating the performance of the business in the execution of its strategy in the context of what is occurring in the external environment (for example, our performance in comparison to our competition), and if necessary, making further adjustments to the strategy implementation process. This is a continuous loop of examination, change, and reexamination—a continuous learning process for the organization.

TURNING CONCEPTS INTO REALITY

The Dynamic Planning Framework, the step-by-step process for moving an organization toward the future, cannot be carried out overnight. It goes beyond conventional notions of strategy formulation, treating the organization holistically, integrating rather than interfacing information technology into all aspects of the organization; moreover, it builds in the mechanisms that will ensure implementation of the plans made and see to it that the organization will be open to, and even search for, further change. As a result, Dynamic Planning can bring order-of-magnitude increases in competitiveness and profitability. The key is learning how the concepts can be turned into reality—ensuring that what appears to be a great idea works in the real world.

We believe that the Framework turns the concepts that make up Dynamic Planning into a logical sequence of activities that when executed properly brings dramatic results. The rest of this book will elaborate on all the activities involved in the Dynamic Planning Framework. First, however, we want to ensure that each of the major activities (Figure 2.3 shows the Framework without the overlay of the Conceptual Planning Model) is understood in terms of its relationship to all the other activities, many of which will actually be done concurrently.

* As with any good planning process, the first activity (Activity 1.0) is to organize the resources required for carrying out the rest of the activities. The most difficult part of this first step is organizing the human resources component. To do Dynamic Planning effectively, the planning team must set up task forces to carry out Activity 2.0, the external analysis, and Activity 3.0, the internal analysis, keeping in mind that these activities are done concurrently and that the task forces will work together to analyze what they have discovered independently. Part of organizing the resources is determining what skill sets are required over what period of time. Then you have to look at your organization and determine how many people you can place on these task forces, given the time needed and the demands of the ongoing activities they are involved in. As part of Activity 1.0, a detailed plan with specific target dates for reporting is developed to ensure that the process is conducted in a timely manner. By informing others in your organization about the team's assignments, the time the members of the team spend on Dynamic Planning is less likely to be regarded as wasted time by those they work for or with.

* The object of Activity 2.0, the external analysis, is to assess the external environment in which the organization must compete. Successfully executing this activity requires that the team address the areas highlighted in Figure 2.4, Environmental Analysis. The focus of the assessment is very context specific; many organizations will choose to examine only those elements (political, economic, technological, social) that could directly impact their industrial sector; others will look only at their direct competitors. The final product of the planning team's assessment should be a list describing the possible scenarios for the business; that is, the possible future business environment in which the business may have to compete.

* Activity 3.0, the internal analysis of the organization, is performed concurrently with Activity 2.0. One of the task forces set up in Activity 1.0 has the goal of capturing information about different aspects of the organization, such as the organization's vision, mission, enterprise

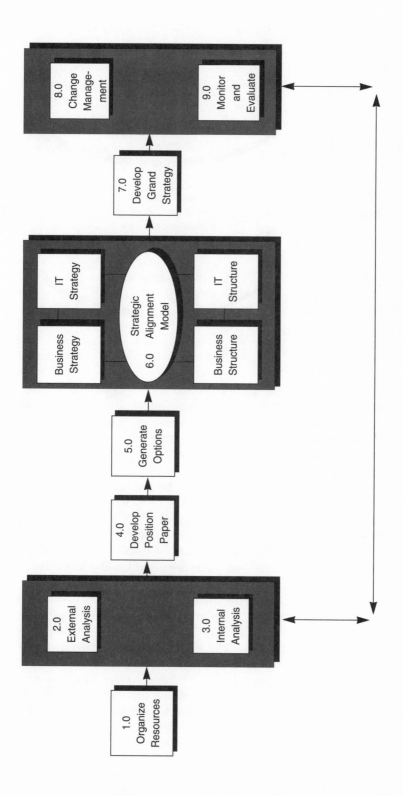

Figure 2.3. Dynamic Planning Framework^{SM}

© 1993 B. Goldberg and J. G. Sifonis

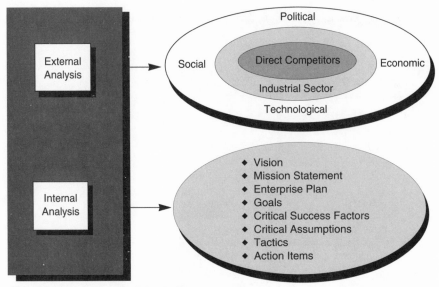

Figure 2.4. Environmental Analysis
© 1993 B. Goldberg and J. G. Sifonis

plan, goals, critical success factors, critical assumptions, tactics, and action items (see Figure 2.4). This information is collected primarily through interviews conducted with executive management and through evaluation of internal documentation such as annual reports and the mission statement.

◆   At the conclusion of Activities 2.0 and 3.0, the task forces meet to prepare a position paper that will serve as the knowledge book for the planning team. The task forces meet with the facilitator to analyze the differences between the business's own view of its position in the competitive environment and the reality of its actual position; in essence, the gap between the two pictures is explored and bridged, resulting in a realistic analysis of its ability to compete in the marketplace. It is critical to the rest of the process that the information in the position paper, which is the foundation for conducting Activity 4.0, be a candid and honest appraisal. Executive management uses the paper as a basis for deciding on the organization's strategic direction; the paper allows management to realistically assess its strengths and weaknesses, compare what it believes is critical to its success given its competition, evaluate its basic assumptions and beliefs about the external environment and available markets, and determine the opportunities it can seize, as well as the threats to its survival, given trends in the external environment. Thus, the position paper provides executive management with the information it needs to begin generating a set of options for the future.

◆   The development of a viable set of options that will allow the organization to enhance its existing competitive position is performed in Activity 5.0. In most instances, performing Activity 5.0 is the responsibility of executive management, since this group is ultimately responsible for the strategic direction of the organization. A key element of this activity is developing evaluation criteria that take into account the realities of the organization's resources—time, money, human, as well as other types of resources—for these will determine which options are most viable. The evaluation criteria not only help narrow the list of options to those most likely to be successfully implemented; they also allow management to assess which options will have the greatest potential impact on the business, given its available resources.

The analysis of the material gathered to date should be performed in a working session conducted by a facilitator, using ground rules that encourage free thinking. If this activity is to produce the desired results, the participants have to feel absolutely safe thinking out of the box. To create this kind of atmosphere, the facilitator has to be sure that no one will feel threatened for making suggestions that are considered unconventional or against company traditions or risky. Ideas cannot be laughed at or shot down the instant they are put forth. Any behavior that inhibits free thinking must be stopped by declaring that it is countercreative. The freer people feel to express the ideas that occur to them in this kind of meeting, the more likely it is that something new will emerge as a possibility. Then, even if the idea doesn't work out, the group has had a degree of success. The more people begin to think about things in different ways, the more likely it is that they will arrive at workable ideas. This new freedom to think broadly is something that tends to carry over into the culture of the organization. Managers who see the positive results of thinking outside the box tend to encourage those who work for them to do the same. Meetings become far livelier, and new ideas tend to emerge at all levels. It is a form of intellectual empowerment that brings great rewards and that makes everyone in the organization much more open to change when it is necessary.

◆   Activity 6.0, running the options through the Strategic Alignment Model—the heart of the Dynamic Planing Framework—to examine and evaluate their impact on the strategy and structure of the organization, can now begin. The Strategic Alignment Model makes explicit the relationship between the business strategy and structure

and the information technology strategy and structure of the organization. In SAM, IT strategy is equal to, not subordinate to, business
strategy. Consequently, each option must be examined with respect to
its impact on both the business and IT strategy and structure—resulting in a more comprehensive, iterative process that recognizes the
role of IT. The Strategic Alignment Modeling process examines the
impact of the options from four views (business strategy, business
structure, IT strategy, IT structure), which will be explained in detail
in later chapters. For now, a brief example of some of the many permutations possible will explain the importance of this process.

Let us say that a strategic option deals with changes in the business
scope of the organization (what it does for a living). SAM will help us
determine the impact of that option on the business structure—do
we need to redesign the existing business processes or do we need to
change how the business is structured or do we need to enhance
employees' existing skill sets? Changes in any of these dimensions
will, ultimately, have an impact on the IT structure—do we need different IT skill sets to support the new structure and scope of business or do we need different technology or do we need to manage
how IT delivers its services differently? Evaluation of a strategic
option to change what the organization does for a living is now made
explicit with respect to the impact on the IT structure.

Conversely, SAM can help us evaluate a strategic option that is
generated by a change in the IT strategy of the organization: What is
the likely impact of a particular IT-generated option, such as changing from mainframe computers to an interconnected network of personal computers, on what the organization does for a living? Does
the organization need to develop or acquire new human or technological competencies? Does it change the business structure of the
organization? What impact will it have in terms of our existing skill
sets? By using SAM, we are able to examine the impact a change in IT
strategy has on the existing strategy and structure of the organization. This gives the business the capability not only to generate strategic options that might be overlooked if IT is not an explicit part of
strategy formulation, but also allows examination of the impact of IT
strategic options.

◆ After completing the appropriate SAM analysis for the various
options, management has some sense of the costs and benefits of
each and can decide which, if any, to pursue. Upon making that
decision, management should launch Activity 7.0—designing a
Grand Strategy. A Grand Strategy is an overarching plan for organizing large institutions—from governments to military forces to
large corporations—that enables leaders to set policies and put in

place strategies for achieving specific goals. In a business, the Grand Strategy is a combination of an organization's vision, mission statement, and enterprise plan, which encompasses everything that will have to be done to complete the mission, as reflected in the goals, successfully.

◆   Once the organization's leaders make this set of decisions and put in place the appropriate management, infrastructure, and resources to carry it out, Activities 8.0 and 9.0, strategy implementation, can begin. This is a two-step activity, consisting of change management, which ensures that the organization's culture can handle the changes being made, and evaluation and monitoring, which puts in place the checkpoints the organization needs to make sure the new mission is moving along successfully and to watch for forces that will mandate future changes.

As will be described later on, the teams put in place to assess and evaluate the external world and to examine the organization are not disbanded when those steps are completed. The work they did made them—and the organization—receptive to the need to keep an eye on the world around them and to the need for change. They remain, in smaller numbers and with less time spent, part of the new organization, serving as change agents and futurologists in a new, more open learning environment.

The discussions that take place between team members and other employees as a result of their involvement in the planning process make it easier to gain acceptance for change. Moreover, employees involved in planning have a vested interest in seeing to the successful implementation of the plan. After all, they were part of the original group doing the planning, and thus its success redounds to them. That is why the first step in the Framework, organizing your resources, especially choosing the right people for the project as will be explained in the next chapter, is so important.

Involving as many employees as possible in the process helps make the Dynamic Planning Framework effective on a scale rarely achieved by plans imposed from above. It also does something else; it creates an organization attuned to collecting information and aware of how information can be turned into knowledge. In the Information Age, marked by extraordinary amounts of available information, such an organization is bound to succeed.

APPENDIX TO CHAPTER 2

USER'S GUIDE TO THIS BOOK

In some ways this is two books: it is a description of a process—Dynamic Planning—that will help you think in a new way, explaining what the process is and what it teaches you. It is also a guide for executing Dynamic Planning.

No matter which road you take, it is important to understand first *what* Dynamic Planning is. If you decide to focus on the what, turn now to the example of Fit & Hearty in Chapter 11; it is an example of how the Framework was implicitly used by a start-up company as it reached a new plateau; then go on to see the Framework at work in a far more complex example in Chapter 12, involving a recently privatized national transportation company. These examples show Dynamic Planning in action. While the CEO may find the Fit & Hearty example somewhat simplistic, like the more complex example in Chapter 12, it reveals the flexibility inherent in Dynamic Planning. Neither example is a perfect match to the activities set forth in the Framework at every point—the companies were real and the Framework is not a methodology. The examples make clear, however, the flexibility of Dynamic Planning.

Given the increasing importance of information technology, we also suggest reading Chapter 8, which is a very basic explanation of Strategic Alignment Modeling, a process for integrating business and information technology.

When reading the book, keep in mind that although there are similarities across industrial sectors in respect to competition, levels of technology, and skill sets, every company is unique. The Dynamic Planning Framework is context specific. It is rare that a solution or experience discussed in an example can be transferred exactly to another company. A company's culture, strategy, structure, and so forth, will dictate the techniques and detailed tasks that have to be completed in the Dynamic Planning Framework; it is a phenomenon known as "sensitive dependence on initial conditions."[1]

Choosing What to Do

If you are going to use the Framework as a tool for planning, you should read through it from beginning to end so you will understand it thoroughly. This user's guide will help you understand *how* Dynamic Planning should be carried out given your specific roles and responsibilities. It is divided into sections, tailored to the needs of someone assigned to a planning team, to someone asked to manage or to facilitate Dynamic Planning for the organization, to the head of the information technology division who has to do an information technology strategy or plan, and to those assigned a specific function, such as membership on a task force or change management or benchmarking, as part of the monitoring and evaluation process.

Each section explains which chapters you will have to focus on and when you need to call in assistance to carry out certain activities.

Members of the Planning Team

As a member of the planning team you share responsibility for the success of the project. You will have to attend meetings and focus sessions and work with the facilitator and project manager. Since you will play a part in setting up the project, you should work through Chapter 3 with the other members of the team (see Figure 2A.1). After considering the role of the facilitator, you and the other members of the team have to decide whether you want to bring someone in from outside to help manage the process. This is usually a wise step if you don't have an individual with the experience or expertise to handle the issues that are likely to arise or the processes involved in-house, or if politics and turf battles are likely to be a large part of the process.

Next you should review the work that the external and internal analyses task forces will be doing, which is described in Chapters 4 and 5. Be prepared to cooperate in the interview process and to help get your peers to cooperate.

Since you will be a critical player in the drafting of the position paper and generation of options, read Chapters 6 and 7 with care. Chapters 8 and 9, which explore the Strategic Alignment Model, are critically important; you must understand these concepts to participate in the sessions in which the options will be analyzed.

The development of your organization's Grand Strategy is the most important work you will do as a member of the team. The first half of Chapter 11 reviews all the components of a Grand Strategy and explains the steps that must be taken to ensure all the necessary elements are in place.

You should read through Chapters 13 and 14, change management and monitoring and evaluation, because an understanding of these

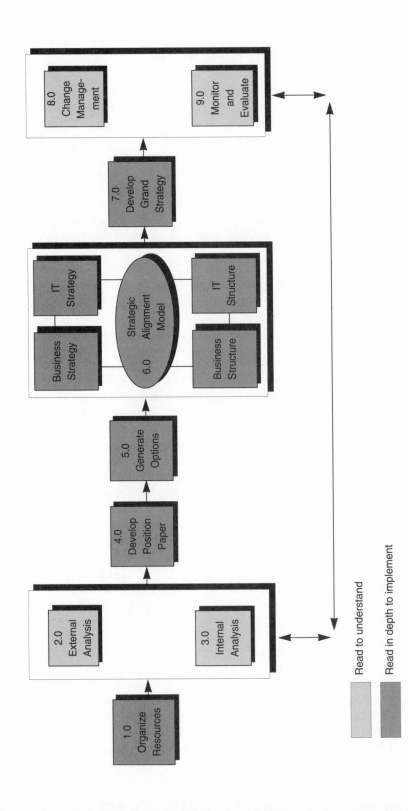

Figure 2A.1. Areas of Concentration
© 1993 B. Goldberg and J. G. Sifonis

processes will help you in reviewing progress in these areas. The chapters are a key to the implementation of the enterprise plan you and your team have developed.

The Internal Planning Project Manager or Facilitator

If you are going to facilitate the planning process, you must be familiar with every chapter in the book—and it is important to also read the notes to the chapters. Whether you are a consultant or an executive assigned to manage the project, as you go through each chapter, you will have to decide when you will call in experts for assistance (see Figure 2A.2). For example, if your organization has never expanded beyond its national borders and is contemplating becoming multinational, you may want to augment the work of the external task force with reports from an organization that is set up to do national analyses. If benchmarking seems advisable as a part of the monitoring and evaluation process and the organization has no experience in that area, read through some of the materials suggested in the notes. At that point you may want to hire someone to benchmark. If you are an internal facilitator and the option generation focus sessions become very political, you may decide to bring in an outside facilitation expert for a few days. The gap analysis that is done as part of developing the position paper is another difficult assignment, one that might benefit from the help of an outside expert.

The area in which it is critical to bring in expertise is Strategic Alignment Modeling. There are so many components to keep in balance, and a deep understanding of business structures and information technology is necessary to complete this stage successfully. An internal project manager or an outside facilitator chosen for, say, expertise in helping lead brainstorming sessions, may not be able to handle the complex issues involved in the SAM analysis.

The Head of the Information Technology Group

There are times when the planning process originates in the IT group in response to a mandate from senior management to develop plans for the future to match possible changes in governance on the business side. When that happens, the IT manager—whether called the Head of the IT Group, the Chief Information Officer, the MIS Director, or any number of similar titles—must think more broadly about his or her role in terms of the business. The book will help you do that. But the work the IT manager must do in terms of IT administrative structure not only involves developing the appropriate IT organization structure, but also involves defining a number of technical architectures that are necessary to implement the IT strategy. Although the definition of these architectures and,

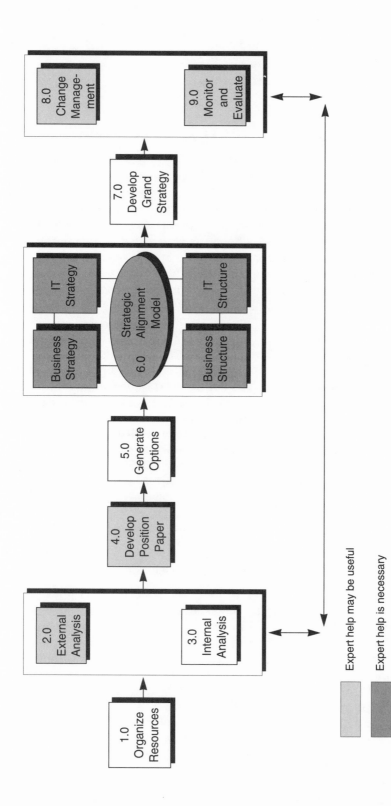

Figure 2A.2. When You Need Assistance

© 1993 B. Goldberg and J. G. Sifonis

ultimately, the decisions made by IT management involve the architectures for hardware, systems software, applications, data, and communications, that is beyond the scope of this book—and we have therefore not explored our experiences in this area here.

You will probably need to bring in expertise to assist your group in understanding the possible governance models the business may select and what it will mean in terms of setting up proper communications networks and other related architectures. It is also often useful to bring in an honest broker—an organization or individual not connected with a specific vendor—to help in the assessment of the platforms, tools, applications, and so forth that will best suit the future IT structure.

SPECIAL FUNCTIONS

Members of the Internal and External Analysis Task Forces. There are specific chapters (Chapters 4 and 5) devoted to the work you are expected to do for the planning team. You will be able to do a far better job if you read through the book to get an idea of how the material you provide will be used by the planning team. The most important chapter in this regard is Chapter 6, which explains how the information will be folded into a position paper that will guide your company through its analysis of the organization and its place in the world.

Change Managers. If you are given responsibility for introducing the changes that are being put in place in an organization as a result of Dynamic Planning, your job will be easier if you collect materials about the organization from the planning team before you begin. You also should find out who was involved in the planning process because many will be able to serve as change agents. Read carefully through Chapter 13 and its notes. If you have problems, you may need to call in a change management consultant to guide you through some of the landmines; you may also want to have a professional writer work on some of the communications materials you will need to develop.

Measurement. This is a difficult process with so many variations that we have just brushed the surface of the techniques in Chapter 14. It is usually advisable to get outside help to develop the tools you need to put in place.

PART I

IDENTIFYING THE PROBLEM

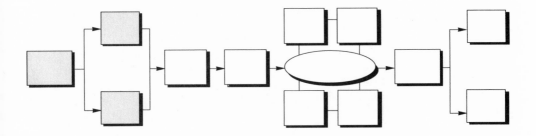

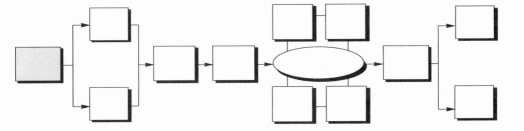

CHAPTER 3

ORGANIZING YOUR RESOURCES

One of the main reasons efforts to change large systems falter is because most people did not know what they were signing up for when they began. We have to learn more about what really happens when we try to change an organization. We must let go of our naive assumptions and our need for immediate action.

Geoffrey M. Bellman[1]

This and the next two chapters show how the first step in Dynamic Planning helps you identify the problems facing your organization. The first of the activities in this step of the Framework (see Figure 2.3) is organizing the resources you need to carry out the rest of the activities that make up Dynamic Planning. It is critical to keep in mind that the very act of organizing your resources is a part of opening your company to change, including changing its culture. The fact that you are embarking upon a new planning process should be communicated to management at the middle and upper levels in all the operational areas that will be involved.

When communicating the fact that you are embarking on Dynamic Planning—or any other kind of planning—it is important to anticipate the question "Why are we doing this?" It is a question asked partly out of cynicism (plans have been developed and not implemented so often that people resent wasting time on what seems to be a pointless effort), partly out of fear (people wonder what the plan will mean to the work they do and the position they hold), and partly out of distrust (there is often a belief that people in the organization are using planning for personal gain, such as increasing their own power bases). The only way to overcome the resistance to planning is to ensure that top management proclaims that Dynamic Planning is necessary to the long-term survival of the organization.[2] This is the start of the change management process that is an inherent part of Dynamic Planning.

LANGUAGE
ONE OF THE CRITICAL PROBLEMS IN DYNAMIC PLANNING

Another problem that must be overcome is lack of communication between different groups within and across the organization: everyone is a specialist and every specialty has its own language or jargon. Yet because one of the keys to Dynamic Planning is integrating business and information technology (IT) strategies, specialists from both areas, each fluent in their own language, must be included in the planning process. In addition, as companies restructure, people are being asked to assume many new functions. A major oil company in the Southwest and a large Midwestern mining company have recently put human resources executives in charge of developing information systems for their divisions. As we worked with them, the problems created by the lack of a common vocabulary became clear.

In the past, the larger a company grew, the smaller each person's area of expertise became. Then add to that the fact that we have abandoned the great humanist tradition of the university: its role as the place where people went to learn how to learn. Today, people are schooled in fairly narrow disciplines: business management, mathematics, scientific disciplines (but not science), technology, or any of hundreds of other areas. The result is that when senior executives meet to develop a plan, they often fail to understand one another. It is as if "an English-speaking general [were] trying to lead troops onto a battlefield with a sergeant who only speaks French; a lieutenant, Spanish; and the rank-and-file, Italian. The army would be in a state of chaos, or at least at a major disadvantage. All the time the soldiers should be planning strategies for winning battles would be spent trying to understand one another."[3]

In fact, poor communication is at the heart of a problem that is preventing many organizations from taking advantage of advanced technology, which is one of the critical success factors for many of the companies we have examined in the course of assisting on planning projects. Harlan Cleveland pointed out in *The Knowledge Executive* that "No one person can know enough to send a team of people to the moon, in the sense that Grandpa and Grandma could know just about everything about managing their corner grocery store. . . . So different types of people, with differing knowledge and skills . . . have to be brought together in organizations designed to transmute their separate expertnesses and their collective insights into wise day-to-day decisions about what to do next, together."[4]

Thus, one of our goals in the next few chapters is to take the time to teach the business side some of the language of information technology, and information technologists the language of business.[5] The result is that some material in those chapters will be all too familiar to some and difficult to others; in the end, however, understanding and a meeting of minds becomes possible.

CHOOSING THE MEMBERS OF THE PLANNING TEAM

Since the planning process itself serves to open your organization to the changes you will be making, a critical issue is the composition of the planning team and the task forces who will be responsible for gathering information for the team. The members of the planning team must be senior management because they will also be the implementors and salespeople for the plan. The definition of senior management will vary dramatically from company to company. For example, a company with gross revenues under $1 billion a year will, normally, have significantly fewer senior managers than companies over this threshold. In general, however, the planning team should include at least the Chief Executive Officer (CEO), Chief Operating Officer (COO), Chief Financial Officer (CFO), and the senior/executive vice presidents of the various functional areas, as well as the Chief Information Officer (CIO) or vice president of management information systems.

Involving the business's stakeholders in the process, those parties whose interests the business is going to serve—for example, the shareholders, the employees, suppliers, customers—may also be useful. For example, in those cases in which customers and suppliers are viewed as critical stakeholders in the ultimate success of the firm, the planning team may want to have them interviewed and surveyed. Often, suppliers and customers can provide candid assessments that are useful in determining the business's hidden flaws as well as highlighting those areas where greater efforts are needed. Shareholders may be involved in planning in much the same way, especially since they often are shareholders in many other organizations and may be able to provide interesting and useful insights on developments taking place elsewhere. In the case of employees at different levels, it may be expedient to place a few representatives on the planning team itself.

Any number of people can be included on the planning team, but keep in mind that the larger the number of participants, the more time and energy needed to achieve the defined outcome. Unless the organization is extremely large (the equivalent of a Fortune 100 company) and the change is going to mean an enormous cultural shift (see the case history of the transportation network in Chapter 12), the recommended upper limit for such teams is from ten to twelve individuals.

THE VALUE OF THINKING ABOUT THE PLANNING PROCESS

From the beginning, all planning team members must agree on the scope of the planning they are going to do. Holistic planning does not always involve starting as if the company had just been formed, although it does require looking at the overall organization. For example, if the intent of the planning process is to reevaluate the progress of the organization in meeting the goals that were established in a prior planning session, the current effort may involve only changing or augmenting the enterprise goals, critical success factors, assumptions, and perhaps some of the tactics and action items that were the basis of the original enterprise plan. (These terms will all be fully explored when we discuss the internal analysis in Chapter 5.) On the other hand, if the objective of the planning process is to start from scratch and develop a new vision, strategic direction, and all of the other elements that constitute an enterprise plan, then the contents of the plan and the requisite effort involved will be substantial.

The defined outcome the planning team is trying to achieve—that is, whether it is updating or modifying the existing plan or developing a new plan—will dictate the techniques that will be used as well as the level of effort and time required of the planning team members. However, based upon our experiences in using the Framework on a number of assignments, we observed some very interesting changes in the mindset of planning team participants (and of those involved in the collection of information for the team members). This was particularly evident on those assignments where the original objective of the project was to use the Framework as a means of examining and updating the existing enterprise plan. Applying the Framework inherently expanded the planning team's understanding of the external and internal environmental factors they had to take into account in the planning process: it resulted in holistic thinking.

For example, in a client assignment with one of the seven sisters oil companies, we were engaged to assist the Chief Information Officer to reevaluate and, subsequently, update the IT function's strategy and, if appropriate, determine how the IT function should be restructured. The meetings held as part of Activity 1.0, organizing your resources, resulted in those involved thinking about the existing environment as well as discussing in detail the activities that are part of the Framework and their interrelatedness; that is, they began to look at the organization to figure out what had to be done, why it should be done, and who would be asked to do it. The purpose of this discussion was not only to identify the players and the time frame, but also to get everyone thinking in a more holistic fashion—looking at the whole organization.

In fact, it opened the team to looking at the impact of strategy and structure on their operations; it brought them out of the isolation of looking at their problem solely from their own perspective. At the end of the day, the team realized that to reevaluate their strategy and structure, they had to gain a better understanding of the business groups they were supporting; that is, they realized that to plan effectively they would have to better understand their users, the business strategy they had, the structure of their organizations, and their cultures. Without such an understanding, they could not develop an IT strategy and structure that would be aligned with and supportive of them. The team realized that they had to consider the broader picture in order to do their jobs effectively.

THE FACILITATOR

In most circumstances, we recommend that a facilitator, either a member of the firm or an external consultant, lead the planning team in conducting the planning process as well as in analyzing the information that is collected. In either case, the requisite core skills to conduct the facilitation process will be the same.[6] If an internal facilitator is used, the facilitator should be someone highly regarded by the planning team members but not a member of the team; the facilitator should know the business and the culture of the company; the facilitator cannot be viewed or perceived as judgmental; the facilitator should be a hard worker, have the capability to pay attention to details, be able to discern the key issues embedded in a complex set of discussions, and have the patience of a saint. (Someone who has been with the company for a long time and reached a senior but not leadership level or someone newly retired might be an appropriate choice.)

The facilitator should guide the group and keep it focused on the objectives. If the facilitator is not careful, the discussion will be taken over by the most vocal or highest-ranking executive on the planning team or the discussion will tend to drift toward a focus on easy issues. The facilitator must draw people out, ensuring that everyone is participating and providing input and that the discussion moves from issue to issue. In many cases, contradictory views and opinions will emerge. When this happens, the role of the facilitator is to record these contradictions and lead the group to an acceptable reconciliation of differences, which is easier said than done. Uncovering contradictions is an important part of understanding and analyzing the business.

As with any group of individuals trying to take an objective, introspective view, issues of pride and turf will emerge. The facilitator must have the requisite skill sets to understand the issues as well as the individual viewpoints and negotiate a settlement while keeping sight of the group's goals and maintaining objectivity. For example, during the facilitation of a focus session at a public utility in the Midwest to determine the final recommendations for a corporate-wide IT strategy, a conflict arose among two of the task force members. After examining the pros and cons of mainframe versus client server computer platforms (two very different approaches to dealing with a company's technology framework), the task force members had concluded that the best option for the company was moving to a client server platform. However, when it came time to formalize a recommendation, one of the team members refused to go along. As arguments and accusations flew across the room, it became apparent to the facilitator that the issue was not only that the person who refused to go along simply preferred mainframes (because of her expertise and the control that kind of system gives to those in charge of technology). Switching would require her unit to make a major investment and adversely affect her bottom line (the return on investment on the mainframe was calculated for a multiyear period). By suggesting the recommendation include timing of the implementation of the switch in technology, and putting her unit last on the list to be switched (this kind of switch takes a number of years), her most recent investment would pay off.

At the end of the day, the facilitator must ensure that all of the planning team members have bought into the final analysis; that is, they all have to agree that the analysis, whether the results are good, bad, or indifferent, is a realistic assessment of the organization.

In some circumstances, the company may elect to have an external consultant act as the facilitator. Turning to an outsider is particularly useful if the firm wants to have third-party input and guidance in addition to a facilitation process. An external consultant is one means of assisting group members to think out of the box or to challenge their assumptions and beliefs. An external consultant also has the objectivity needed for this type of analysis.

In many cases, the external consultant also can provide competitive insights (but not inside information because consultants guarantee their clients confidentiality) based upon experiences with other companies within the same industry that an internal facilitator might not have. In addition, an external consultant can also bring experiences from other industries in terms of presenting different views of the same problem. Again, the choice of internal or external facilitators depends upon the planning team members and what they want out of the internal evaluation; however, the best means to attain an objective evaluation is through external parties willing to challenge planning team members without fear of damaging their own careers.

The facilitator must prepare a detailed agenda for the working sessions. The difficulties inherent in running meetings in which the goal is to get everybody to participate are such that the facilitator cannot wing it—having a thorough understanding of the organization and its culture is critical because the facilitator's job includes having enough information to be able to introduce ideas whenever the group begins to falter.

Moreover, the kind of brainstorming that leads to thinking out of the box is only possible within a structure that allows everyone to feel free to participate, where the quietest are encouraged to speak, and where no one is allowed to belittle another's ideas. Thus, the facilitator must be quick to repair damage, saying, for example, after someone shoots down an idea that an aspect of it is well worth exploring.

The facilitator is also responsible for moving the session along, keeping in mind the fact that the time of the planning team is valuable. The agenda must set forth specific goals or targets to accomplish in a given time frame. If the members of the planning team do not come away from these sessions with a feeling that they learned something or that there was value added in the process, it will be extremely difficult to persuade them to continue to devote time to such meetings. In order to ensure the success of the planning project, the facilitator must have an appropriate administrative infrastructure in place. Depending on the size of the company, the number of people involved, and the scope of the project, this can range from a room to work in with a single point person from the company assigned to help arrange schedules, to team offices, computer support, company librarian on call, and a team from the company assigned to work with the facilitator.

As the planning process enters the later activities that comprise the Framework—change management and monitoring and evaluation—different facilitators will probably be needed. In the change management phase, for example, if an internal leader is chosen, the best choice would be a senior manager in the human resources or communications area. The general skill sets—ability to work with people, nonjudgmental approach, being perceived as above the fray—will be similar to those of the earlier planning process facilitator. Here, however, specific knowledge about the parameters of jobs, reward systems, psychological insights, and knowledge of educational techniques is extremely valuable, as is an ability to use internal communications to reach people with messages that will ease change. For the monitoring and evaluation process, the facilitator needs to have an understanding of business processes and costing, as well as general management skill sets. In either or both instances, a consultant may be the best choice.

LOCATION

The planning process is, by tradition, a yearly off-site ritual driven more by the need to spend time arguing through budgeting issues than by the need to rethink the competitive position of the company. (Although planning should also include budgeting, in most companies planning is merely budgeting, because it does not take into account the nonfinancial external events that may impact the industrial sector or the direct competitors within the industry. Even worse, the planning process may be nothing more than rolling forward, in a linear fashion, another year in an ongoing multiyear plan [that is, adding to the original projection of profits for each upcoming fiscal year increases for inflation and growth]. In these cases, today is an extension of yesterday, and tomorrow is a linear extension of today. In the environment of the 1990s, this type of planning process, and the plan it produces, is likely to prove worse than useless.)

The off-site tradition is valuable. During the planning process, some time will be needed for intensive analyses of the information that has been collected by the members of the task forces. This analysis is most likely to succeed if it is conducted during a two- to three-day session (depending upon the experience curve and culture of the firm with respect to the planning process, it could take more than one of these sessions), preferably at an off-site location so that the team can work without the interruptions and daily pressures of the office.

Holding the meetings off site allows the planning team members to focus on the large body of material they must understand and internalize in the course of performing the evaluation. Bringing together the key players also allows you to augment the body of information collected because it provides an opportunity for senior managers, who usually do not spend a large amount of time together as a group, to talk about the business, their markets, and their competition, and thus learn a great deal about the business as a whole.

SPECIAL TASK FORCES

After the planning team members are selected, they should set up task forces to do some of the research and interviewing necessary to gather enough information about their company and their competitors to do the job of planning thoroughly. One task force, usually guided by the facilitator, should conduct interviews (and perhaps send out questionnaires) to collect information from senior management and perhaps a level below. At the same time, a task force should be set up by the planning team to gather information about the external environment. The goal of some of the members of the task force charged with exploring the external world is to gather pertinent information about the social, economic, political, and technological factors that may have an impact on the business. Other members of that task force should be preparing an analysis of the industrial sector in which the company competes and an analysis of its direct competitors. (These techniques—and the need for doing this concurrently—will be described in detail in the next two chapters.)

The task force involved in this effort has to understand what the information means in order to use it. The intent of the analysis is not to collect every possible bit of available information, but rather to develop an awareness of the factors that could realistically affect the organization's competitiveness in the marketplace. The task force members involved in the external analysis are the seed for ongoing groups that will help create the open, continual learning environment that is necessary to understanding subsequent changes—and to accepting the fact that changes will keep happening.

ANALYTICAL TOOLS

As noted, collecting information from senior management for an internal analysis (Activity 3.0) may involve, in addition to interviews, survey tools. Personal interviews bring out the intangibles that cannot be garnered from a written response—the meaning behind the responses. At the same time, people tend to be very cautious in an interview setting and often respond in the most noncommittal way possible. The survey tools thus supplement the interviews. In fact, checking one against the other provides the most comprehensive picture possible. (This kind of interactive analysis technique will also be used later in the benchmarking that is done as part of the monitoring and evaluation process.)

Once the resources are acquired and everyone agrees that the process can begin, the planning team should meet to review the task forces' assignments and time frame for doing them and discuss the kinds of problems that are likely to occur. By anticipating the problems, the team will be able to circumvent most of them. Those that pop up unexpectedly will be fewer—and if they keep in mind that unexpected problems will emerge, they will be better able to deal with them when they do: holistic planning in a microcosm.

THE MEANS TO THE END

The planning process is a means to the end, which is the development, implementation, and evaluation of the new enterprise plan. In effect, the end is the commitment to a dynamic process of adjustment and review. It is not a finish line that entitles you to rest after you cross it.

For the planning process to be successful, a number of critical success factors must be met. (A detailed discussion of how to discover an organization's true critical success factors, or CSFs, appears in Chapter 5.) At a minimum, a necessary set of CSFs for planning are the following:

- Commitment of senior management to the planning process. The planning process can be a difficult, exhausting, and frustrating experience. At times, progress can best be described as glacial. All too often, senior management will vigorously participate in the initial stages of the process, but will lose interest because of the amount of time and effort required to complete it or because there is a need to put out fires elsewhere in the organization. The temptation for distraction is enormous. The problem is that for planning to be successful, there must be a visible demonstration of the commitment and involvement of senior management throughout the process; without it, the planning process will not be viewed as relevant by the other members of the planning team.

◆   Involvement of senior management in the planning process. In addi-
    tion to being committed to the planning process, senior managers
    must be involved in the process. Their input is critical in a number of
    areas: they are responsible for setting and articulating the future direc-
    tion of the firm (indeed, senior management is the only group
    empowered to perform this task); they are responsible for defining
    and developing the enterprise goals; but more important, they are
    the individuals who can articulate the assumptions and beliefs that
    underlie the CSFs and tactics of the organization.

◆   The mission and strategic direction of the organization formulated
    during the planning process must be shared by all planning team
    members. The planning team should collectively develop, share in,
    and ultimately be driven by the same set of values and beliefs; they
    must all be reading from the same page of the book. A shared set of
    values and beliefs literally bond the company. If these values and
    beliefs are not shared, or if the planning team does not buy into these
    common values, the plan will not be successfully implemented: divi-
    siveness between and among those who do not share the common
    set of values will, at best, significantly slow the implementation of
    the plan, and will, at worst, prevent its adoption. The value of having
    senior managers formally and constantly communicating the vision
    and direction of the company should not be underestimated.
        Moreover, it is senior management that is the primary vehicle for
    communicating the plan to operating management and operating
    personnel within the organization. This communication process is
    essential if the organization is to think holistically instead of taking
    the conventional wisdom view of the organization as a set of func-
    tional silos—that is, a view of the firm focused on each manager's
    functional responsibility. The concept of thinking across functional
    areas will be a critical element for the survival of the company dur-
    ing the 1990s.

◆   The planning process should be done within a framework that
    includes dates for deliverables. There should be a structured mecha-
    nism for conducting the planning process—structure is necessary to
    define the goals that must be achieved. The planning process should
    not be viewed as an informal gathering that, inherently, will yield
    results because the members of the planning team are bright, articu-
    late, know the business, and can intuitively achieve a set of goals
    without some structure. It simply doesn't work that way in practice:
    a framework not only assists the planning team in focusing on a set of
    goals, but also provides a structure to ensure that the critical elements
    necessary for plan development are not overlooked and that the
    process does not drag out over too long a time.

◆   Planners should also be implementors. The members of the planning
    team should be the doers of the company. The individuals involved
    in the planning process should be the senior managers who are
    responsible and accountable for implementing the plan: they are the
    stakeholders of the plan. All too often, planning is relegated to a staff
    function whose purpose is to develop the plan and budget for the
    business. Although they play an important role in terms of collect-
    ing and developing the needed information for preparation of the
    plan, ultimately they are not the individuals who will be responsible
    for its implementation. In circumstances such as this, the realities of
    executing the plan from an operational perspective are missing.
    Eventually, the planning process will end and the real work of imple-
    menting the plan within the organization will begin.

◆   Planners should be strategic thinkers—people who have already
    demonstrated their ability to think beyond tomorrow. This does not
    imply that only strategic thinkers should be members of the planning
    process, because the team also needs members whose primary com-
    petence is their understanding of the day-to-day realities at an oper-
    ational level. Achieving this balance between operational considera-
    tions and strategic thinking is a critical element in successfully
    implementing the defined enterprise plan.

◆   The plan must be achievable. The plan must not only be logical but
    also practical: it must consider the business's resources, time frame,
    and culture. All too often, the planning team will get carried away
    and overestimate the business's resources. Without a realistic assess-
    ment of the strengths, weaknesses, and core competencies of the orga-
    nization, an apparently logical plan will be impossible to execute. The
    culture may not buy into the plan, because "it's not the way things are
    done" in the company; the firm may have the right number of people
    to implement the plan, but they may not have the right skills neces-
    sary for executing it; the time frame for implementation may be longer
    than the window of opportunity within the marketplace—in other
    words, if it can't be put into place fairly quickly, it may not be worth
    doing; and the funds necessary to implement the plan may be more
    than the organization can afford to spend.

◆   There must be only one plan. The plan that emerges from the planning
    process must articulate and define the mission and strategic direction
    for the entire organization. Although there can be multiple plans and
    strategies for different business units within the firm, there can be only
    one statement of strategic direction; the other plans should be subor-
    dinate to, as well as supportive of, that strategic direction. In some
    instances, a plan may be developed as a group activity, only to be

ignored as each business unit or group develops its own way of doing business. Under these circumstances, there can be no cohesive view or driving force that binds the firm to a common vision, set of beliefs, or values. The result will be a lack of focus and direction, and a mismatch of resources as the organization attempts to achieve its goals.

- The company must be able to change the manner in which it conducts business. If the company's environment (that is, its values, beliefs, and the way it operates) cannot adapt to the plan, implementation will never take place. Establishing a new strategic direction is difficult enough—overcoming the inertia of a company is even more daunting. Changing what the company does for a living or changing how it does it requires changing the values and beliefs of the company, the required skill sets of employees, and the way the business is managed. Ensuring that these kinds of changes occur often requires establishing a change management program that can transform the values, beliefs, and behavior of people—the way the company does business today—to a new set of behaviors. The beginning of the change program lies in the learning done by the members of the planning team, which makes them the visionaries needed to begin the change management process. (The way change can be brought to an organization is explained in Chapter 13.)

- The last planning critical success factor is a well-defined measurement program. Mechanisms are needed to monitor, control, evaluate, and, if necessary, change the direction of the organization as the plan is implemented. Not all things will proceed according to the plan—no matter how well thought out the plan may be. Social, political, economic, or technological changes outside the control of the organization may occur. Once the impact of such additional changes are evaluated, the organization may have to change how it intends to implement the plan currently being put in place.

  Another aspect of a plan evaluation program is the establishment of performance measures. In many instances, the planning team members will ignore this, arguing that they inherently know what the criteria are for success. In other cases, they may argue that some parameters allow only for soft measures, especially in areas such as quality improvement. For example, the typical response of senior management in setting quality improvement performance measures is: "I'll know how much quality has improved when I see it." But quality can be measured in a number of ways: customer surveys conducted over a specified time period to measure how customer sales and service representatives treat customer inquiries or how they handle customer complaints; a more obvious measure is the number of product complaints received over a specified time frame; and some performance measures may even include minor items such as the number of times the telephone rang before being answered.

Sometimes the planning team knows what should be measured, but has to figure out how to define the metrics or values to be used in the measurement process. Without an evaluation program and rational performance measures, attempting to assess the implementation of the enterprise plan is analogous to driving forward at ninety miles an hour by looking in your rear view mirror to see where you have been.

CONCLUSION

Now that you have organized and put in place the resources you need for your journey, it is time to execute the remaining activities that make up the Dynamic Planning Framework. However, keep in mind that many of the subsequent activities in our Framework take place concurrently. For example, while the planning team is busy exploring the world in which the organization lives (Activity 2.0, external analysis), another group is doing the work that goes into determining what senior management believes the company is and can be (Activity 3.0, internal analysis). These two activities are done at the same time, although the next chapter will concentrate on the external analysis. And after each is completed, the results of each is measured against the other in a step that begins the search for solutions. The fact that many activities are done concurrently is sometimes lost in reading a book where what must be done is related one step at a time; in real time, it is much easier to deal with concurrency.

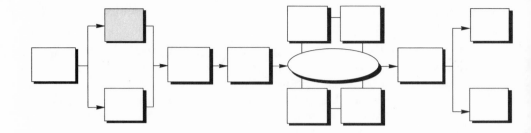

CHAPTER 4

THE EXTERNAL ANALYSIS

There is no magic in planning. . . . More than goals, materials or objectives, and far more than any elaborate or simple concepts, planning, to be effective, requires context.

Max Dublin[1]

In order to get a good picture of your organization and its place in the world, two very different types of examinations have to be done concurrently. As part of Activity 1.0, organizing your resources, a planning team was established that, in turn, set up task forces to do two things: determine your company's place in the universe (the external analysis, Activity 2.0) and gather executive insights (the internal analysis, Activity 3.0). One task force will examine your firm in terms of the world in which you live; the industrial sector you are a part of; and your direct competitors. At the same time, the other task force will be looking at what those who lead the organization are doing and why they are doing it; that is, the task force will be interviewing the leaders to determine the company's goals, critical success factors, and assumptions (all of which will be described in the next chapter).

This part of Dynamic Planning, which is aimed at identifying the problems your organization faces, centers on Activities 2.0 and 3.0 of the Framework, the activities that comprise the Environmental Analysis (see Figure 2.4). The picture of the external world will be folded together with the information the task force charged with the internal analysis is building as it conducts senior management interviews in a process known as gap analysis (that is, the reconciliation of the differences between what your company's executives think the company is and what a more objective outside view perceives it to be). The gap analysis provides the material for the position paper, the initial step in that part of the conceptual model in which the search for solutions takes place.

Some of the material in this and the next chapter will be very familiar to some, less familiar to others. It is important, however, to establish a common vocabulary early in the Dynamic Planning process, thereby ensuring understanding between the business and information technology sides when the time comes to perform the in-depth analyses of the options available to an organization using the Strategic Alignment Model. Moreover, it is important to remember that the members of the task force doing the external analysis will become the seed of an ongoing group of information collectors.

DISCOVERING YOUR PLACE IN THE UNIVERSE

The first step in the external analysis is looking at the world around you in order to become, as Edward A. Filene, a noted American retailer and philanthropist, said, "something of a prophet . . . cultivating the habit of looking ahead to be sure that [you] have taken into account all of the factors that will determine future conditions."[2] That statement was made in 1926—before Lindbergh, before Bretton Woods, before World War II. How much more important is an awareness of technological, political, economic, and social possibilities today when global and economic downturns affect your ability to sell your products and finance growth; when regulatory changes due to environmental concerns make it necessary for you to find new—and more expensive—ways to package and ship products; and when events in foreign countries often make it dangerous to site plants close to natural resources?

As you think about the answers to these questions, keep in mind that it was almost fifty years between the introduction of typewriters to offices to the large-scale introduction of the electric typewriter—and then just twenty-five years to having computers on almost every desk. Moreover, the differences that resulted from each development were even more dramatic than the compression in time between the introduction of these technologies. The introduction of the electric typewriter increased typing speed; the introduction of computers changed the shape of business.

THE FIRST STEP
ORDERING YOUR UNIVERSE

Understanding the world, the industrial sector in which your business fits, and your competitors, as well as the time compression that is now a norm, are necessary to Dynamic Planning. After all, no company does what it does in isolation. The question is, How much and what kind of attention do you have to pay to outside events? Of course, you cannot decide to watch everything—but neither can you afford to ignore everything.

Keep in mind that the goal is not to watch the world to decide what the future holds. Those who think that there are only one or two possible scenarios for the future are in as much trouble as those who think the future will be the same as the past. The problem with this kind of scenario building is that those who believe that the future is likely to be one thing or another, based on major events or developments they can imagine, tend to put on blinders to what is happening around them in their focus on building toward the future they have decided is most likely.

Such a use of scenario planning creates a narrower focus than we are advocating. In *Competitive Advantage*, Michael Porter says, "Scenarios are not needed every year for every business unit. They are necessary only when significant uncertainties are present in an industry."[3] The key phrase is "when significant uncertainties are present." Today, uncertainty is a given. Nothing is static for long. Change is constant and inevitable. But perhaps more important is that the things that cause change look so small. Chaos theory explains that "tiny differences in input . . . [can] quickly become overwhelming differences in output—a phenomenon given the name 'sensitive dependence on initial conditions.' In weather, for example, this translates into what is only half-jokingly known as the Butterfly Effect—the notion that a butterfly stirring the air today in Peking can transform storm systems next month in New York."[4]

The enormous number of uncertainties becomes clear when you begin to keep an eye on world, national, local, and business-specific events. It is important to do this because an awareness that change is all around you and that you will have to deal with it—and that others have successfully done so—makes it far less likely that you will be paralyzed by change. Moreover, by studying the effects of different types of events, you can begin to draw analogies between events and their likely effects; that is, you can develop anticipatory capability. By that we mean the capacity to have some idea of which developments in the world outside your organization may affect you while you still have time to develop contingency plans for dealing with them. That takes an extraordinary organizational mindset, one that encourages the study of the world, is willing to listen to warnings, and supports the education and growth of employees to prepare them for what might happen.

In *The Fifth Discipline*, Peter Senge writes that "organizations learn only through individuals who learn. . . . A small number of organizational leaders are recognizing the radical rethinking of corporate philosophy which a commitment to individual learning requires."[5] The result of this mindset is flexibility, a willingness to think about the unknown and to accept the fact that change is not a threat, but an opportunity.

And yet given the enormous scope of the available information about the world, clearly everything cannot be examined. To make it easier, we have developed a framework that will help you analyze the relevant aspects of what you see and hear and read. The framework, which will be described in detail later, is a formal way of dealing with the elements of the external analysis shown in the Environmental Analysis (Figure 2.4). Remember that your firm works within a global environment, an industrial sector, and faces direct competition. It also has its own body of rules, regulations, and values that it abides by—its mission. Each of these elements impacts on the others and in turn is impacted upon by them. A world event such as the military action in the Persian Gulf may, at first sight, have little to do with your business; that is, unless you are located in a small town near a military base and many of your people are reservists, or unless your business relies on oil supplies, or unless you are engaged in a business that is affected by people's fear of terrorism. In the same way, you must look beyond the obvious every time there is a major sea change in the world. The end of the cold war did much more than stop the threat of a Soviet nuclear attack. By reducing the need for a large standing army, the cold war's end created an enormous number of layoffs in the defense industry, worsening an already poor national economy. The cuts in the military research and development budget also will have long-term effects on American civilian technological developments if the research into, say, aeronautics, isn't continued. It will also, for example, affect the Turkish economy; Germany depended on Turkish guest workers to supplement its small workforce. The reunification of the two Germanys means that guest workers aren't needed as the underemployed Eastern Germans fill the jobs once filled by Turkish workers.

Of course, it is somewhat easier to see how events in your industrial sector could impact your business. For example, events in any number of areas could affect a company involved in transportation directly or indirectly. If the government decided that it was going to subsidize rail service in order to save the railroads, an airline or a car rental company could lose a great deal of business to lower rail fares. In the same way, if a new airport was built in a region that couldn't handle large aircraft before, rail and other transportation to that region would be adversely affected. Businesses watch for these kinds of developments to try to counter them, say, by joining a lobby against the airport, or to promote them, say, by advertising the merits of an airport in terms of the extra jobs it will bring into the community.

Events in the competitive environment in which you function are the most obvious source of interest and concern. A recent case involving Boeing demonstrates how critical it is to keep up with developments. Boeing, which stays attuned to developments in technology and, indeed, supports a considerable amount of R&D, turned to a new technology to develop its latest plane, the Boeing 777. The computing technology involved using three-dimensional design workstations and putting all of the information about the new plane in one database that could be accessed by all designers in eighteen different locations. The computing technology that was put in place makes possible designing the plane on a computer screen, thus making the Boeing 777 the first "paperless" airplane. The technology makes it unnecessary to build a full-scale mockup of the plane—thus saving significant cost, but more importantly, saving the time to certify and deliver the aircraft. Boeing reports that "even though the 777 will not begin carrying passengers for almost four years, it is getting substantial orders."[6] Boeing's competitors, engaged in designing a similar plane, are finding out that Boeing's unexpected shift in technology, which is allowing it to promise earlier delivery, is costing them market share.[7]

But looking at each of these and how it impacts you can be simplified somewhat by learning to watch them in a different sequence. For example, you can look at a development in the industrial sector and see what it stemmed from; that is, you can see if an event in the external world caused it. This provides information about which events in the external world might affect you in the future and allows you to prepare for changes before your competitors even realize that something is happening. Examining one aspect of the communications sector, publishing, for example, can be very useful. Magazines and newspapers suddenly found sales and advertising revenues slipping dramatically in the early 1990s. The trend followed the general fall in business revenues and unemployment. (When companies are having trouble with their bottom line, they advertise less, and people who are out of work don't buy as many magazines or papers.) The last group in the communications sector to be affected by the problem turned out to be book publishers. Book returns in the summer of 1991 were far heavier than usual. (Stores and distributors can return unsold copies of books to publishers for several months after they accept them.) A look at developments in their industrial sector—communications—should have alerted publishers to the fact that sales might be heavily affected. But they were so taken with the stories about the loss of advertising revenues that they did not pay enough attention to the fact that magazines and newspapers were hurting because sales, as well as advertising, were falling. If they had paid more attention to that aspect of the problem, they might have decided to advertise more, since they could get advertising space at a lower cost given the problem magazines and newspapers were facing.

THE INTERACTIVE FORCES MODEL (IFM)
PATTERNS OF IMPACT

The Interactive Forces Model (see Figure 4.1) clarifies the interaction of these concurrent forces; it is a model rather than a methodology because a less structured approach to analysis is critical to innovative thinking.

Flux: The Global and National Environment

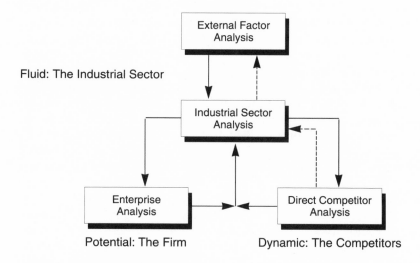

Fluid: The Industrial Sector

Figure 4.1. Interactive Forces Model
© 1993 B. Goldberg and J. G. Sifonis

Indeed, rigid processes restrict and restrain imagination and creative thinking. Coping with a turbulent environment requires thinking about things in new and different ways, combining bits and pieces of information to determine evolving patterns, noticing odd things that may signal something, thinking abstractly and broadly, all of which are the antithesis of a systematic and formal set of directions.

The Model addresses the interaction of concurrent forces; it should be reviewed, thought about, internalized—and tucked somewhere in the back of your mind. Do not treat the Interactive Forces Model as a bible. The IFM is a framework for thinking about thinking—a way of pointing out possibilities and making you think. As you encounter information, you should study it, looking for parallels, connections, and analogies. The key to the kind of thinking that is at the heart of Dynamic Planning is freedom within context.

The IFM asks you to think of the world in which your business functions as being composed of four boxes:

◆ *External Factors.* The first box represents the global and national environment. This box is the external world, the place where large events occur and major policy changes take place—wars, political upheaval, famine, elections, laws and regulations, advanced R&D, space travel, educational systems, taxes. This is an environment in *flux*, one in

which changes on a massive scale take place: the end of the cold war
and the dissolution of the Soviet Union as we knew it, the development of superconductivity, the globalization of financial services, the
development of new trading blocs, the failures of America's public
educational system, particularly in large urban areas. It is an environment in which you and your firm are, for the most part, small
players with limited power. You have little effect on that environment, and its effects on you are usually long term. Moreover, external
factors tend to impact everyone in your sector equally. As a result, the
only way to gain a competitive advantage in this box is to recognize
the likely effects of changes before your competitors do and put in
place plans to overcome those effects.

♦   *Industrial Sector.* The second box represents the industrial sector in
    which you operate. It is a *fluid* environment. Changes take place in an
    industrial sector as a result of changes in the world—say, deregula-
    tion as a result of an industrial policy decision or energy shortages
    because of a war—but they are less random and usually less sud-
    den than changes that occur in the external world. Developments in
    the industrial sector can also have some impact on the world; for
    example, developments in computers can change the way informa-
    tion moves globally. The next set of impacts are those within the
    industrial sector on the various groups of companies that make up
    the sector. Changes that directly impact a group of companies (direct
    competitors) within the sector may have indirect effects on other
    groups of companies within that sector; for example, a shortage of
    crude oil supplies among oil companies may favorably affect natur-
    al gas companies in the energy sector in which they both play. Given
    the speed with which developments take place today, the time com-
    pression that has affected our world, the more you can anticipate
    what external events are going to affect your industrial sector, the
    more you can do to take advantage of them before your competi-
    tors, both direct and indirect, do.

♦   *Direct Competitors.* The third box represents your direct competitors.
    Here, the environment is very *dynamic*, marked by jockeying for posi-
    tion. You need to know what your competitors are doing in order to
    prevent them from grabbing too great a share of the pie. These are the
    firms you fight against for market share. You try to match their prod-
    ucts and services and develop long-term customer commitment to
    ensure that if you temporarily fall behind, you have a chance to catch
    up. It is a game of positioning, advertising, marketing—and, of
    course, price. In addition, it involves providing customer satisfaction
    and meeting and even anticipating customer expectations.

♦   *Enterprise.* This is your firm and its current and *potential* place in the
    world. If you plan intelligently, you will have the capability to move
    from where you are today to a point in the future that provides your
    organization with a significant competitive advantage. Looking at
    the IFM, it should become clear that you and your competitors will
    usually affect one another, and that together, you can affect what hap-
    pens in your industrial sector. Consider the baseball analogy:
    Geography helps you the most, but that loyalty is tested when, for
    example, a major network broadcasts the games of the teams vying
    for the lead in your division at the same hour a game your team,
    which is not in contention, is playing is being broadcast on a local
    channel. At the same time, as part of the Major League Baseball
    Association, you are vying for loyalty to your sport over others in the
    industrial sector known as sports/entertainment, striving to gain an
    image advantage over another sport by publicizing yourself as the
    national pastime or the family game.

   These are the usual interactions among the four boxes, but not the only
ones. Things can change when, for example, a single firm achieves dominance (such as IBM in the 1960s and 1970s) or when a sector has unusual
dominance that gives it a chance of impacting heavily on the external
world. In the latter case, the government often intervenes, as it did in the
AT&T antitrust case. In these circumstances, it is government's responsibility to ensure that the influence of companies does not supersede the
national responsibility for ensuring economic and social order.

   Now that you understand what you need to be aware of and why, you
can explore how to look at these things, including some of the tools you
will need. But remember to approach all this with an open mind. Violate
the rules, follow your instincts, and use your imagination. If you have
internalized the information, you are likely to include the right material,
but not be limited to what someone else has told you is right.

THE WHY OF THE EXTERNAL ANALYSIS

Everything that happens in the world affects your business in some
way—even those things that seem most removed from your concerns.
For example, absenteeism increases because of inclement weather or the
opening day of the baseball season. A global economic downturn will
affect even such local businesses as restaurants; people disturbed by
fears of a recession hesitate to spend as freely on such nonnecessities as
eating out. A strengthening of the environmental movement may
increase energy costs. A change in immigration law may make it easier
to hire low-level service workers, or it may increase taxes in order to

cover welfare payments to immigrants until they get established—or it may do both those and more depending on the nature of the immigration bill. Foreign policy has repercussions: sanctions against trade with particular countries may make raw materials more expensive or it may cut off markets. Changes in other countries have enormous effects: an end to Soviet control in Eastern Europe may create a new trading bloc and place for investment, or it may end up creating a massive new competitor along the lines of a Japan or Germany. A political change can have enormous effects that vary over time: higher taxes to promote social programs may hurt at first by cutting the amount of money people have to spend. But if it ends up producing a better educated workforce and fewer people on welfare, it could have the opposite effect in the long term. Demographic changes have impacts: Gerber baby foods reacted to the baby boom by expanding, then when the baby bust followed, it diversified into other areas, such as life insurance, that allowed it to take advantage of its image as a protector of the young by focusing its advertising of the new product on its value as a means of protecting the child in case something happened to a parent. As a result, it quickly gained a foothold in the very competitive insurance industry, which not only ensured its survival, but led to its growth.

PERFORMING AN EXTERNAL ANALYSIS

How can you deal with changes? How can you know what effects changes will have on your company? The simple answer is, There is no way to know exactly what will happen and exactly how it will impact your business.[8] But you can spot trends and try to determine what effects those are likely to have on your company. The importance of looking outward was realized early in the Industrial Age. For example, in 1919, Edward Filene set up the Twentieth Century Fund, a not-for-profit research foundation that would help him and other businesspeople "discover and understand *all* the forces, local, national, and international, that promised to react upon and determine future business conditions."[9]

The way in which you "discover . . . the forces" at work can—and should—vary. It is important to find a happy balance between what you need to know, want to know, and can afford to spend. There are a number of ways to approach this problem. You can hire an outside organization to do formal scenario planning; you can put a firm that does specific kinds of forecasting on retainer; you can hold regular conferences with experts you hire for that purpose or with board members selected for their general expertise; you can employ someone to collect and disperse information (a superlibrarian/thinker); you can set up teams of employees to do the job. Some combination of these is probably the most efficient and expedient way to handle the problem. Deciding which way to go is one of the tasks that, when implementing the Framework, is the responsibility of the planning team that was set up as part of Activity 1.0.

The tasks involved in performing the external analysis should not tie up people in endless meetings. The job of collecting information is ongoing and should be secondary to doing the business of your business, but it must not be ignored. The value of performing the tasks is enormous: doing them broadens your view of the world and your firm, opening the door to possibilities. They help you think without the usual constraints that keep businesses from reaching their full potential.

CHOOSING THE BEST METHOD

The first step is determining what level of knowledge your company needs, given that the rapid changes and ever-increasing complexity and uncertainty that have marked the past decade are likely to continue. Anticipating the trends that will affect your company tomorrow requires not only information but a new kind of thinking. John Clendenin, Chief Executive Officer of Bellsouth Company, warned his employees in a special message in 1987 that "straight-line projections won't work anymore. We've got to do a better job of anticipating the outside influences—competitive, regulatory, etc.—that five and ten years out will disrupt the linear projections we've all been accustomed to."

The first step is determining what questions you want to be able to answer. For example, if you want to set up a manufacturing plant in a foreign country, you need to know what is likely to happen there. What new problems, say, with energy sources, are likely to develop? What human resources are likely to be available, and what will it take to attract and train them? Figuring out what will affect you helps you to decide what information to track. The external analysis task force should devote a few sessions to thinking through the questions your company needs answered and then rank them in order of importance. The list should be built in a meeting with the task force members conducting the internal analysis; as they work through interviews with senior management they will be uncovering what kinds of information those executives depend on for their decisionmaking. That information must be included in the list. The list can then be presented to the planning team members for use in deciding what trends will be followed over time. They have to make choices depending on resources (human and money) and the eventual direction they decide to move in.

The decisions made now are important because they will determine to a large extent the shape of the ongoing "future watch" task forces that will be set up to ensure that you don't lose ground in the future. These ongoing activities will be discussed further in Chapter 12, which explores monitoring and evaluating within the Dynamic Planning Framework. The external world can be monitored in a number of different ways.

Employee Task Forces

This solution, the least expensive and most useful in terms of employee development, requires establishing an in-house task force charged with trend watching. The members of such an internal task force can discover a great deal at little cost—and in the process enrich their own knowledge and awareness of the world around them.

There are many ways for such groups to keep abreast of developments. If such a group is to succeed, however, its members must be selected carefully. Choose people with diverse interests and backgrounds. Provide them with a budget for materials, including subscriptions to important national and international papers, journals, and magazines. Also subscribe to a database, one that will allow access to a wide variety of specialized sources. In addition, encourage the members of the group to attend association meetings, seminars, and meetings held by expert groups. Encourage them to follow the work of think tanks, which tend to house many leading-edge thinkers.

For example, in 1980, an organization that required truck deliveries was contemplating moving a part of its business to New York City; it could have learned from a research report published by a think tank that, if something weren't done about the city's infrastructure, relocating to the city would not be advisable. (New York permanently closed a number of its bridges and is in the process of doing patchwork repairs on many others, making traffic in and out of the city more of a problem than ever before.) The cost of the report was less than ten dollars.

In 1983, organizations dependent on skilled employees could have discovered from three different reports that unless something were done quickly about the national education system, they would have problems finding skilled employees at all levels, especially entry levels. (These reports were issued by a presidential commission, the Carnegie Endowment, and the Twentieth Century Fund.) Although piecemeal attempts were made to do something as a result of these reports, no set of consistent, well-funded programs were put in place. Today, our educational problems have reached such massive proportions that some insurance companies, for example, have had to move their back offices to Ireland, where support staff with computer skills are available to handle the massive amounts of paperwork that have to be converted. Again, the cost of buying the publications was minuscule.

The work of the task force examining the external world soon gets down to a routine of scanning documents. For example, much specific information about companies is easily available from annual reports. In addition, your organization can get on mailing lists of agencies and think tanks that are likely to be looking at subjects that might affect your business. Read the publication summaries in the catalogs put out by these institutions. The catalogs of recent publications of university presses and publishers are very useful as well—they contain summaries of new books. Reading the book review sections of newspapers and magazines can also provide valuable information about emerging issues and trends.

If your task force is having a problem deciding where to start, there are experts who can be hired for a few days to help develop lists of what you need to track. (Keep in mind that a lot of the tracking that has to be done in the industrial sector can be done through the same materials and databases.)

HOLDING CONFERENCES

One way of dealing with these questions would be to bring together, on occasion, groups that, if large enough and selected from the right lists of specialists and asked the right series of questions, might derive some of the answers. But gathering such groups is very difficult and very expensive. However, a form of conference may be possible. If, for example, you wanted to track certain demographic trends, you might want to augment research you buy and/or conduct with yearly conferences of academics. For example, you might decide to invite professors from universities in your region to spend a day discussing these issues with senior staff.

HIRING SCENARIO PLANNERS

Another solution is turning to experts who can help you overcome the tendency to predict the future simply by extrapolating from the past, thus making it easier for you to deal with the uncertainty brought about by the discontinuities that mark the modern world. But hiring these experts is, as noted before, expensive. Scenario planners use complex technologies to show how a company and industry would behave in various situations. These technologies rely on a sequence of steps:

- Creation of a knowledge base through:
  - Interviews, dozens of interviews with international government and industry experts
  - Extensive research, in hundreds of books and articles

- Creation of thousands of possible scenarios using artificial intelligence-based technology to generate all the possible scenarios that a country or an industry can manifest

- Reduction of these thousands of scenarios to a manageable number (four or five) by applying a rigorous set of rules housed in the computer database pertaining to the specific industry or country being analyzed

This is an extremely complex, highly technical, and continual process involving consultants who know how to apply this kind of analysis—they examine your business and conduct both internal and external interviews that provide the information they need to add to the enormous data banks they have built up in order to develop your specific scenarios.[10] What you get are those scenarios, and then the advice you need to help you determine what the scenarios mean for your business and what steps you should take to be prepared for the future, much as a doctor tells you what to do, for example, to lower your risk of a heart attack. But unless you are a multinational company of huge dimensions, hiring people at this level may be too costly to even contemplate.

USING EXPERT ADVICE

There are many consultants who provide specific information, say, economic or political trends in various countries, in the form of advisory newsletters or specially tailored memos. You can subscribe to their services for a fixed fee. Many of these experts have had years of experience and built up enormous networks that they can draw on to provide advice that is not available to the general public.

HIRING AN INTERNAL EXPERT

A specialized librarian (law firms have been using law librarians for this kind of help for years) can be the source of information about future trends. It is useful to have such an individual in the organization, but it is economical only if there is enough other work to keep the person occupied. Since most organizations do not need a full-time person of this caliber on staff, a part-time or free-lance arrangement may be useful.

Each of the above has an additional down side; your employees do not receive the benefit of learning that change is constant and inevitable. Having employees do this work in a team that crosses functional and hierarchical lines helps open the organization to the changes that are bound to take place.

TAILORING THE PROCESS TO YOUR ORGANIZATION

You can adopt the various techniques outlined to develop a form of scenario planning that will meet your needs. As Peter Drucker has said, "The greatest danger in times of turbulence is not the turbulence; it is to act with yesterday's logic."[11] One of tomorrow's techniques involves the creation and then the analysis of an organization-specific vocabulary—a small dictionary of the words that appear over and over again when you and your direct competitors and the industrial sector in which you compete are described. For example, if you are in the fast food industry, *location, customer recognition, service, speed,* and *price* are words that are heard over and over again as you examine your sector and your competitors. As you go through each stage of the external analysis, it is important to add to your organization-specific vocabulary. (The way this vocabulary is used will be explained in the next chapter.)

INDUSTRIAL SECTOR ANALYSIS

An examination and analysis of the external environment helped you identify those factors that could impact the world in which you play. However, in most cases, the factors that you have identified may not be within your control—they are external factors that potentially drive and impact your industrial sector and are broader than you or any firm can, singularly, control. An examination and analysis of the industrial sector that your firm and its direct competitors are part of, on the other hand, yields those drivers (also known as triggers) that, in most cases, you, in conjunction with your direct competitors, can monitor and to some degree influence. (Remember that we are here talking about, say, automobile manufacturers in the transportation sector or baseball teams in the sports/entertainment sector.)

There are several key questions that have to be answered. How does a firm go about collecting the necessary information to understand the industrial sector it is a part of? Why is it important to understand the movement of the industrial sector? If obtained, can this understanding bring some form of advantage? And if the business does not have a mission statement or if it is trying to develop a new mission, how can the information and subsequent analysis assist in the development of the mission statement and, ultimately, a new enterprise plan?

Collecting and analyzing information about the industrial sector are key elements in understanding what is driving the sector. These factors or triggers are important because they provide valuable insight into the potential movements of competitors as well as an understanding of the direction in which the industrial sector is moving over time.

Much of the work involved in collecting information about the industrial sector is done at the same time information about the external world is collected. One difference is the nature of the material that has to be scanned. If your industrial sector is information and communication technology, you would, for example, add journals such as *Chief Information*

Officer, Datamation, Computerworld, and *Information Week* magazine to your reading list. When working on a database, you would broaden your search—by in a sense narrowing it. If you are in the sector known as leisure/travel you would track demographics for retirement and age and income. Now, even though you are a car rental company and for your direct competitor analysis track other car rental companies, you would also look at airline information, since it also affects your sector. For example, if you think an airline is likely to buy gates from another airline in a city where you are strong, you might want to establish a companion program (a variant of frequent flyer programs) in the local market with that airline before your competitors can.

You will also be doing a lot of very basic networking to obtain information about competitors in your industrial sector. This is more difficult than building similar contacts with direct competitors because it is harder to get to know the players. The information you can collect about the sector is, at best, imprecise. You are analyzing information that is based upon data that have been gathered and collected from annual reports, newspaper announcements of personnel changes, publicity releases, and various materials accessed through literature searches. What you are looking for is information to help identify and track the triggers that could change the directions of the sector.

At this point, remember to note those words that seem to be specific to the industrial sector, so you can add them to the organization-specific vocabulary you are building.

DIRECT COMPETITOR ASSESSMENT

When it comes to the analysis of your direct competitors, the research techniques are again similar. In addition, at this stage you should be collecting information about your competitors' critical success factors; emerging issues you are likely to face, many stemming from changes within the industry; market shifts; changing characteristics of the customer base; new entrants; the development of new or substitute products; shifts or changes in the assumptions of competitors, suppliers, or customers; and changes in the growth patterns of direct competitors.

Businesses can use a number of different mechanisms to collect and analyze information about direct competitors. They can establish study groups comprised of operational-level personnel who have contacts and deal with field-level issues on a daily basis. These individuals have useful insights into to competitors' products or services, changing trends in the customer base, as well as the very nature of how competition is changing. In many ways, they have a much better focus on the way competition is changing than senior management does—they are the people in the trenches who must compete on a daily basis.

Another useful mechanism for obtaining information is to attend seminars and be involved with industry organizations and associations. Information gained through these mechanisms could be very valuable. Meetings and networking often provide insights about changing landscapes. The object is to gain insight about changes in products and services offered, about advertising campaigns being launched, about new companies being formed—anything and everything that will directly affect your business.

THE TECHNOLOGY FACTOR

One of major changes in the structure and operations of businesses today, as noted earlier, is the new, critical role of information technology (IT) as a cornerstone of the business. Therefore, the task force charged with collecting information about the external world must pay particular attention to the use of technological developments by key competitors. Although getting precise information about what your competitors are doing in this area is almost impossible, and even general information is difficult to find, there are ways to gather insights that can keep the competition from advancing so far ahead of you that you cannot catch up.

Scan articles in IT-specific trade journals to see what general developments are taking place that might be useful to you or your competition, but remember that these are, at best, six months out of date. By the time such information is written about in, say, a case study, your competitor would have already gained an edge. But listening to what vendors have to offer, attending meetings of information technology groups, and scanning the academic journals will often yield valuable insights. For example, you may be able to learn that the Chief Information Officer just hired by the competition is known for jumping to leading edge technology while your organization prefers to stay with state-of-the-art technology; you may learn that your competitors have teamed up with a vendor to develop a proprietary system; you may be able to learn from an article that they are among the companies moving to a network of personal computers instead of remaining on mainframe computers. It is important to be inventive when looking for clues; for example, even though it may be impossible to get detailed information about what the competition is doing, a large number of help-wanted ads for computer experts may be an indication that they are placing increasing importance on IT as a competitive factor for success.

THE ADVANTAGES ACCRUED

With the capabilities that exist today to access the large number of publicly available databases, it is amazing how much information can be readily obtained. These data, if analyzed creatively and innovatively, can lead to insights that can help your business gain a competitive advantage. For example, if you analyze the growth patterns in your industry over time, you could determine when the market is likely to mature—that is, reach the point where, demographics and income levels aside, there is no likelihood of significant new growth. Potentially, this could give your company enough lead time to diversify or put in place new technologies, processes, products, or services to extend its life cycle. In other cases, understanding the shifts or changes in the customer base could give your firm an early warning of the changes it may have to make to compete in a new environment. In today's business arena, scanning the technology environment might lead to the early development and implementation of a technology that could give your firm an early mover advantage. These are some of the ways in which an in-depth analysis of the industrial sector and of your direct competitors, coupled with scanning the external environment, could lead to some form of competitive advantage.

THE FORMAL SUMMARY OF THE EXTERNAL ANALYSIS

The information gained from the in-depth external analysis (Activity 2.0 of the Dynamic Planning Framework) should be pulled together into a formal summary. This summary may be prepared by the facilitator, a consultant, or the task force itself. The summary will be used when the task forces responsible for the external and internal analyses formally meet each other to prepare the gap analysis for the planning team. (Again, keep in mind that the organization-specific vocabulary that is emerging in the course of this analysis will be formalized for presentation to the planning team at the same time the gap analysis is given to them.)

Concurrency is a key here. It is essential that what emerges from the external analysis has been checked periodically against the information garnered from the internal analysis. As you will see in the next chapter, to a large extent your decisions about what to examine in the external analysis will be based on the kind of information management uses in its decisionmaking.

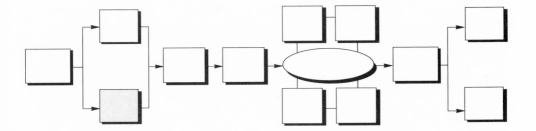

CHAPTER 5

THE INTERNAL ANALYSIS

[O]ur goal is nothing less than a complete description of the universe we live in.

Stephen Hawking[1]

Until we know and understand our business—that universe that we spend our days in, that pays our wages, that in many ways controls our lives—we cannot make it the most successful and rewarding place it can be, in either financial or psychological terms. As part of learning about that universe, at the same time that the task force assembled by the planning team is examining the external world in which our firm functions (Activity 2.0), another team, working closely with the facilitator, is examining internal documents and surveying and conducting interviews with senior and operational management (Activity 3.0). It is critical that the picture of the organization that is being sketched include as a centerpiece both the business side and the information technology (IT) side of the organization—the areas that are its cornerstones.

All of this information, which is necessary to identify the problem (the first step in the Dynamic Planning Framework), will then be used to build an accurate image of the firm for the position paper (Activity 4.0) and to aid in the generation of options (Activity 5.0). These activities comprise the second step of the Framework, the search for solutions.

THE BASIC STEPS TO ACCUMULATING INFORMATION FOR THE INTERNAL ANALYSIS

Since the goal of Activity 3.0 is to derive a careful and true picture of the business and the way it functions, the team must spend more time than would seem, at first glance, necessary to ensure that the business really is what senior management thinks it is. Because instinct says that you could find out what the business is by simply asking those who have been with the organization for a long time, a cautionary tale from an assignment seems in order.

Often changes occur over the years that subtly transform what a business believes it does for a living. In the case of a natural gas company in the Midwest, almost every senior executive we interviewed described the company's scope of business as the marketing and trading of natural gas. Indeed, the company had been founded by a small coterie of individuals who did just that. The assets required to start the business were small, they found a large company that would guarantee a line of credit to support their endeavor, and for a number of years they successfully marketed and traded natural gas. In fact, they were so successful that in less than five years, the company had become the number two player in the sector.

As time went on, the company discovered that to grow the business, it would have to find a way to reassure customers that it would always be able to supply the amount of what was sometimes a scare commodity, natural gas, that was promised. So the company acquired some gas-producing properties in order to alleviate customers' concerns. In essence, acquisition of these properties reduced the company's dependence on sources of natural gas over which it had little, if any, control. Once the customers knew that the company had its own source of supply, the level of confidence in its ability to deliver as promised went up substantially. This translated into increased market share and increased revenues.

The company then seized on some opportunities to buy natural gas-processing plants. This decision was prompted by a very interesting property of natural gas—the fact that a number of chemicals are inherently embedded in it. When the gas is processed in these plants, the residue is in the form of natural gas liquids that can be sold in a number of markets. The beauty of this process is that it is the result of doing what has to be done to produce usable natural gas. The company incurs no additional cost in generating these marketable by-products.

The natural gas assets the company bought proved enormously profitable. Moreover, they were very cost effective assets, requiring less than 5 percent of the total staff of the company to run. At the time we came in to help devise a business resumption plan for the company, it considered itself a seven-year-old gas marketing and trading company. However, from our examination of the company's financials, it became clear that there was more to the story than that. The numbers indicated that a large percentage of its revenues were from the assets—the processing and sale of gas and natural gas liquids.

As we conducted the interviews necessary to determine the critical business areas to protect and rebuild in the event of an interruption to the ongoing activities of the business, it became clear that the company was using the information gleaned from the marketing and trading operations to purchase and manage its assets in natural gas. The business had been transformed into a small marketing and trading company within a larger company that held and managed assets that happened to be natural gas.

Confirming this impression of what business the company was really in was, however, a problem. The executives, most of whom turned out to have been with the company since its earlier period, were unwilling to relinquish the image that stemmed from the company's founding—an image that recalled what were to many of them the best of times, the days marked by the challenge and excitement of building something new. This is an example of the danger of relying on any single source, even the proverbial horse's mouth, for your information.

DATA GATHERING

Gathering information from a variety of materials is the first and easiest step in preparing for the interviews with management that are the key to understanding an organization. The task force members assigned to do this usually spend a few days collecting annual reports, financials, organizational charts, the existing mission statement, newsletters and news releases, and stories in the press, then, after perusing them, they prepare fact sheets that the other team members can use as a starting point for discussion. The discussions will help the task force pinpoint information that seems contradictory.

The next step is to develop the questionnaires that will be distributed to senior management and selected operational management and to decide on the interview questions. There are generic sets of questions (see Tables 5.1 and 5.2) usually asked of executives in order to understand an organization's business and information technology components—the business's cornerstones. But the answers to these questions should always lead to further questions based on specific information that is collected from documents about the company. In this step, the survey tool is sent out and the interviews with senior management are scheduled.

The most important source of information about a business is senior management. They know the industrial sector (most executives work in the same sector for a long time before reaching management level) and have some insight about the direction in which it is moving; they understand the competition; and they are aware of the critical success factors (CSFs) driving the business (keep in mind, however, that the perceptions of CSFs held by senior management can vary, particularly in companies that are having problems).

The internal analysis should reach out to as many executives on the business and IT side as possible because the planning process will take time

Table 5.1. Executive Management Questionnaire

1. What are the goals of the enterprise?

2. What are the critical success factors (CSFs) for your organization, and why do you think they are critical?

3. What is your area of responsibility?

4. What are the goals for your area of responsibility?

5. What are the CSFs for your area of responsibility, and why do you think they are critical?

6. What takes up most of your decisionmaking time?

7. What information do you need that you find difficult or hard to obtain?

8. What do you perceive as the role of information technology and systems within the enterprise: providing "back office" or administrative support; enabling new areas of opportunity; necessary to remain competitive?

9. What do you think are the core competencies or strengths of your business? What are the weaknesses?

10. Who are your major competitors today? What are their strengths and weaknesses?

11. Where do you see the industry going over the next three to five years?

12. Who do you envision will emerge as your major competitors over the next three- to five-year horizon?

13. What potential threats do you see to the enterprise over the next three to five years?

14. What potential opportunities do you see over this time horizon?

15. Are there any other problem areas or other concerns that could impact the enterprise's ability to achieve its goals?

and effort and the more that senior managers understand the purpose of such planning and its eventual business applications, the more they will be willing to accept the time and effort involved and, in the end, will buy in to change. In addition, the steps involved in Dynamic Planning are themselves a tool for opening the business to new ideas. By forcing executives to think deeply about the way the business works, especially the interactions between the business in general and IT and between and among functions, you can push them to reexamine the things that they take for granted.

Management is often so caught up in immediate problems, in dealing with putting out fires, that they lose sight of the big picture. They do not have the time to reevaluate business processes, to understand the possibilities of technological advances, to think about the way some new innovation they have heard about could be adapted to their business, to meet the needs of increasingly resentful and disaffected middle managers who find themselves putting in extremely long hours in an era of downsizing.

Table 5.2. Senior Information Technology Management Questionnaire

1. What are the goals of the IT organization?

2. What do you see as the role of IT in the enterprise and why? And how has the role of IT evolved?

3. What is your area of responsibility?

4. What are the goals for your area of responsibility?

5. What are the CSFs for your area of responsibility, and why do you think they are critical?

6. What takes up most of your decisionmaking time?

7. Is there a formal IT Strategy in place? How was it developed?

8. What are the distinctive competencies of IT?

9. Are there alliances or joint ventures in place with vendors, and how are they structured?

10. Is there a formal IT Plan in place, and is the planning process driven by the IT Strategy?

11. Which competitors do you respect most in terms of using IT and why?

12. What do you perceive to be your company's IT strengths? Its weaknesses?

13. What IT advances on the horizon will give your enterprise some form of competitive advantage?

14. What is the operating budget for IT? (Current fiscal year and five-year history broken out by operations, application maintenance, application enhancement, new systems development, hardware, telecommunications, and personnel.)

15. What is the state of IT in your organization? That is, create a picture of the existing hardware (mainframe to PCs), software, telecommunications (phones, faxes, video), applications, and data architecture.

In the end, those executives on the planning team will, in all likelihood, be forced to confront the fact that the leaders of the business do not all have the same view of the business's goals, what they think is critical for it to succeed, or even share the underlying assumptions about the business and its competitive environment. This process also offers the business the opportunity to really understand how well its executives are functioning as a team, whether everyone is focusing on the future of the business, and if they are ready to think about the business in long-range terms.

But keep in mind that internal interviews can be trying in the best of times. Therefore, when a business is having problems, it is critical that the interviews be conducted by the facilitator rather than by task force members. The task force members will find it difficult to deal with contradictions, hesitating to probe beyond the questions formally presented because of their positions relative to those of the executives they are interviewing. But personal interviews are important to the internal examination because they bring out the intangibles that cannot be garnered from a written response—the meaning behind the responses.

Over the years, we have found that it is important to both conduct one-on-one interviews and use survey tools, matching the results of one against the other and then probing discrepancies. In this step, the results from the questionnaires filled out by the executives responsible for the various functional areas of the organization are checked against the information from the interviews; among other reasons for checking questionnaire results is the tendency of many executives to pay scant attention to them or to shade the truth because of fear of a written record of their real opinions, especially if those opinions are negative.

In most companies, those interviewed would include the Chief Executive Officer, Chief Operating Officer, Chief Financial Officer, and Chief Information Officer, as well as the heads of each of the administrative areas that support them, such as research and development, engineering, manufacturing, distribution, marketing, sales, and human resources. The questionnaire, which reaches many more people than most companies can find time to interview, also informs every manager who fills it out that planning is being taken seriously, thus opening more executives to thinking about the business and what it is doing and how well it is doing it. The questionnaire also provides a means of probing initial responses to interviews in a nonconfrontational way. For example, say that the questionnaire reveals that most executives believe communications within the business are not working well. During an interview, the respondent answers the question "Do you have a good idea of the plans the information technology department has for next year?" by saying "Yes, a pretty good idea." If the person conducting the interview can follow up with "That's good—a lot of other people seem to have a problem understanding what the department is planning, according to the results of our survey," the person being questioned can expand on the first answer without becoming defensive. The response was not being questioned; instead, other people's impressions were mentioned. The interviewee is free to say, "Well, the information I have is really just from the grapevine," or "Oh, that's because I play tennis with the head of the IT department."

LEARNING THE BUSINESS

The overview of the basics just presented does not explain some of the detailed work that goes into collecting material from senior management in cases of a very intense examination required by the Dynamic Planning Framework. But the basic process should result in, at the very least, a collection of information encompassing the following:

◆ The current goals of the business.

◆ The factors critical to the success of the business (CSFs).

◆ The assumptions underlying the CSFs about the environment, competition, and the industry (these reveal a lot about what shapes the thinking of the executives as a group).

◆ Information related to the running of the business; that is, any anticipated changes within it that might impact its goals or CSFs; the critical decisions senior management makes; what information they find difficult to obtain regarding the decisionmaking process.

◆ Information regarding the firm's position in the world; that is, what they perceive as the competitive advantages or distinctive competencies of the organization as well as its weaknesses. (It is also useful at this point to check what the executives see as the strengths and weaknesses of the competition, where they see the industry going over the next three to five years, what they think the drivers of the industry are, who they perceive as future competitors, and any problem areas or concerns that could prevent the organization from reaching its goals. This will help the task force doing the external analysis to narrow the focus of its research.)

The task force must also keep in mind that the information needed about the information technology side of the firm must be collected in as much detail as the information on the business side. This sometimes poses a problem because fewer senior executives are found in IT departments. However, the direct reports of the CIO or the manager of information systems can provide the needed information about the information technology strategy in place, the kinds of technology in use and planned, the budget for technology, and the skill sets of the personnel in the information technology organization.

Once the information from the internal analysis is collected, it will be weighed against the knowledge gained from the external analysis in a process known as the gap analysis; that is, through a discussion and interpretation of the discrepancies between the internal and external views of the business, a valid picture of the business can be developed. The task force, the facilitator, and some members of the planning team will pull the information garnered from the gap analysis into a position paper (Activity 4.0 of the Framework); that, in turn, will be used by the planning team to generate the options the company has for moving into the future (Activity 5.0).

THE TECHNIQUES FOR CONDUCTING INTERVIEWS

Senior management's views of the business can be collected through interviews based on questions such as those in Tables 5.1 and 5.2, but a variety of analytical techniques can be used to probe more deeply.[2] As a general rule, the more complex and larger the business, the more divisions and units and functions, the more sophisticated the techniques. (In Activity 7.0, the development of the Grand Strategy of the business, the business's current mission will be reexamined. Here, as part of the work to measure the business's current state, some of the same analytical techniques are useful: particularly those that help in determining the business's goals, the critical success factors necessary to realize those goals, and the critical assumptions [CAs] underlying the critical success factors. An understanding of these concepts and the techniques used to derive them is vital at this stage of Dynamic Planning.)

GOALS
HOW HIGH DO YOU WANT TO JUMP?

A goal is an objective that an individual, group, or firm has set out to achieve within a specified time frame. Business goals, which are defined and developed by senior management to support the mission of the company, have to be precise. Suppose, for example, we interview senior management and the one business goal that is stated consistently is "make more money." Although this is a noteworthy goal, it is not well defined, neither stating what is meant by how much money nor over what period of time. However, more often than not, senior management will insist that this is a valid goal, excusing its lack of precision by explaining, "We know how much more we want to make, but we have never formalized the specifics.

We all know what we mean." In most instances, not all members of senior management have the same notion of how much is more, nor do they have the same ideas about how it should be made. A more precise business goal would be: "Achieve a 10 percent profit before tax by the end of fiscal 1995."

Senior management's role is to articulate the business's goals, that is, those goals that pertain to the business as compared to an individual or group, and to determine if the business's goals are logical; that is, can they be achieved in the time frame set, in the context of the resources of the organization, and given the realities of the environment? In many instances, senior management may set forth "stretch goals" (goals meant to make employees try harder, to stretch themselves); these goals, while seemingly impossible at first sight, can be justified because they can, in fact, be achieved if everything goes right. Unfortunately, in the turbulent environment of the 1990s, they may be too great a stretch, discouraging rather than motivating employees. Indeed, in an environment such as that in the beginning of the 1990s, many businesses may have only one goal: "To be in business at the end of the fiscal year."

The business goals aimed at supporting the overall mission of the business are the highest-level goals. At the same time, the various members of senior management responsible for the functional areas of the business also have goals; these goals represent what each of the functional areas has to achieve to ensure that the goals of the business are met. They must be in alignment with and supportive of the business's goals. For example, a specific goal of the vice president of manufacturing in a company may be: "Reduce manufacturing costs 5 percent during the fiscal year." This goal is supportive of the business goal, "Achieve a 10 percent profit," because a reduction in manufacturing costs will, more than likely, increase profitability. All too often, however, the functional area goals have very little, if any, impact on the business goals because the business goals were not defined at all or they were poorly defined and communicated. In either case, the result is that the various functional vice presidents perform their responsibilities in a nonaligned and uncoordinated fashion—they compete with one another instead of focusing on moving the business forward.

How do you go about avoiding this so that everyone is trying to achieve the business's goals? First, be sure that everyone understands what the business's goals are, and then make clear that they can be attained by achieving critical success factors.

CRITICAL SUCCESS FACTORS
KNOWING WHAT YOU HAVE TO DO

In the late 1970s, a new approach to providing information to top management was developed. The concept involved discerning an organization's critical success factors,[3] "the limited number of areas in which results, if they are satisfactory, will ensure successful competitive performance for a business. They are the few key areas where 'things must go right' for the business to flourish."[4]

What factors are critical to the success of an organization, a group, or a given manager? It may be easier to define critical success factors by explaining first what they are not. They are not those standard measures, often called key indicators, that apply across the board to all divisions of a company. They are, rather, areas of major importance to a particular manager, at a given moment in time, in a given spot in the company. They are those things that help the executive and, by extension, the business achieve its goals. For example, in the automobile industry, styling is a CSF that will help achieve the goal "increase market share." In other words, CSFs are "those characteristics, conditions, or variables that . . . have a significant impact on the success of a firm competing in a particular industry. A CSF can be a characteristic such as price advantage, it can also be a condition such as vertical integration."[5]

Learning the CSFs is thus an essential part of learning about the business, uncovering the information that will be folded together with information about the world outside the organization to pursue the planning necessary to long-term success. But keep in mind while working on this aspect of the internal analysis that managers do not develop CSFs in isolation. Although defining individual goals and CSFs has merit and must be done throughout the organization, there has to be a common focus or set of business goals that the individual or group is trying to achieve. Without such goals, each individual or group will do what it perceives as important, but the collective effort may not support the mission of the business.

Assuming, however, that those goals are clear, a manager must know in which areas it is critical that things go right and what things must go right in order to achieve them; those are the critical success factors that everyone must try to achieve. Moreover, as stated previously, the planning process is an iterative as well as collaborative process. The definition of business CSFs may take several iterations before all those involved in the planning process can agree and buy into the CSFs, but the buy-in process is essential if the planning process is to move forward.

DEFINING AND DEVELOPING CSFS

One of the most common problems encountered by those conducting extensive executive interviews for a thorough internal analysis is discerning the difference between a goal and a CSF; indeed, one person's CSF may be another person's goal. Examples may help: let us look at a company that manufactures high-technology products. If the stated business goal is "to increase gross revenues to $700 million by fiscal year 1995," the business CSFs associated with this goal may be "reducing the number of

suppliers we use by 20 percent by fiscal year 1995," and "reducing product development cycle time from eighteen to six months by fiscal year
1995." In this example, the first CSF would become the goal of the vice
president responsible for manufacturing. She would have to define and
develop a set of CSFs to achieve what has now become her goal—"reduce
the number of suppliers." The CSFs necessary to accomplish her goal may
be "developing and implementing a quality assurance program to track
and evaluate the performance of our suppliers within the next three
months," and "negotiating long-term commitments with those suppliers
that meet our performance criteria, within the next six months."

In the case of our second business CSF, reducing the cycle time for product development, this would become a new goal for both the vice president
responsible for research and development as well as the vice president
responsible for manufacturing. Although the goal is shared, their respective CSFs may be different. For example, a CSF for the vice president of
R&D may be "achieving a 50–50 balance between new product research
and continuous improvement on existing products within the next fiscal
year." For the vice president of manufacturing, a CSF to achieve the new
goal may be "establishing a task force with personnel from R&D, engineering, and manufacturing to redesign the existing business processes to
implement a 'design to build' program within the next six months." These
CSFs, in turn, may become the goals of other members of the respective
groups. However, they will all be derived from the initial starting point:
the organization's goals and CSFs.

How do we define and develop CSFs such as those discussed in the
example? How do we know if these are the right CSFs? In the majority of
cases we have studied, successful senior managers have an almost intuitive
sense for those few things that have to go right. They may not have articulated or formally written down what their CSFs are, but they do, in fact,
run the business, make decisions, and achieve their goals by understanding and achieving them. The major problem faced by those charged with
the internal analysis, as stated previously, will be to articulate and formalize what is for the most part already being practiced intuitively by
senior management.

Formalizing a process for articulating CSFs is more of an art than a science—for example, defining CSFs and defining strategy have a lot in common: almost everyone knows what they mean, but there really isn't a good
definition that everyone can agree with. There are, however, four guidelines or rules of thumb that can be used in identifying a CSF:

1. A CSF must be achievable—the CSF examples discussed previously are all achievable. The individuals may not be able to achieve the
CSFs in the time frame stated, but there is nothing (that we know of)
that will prevent them from eventually achieving them.

2. A CSF must be controllable—the individual, group, or business has to have some degree of control over the CSF. For example, the CSF "interest rates must remain fixed over the next twelve months" cannot be controlled—only managed. There is no way that the individual, group, or business can take action to ensure that interest rates will not fluctuate. Therefore, a better CSF would be "attaining $10 million of new funding at current rates within the next three months."

3. A CSF must have a time frame for completion; three months, one year, or whatever the most appropriate time frame is. It cannot drag on indefinitely. If it did, it would not be a CSF.

4. Information must exist to track the achievement of the CSF. In essence, there must be performance measurements in place. Referring to our business CSF reducing product development cycle time, the progress and achievement of the CSF can be fairly easy to track. In the worst case, if at year end we are still not able to design and build new products more rapidly than before, we will know that we have failed in achieving our CSF—either we did not allocate enough time to achieve it, or it is not currently achievable within the context of the firm and the world in which we have to compete.

CSFs can, in many instances, support the attainment of more than one goal. For example, referring to our business goals: "to increase gross revenues to $700 million by fiscal 1995" and "to achieve profit before tax of 10 percent by fiscal 1995," the business CSF "reducing the cycle time for product development" supports the attainment of both. The CSF will directly support the first goal, but it only indirectly supports the second. The CSF is important, but not critical to the attainment of that goal. If it isn't critical, then why is it a CSF? As stated, a CSF can support more than one goal. It may not be critical to each particular goal, but it must be critical to some goal.

If those in charge of the internal analysis define and develop CSFs that are neither important nor critical to the attainment of a goal, then, more than likely, the CSF is either not well defined or it is not a CSF. This is one of the reality checks the facilitator can lead the internal analysis task force members to apply to determine if they have properly defined the CSFs. Knowing if it is the right CSF is a different issue. The derived CSFs can be compared with those of a direct competitor or industry. For example, automobile manufacturer CSFs would include quality, performance, technology, style, and cost. If the CSFs dealt with everything but quality, then the facilitator should suggest a reexamination of why that CSF was not included. All the CSFs need not match competitor CSFs, but those CSFs that emerge from the analysis with competitors must be included in the CSFs that result from the internal analysis.

How many CSFs should the organization have? Are there guidelines for the types of CSFs that should be considered? Normally, a business has between twelve and fifteen CSFs. If there are more than this, the defined CSFs should be examined for similar meaning and content in order to collapse or combine them. For example, two of the most common CSFs that appear in virtually every for-profit company are "recruiting and retaining quality, competent people" and the need to have "timely, accurate, information available." There could be many variations of these CSFs—for example, the CSF "hiring three new product managers in fiscal 1991," although a valid CSF, could be aggregated with the primary CSF dealing with people ("recruiting and retaining quality, competent people").

The CSF would be written as follows:

CSF: Recruiting and retaining quality, competent people
  —Hiring three new product managers in fiscal 1991

The objective of this exercise is to aggregate similar words and meanings into categories of CSFs so that they can be more easily examined and dealt with; the intent is not only to deal with categories for discussion purposes, but also to include the detail for subsequent action items. One of the most common problems that the task force members will face is assuming that they will remember the details associated with all of the CSFs; unfortunately, after several months of dealing with a variety of implementation issues, most people forget the details associated with the meaning and why they expressed the CSFs the way they did.

If the CSFs were discussed in depth by senior management, more than likely it would become clear why the CSF is a CSF—that is, the underlying belief or assumption that makes the CSF a valid CSF from their perspective would emerge. This is the subject of our next section—surfacing and discussing critical assumptions.

CRITICAL ASSUMPTIONS
MAKING THE UNCONSCIOUS CONSCIOUS

Critical assumptions are the values and beliefs (stated by senior management) that underlie the CSFs.[6] These assumptions usually reflect senior managers' beliefs about external factors that could affect the strategic direction of the business—the industrial sector, competitors, and their own organization.

Some of the questions raised in the internal analysis when dealing with assumptions are: "Why are critical assumptions critical? What do they have to do with the planning process? Why do you track assumptions? Which assumptions do you track?"

- *Critical assumptions are critical because they have an impact on the CSFs and tactics of the organization.* The best way to explain this statement is through an example. The senior management of a major soft drink company in the southwest is going through its annual planning process. This year, however, the firm has a new CEO who was handpicked by the Chairman of the Board. The CEO had significant experience with other, major package goods companies, one an extremely large international company. He is recognized as an aggressive player in the industry, which was why he was brought in. With the addition of this major new member of the senior management team, a new set of goals and critical success factors were defined and developed during the planning process. One of the CSFs defined was "achieving product diversification through acquisition of a another soft drink product within the year." This was a well-defined CSF that was bought into by all members of the planning process—that is, senior management, including the Chairman of the Board.

  Problems emerged, however, because senior management neglected to determine the assumptions being made about the CSF. They all believed that each of them had the same mental picture of what the CSF meant. In reality, the Chairman of the Board and the CEO had contradictory assumptions about its meaning, and consequently, about how to achieve it. In this case, given the international mindset of the last corporation he had worked for, the CEO assumed: "The way to achieve diversification was to acquire a product that would give the company a new line while allowing it to expand internationally." The Chairman of the Board assumed: "The product would be domestic, allowing the company to penetrate new domestic markets and reducing domestic competition." The chairman had never thought about going global; the CEO assumed that the best way to diversify was to add a new product to enhance domestic share and allow for growth—after all, that was his area of expertise, and why else would the company have worked so hard to convince him to join their ranks? The result was that both the acquisition targets presented to the Chairman of the Board after months of research were rejected. The CEO resigned on the spot, unable to understand the chairman's refusal: he felt the refusal signaled a lack of faith in his judgment. The chairman accepted the resignation because he felt the CEO had failed to find a domestic target and so was attempting to go international, something the company would never be able to handle successfully, in order to save face.

  Referring to one of our defined CSFs in the previous section, "attaining $10 million of new funding at current rates within the next three months," a critical assumption is: "Interest rates will remain stable over the next three months." The assumption provides the rationale for the CSF: it is the underlying meaning or belief held by senior management about the CSF. In this example, the difference between a CSF and an assumption is the difference in what can and can't be controlled. This CSF can be controlled and achieved by monitoring the trends in interest rates—that is, monitoring the assumption about the CSF. Assumptions involve external factors that can neither be controlled nor, in most cases, influenced, but they can be monitored, and the information collected can be used by the company in its effort to achieve the CSF. For example, if monitoring interest rates indicates that the trend is for higher rates, the time frame for the CSF may have to be shortened or the CSF may have to be abandoned—at least for the next several months.

An additional CSF defined and articulated by the soft drink company was "developing an in-house marketing and sales support system over the next ten months." Let's assume now that the lesson had been learned from the initial problems. The CSFs are then challenged, which leads to the identification of the following critical assumptions behind the CSF just cited: "A marketing and sales support system will provide the necessary information to support our acquisition efforts; the system will help us develop a better awareness of markets and consumers; and the system will help us identify which products, in which markets, will give us a competitive advantage." Everyone is now reading from the same page; they all understand the CSF and the assumptions related to it. The marketing and sales support system will be the mechanism for tracking various sets of assumptions about customers and markets as the planning process continues.

◆ *What role do assumptions play in the planning process?* The set of underlying assumptions provides the backdrop for the CSFs and for the eventual development of the Grand Strategy. Changes in the assumptions will lead to changes in the CSFs—and thus in the Grand Strategy. Monitoring and evaluation of assumptions can, therefore, help to identify when CSFs, and thus the subsequent tactics of the business, require change.

◆ *Why do you track assumptions?* You need to track assumptions in order to determine how stable they are and how important they are. If an assumption is not important and not very stable or not important and very stable, there is no apparent need to track it. If the assumption is very important, but stable, the assumption should be tracked, but there is probably no need to invest a lot of resources in tracking it. However, if the assumption is very important and is believed to be very unstable, then resources should be made available to track it on an ongoing basis. For example, proposed changes in business tax write-offs must be seriously tracked because of the potentially significant consequences of even small changes, but a fast food company's assumptions about demographics, while very important to the business, are less of a problem because demographics tend to be fairly stable. Consequently, the level of effort necessary to track information pertaining to assumptions about tax write-offs is different from the level spent tracking demographics.

◆   *How do you determine which assumptions to track?* There is a well-established process that is meant to aid you in making these decisions. The first step is to list the critical assumptions underlying the critical success factors you have decided are most important. A rule of thumb is that there are usually two to four assumptions for each defined CSF. In some cases, one assumption may be relevant to a number of CSFs.

An example of how this works can be derived from a major energy company in the Midwest. (Although there were actually eight CSFs, we are here selecting three and combining some critical assumptions under the first CSF.) In the course of developing the enterprise plan, those on the planning committee determined that three important CSFs were *"adding profitable reserves economically," "improving cash flow,"* and *"acquiring and retaining quality human resources."* In further discussions, the group surfaced thirteen (again, remember this is a limited example; there were actually twenty-four) CAs underlying these CSFs. The critical assumptions the group agreed upon for these three critical success factors were the following:

Adding profitable reserves economically:
    1. The exploration process can be managed—it is not an art.
    2. All projects can be compared on an equal, rational basis.
    3. We will stay in geographic and technical areas where we have a competitive advantage—we will explore in areas we know.
    4. There are no restrictions on approaches to adding oil and gas reserves—we can buy reserves as well as explore for reserves.
    5. The total exploration and development program will be funded by cash flow and asset sales—not by adding debt.
    6. The stability of price, cost, and demand for oil and natural gas impacts our ability to profitably add reserves.

Improving cash flow:
    7. We will use cash flow to reduce debt.
    8. Cash flow is the most significant restriction to growth.
    9. Equity through the stock market will not be available.

Acquiring and retaining quality human resources:
  10. Quality people will make a difference to our future success.
  11. Technology cannot replace highly skilled people.
  12. The market for highly skilled people continues to be strong.
  13. The bonus program will impact performance and increase the retention of highly skilled people.

The members of the group were then asked to choose the six they considered most important and rank them on a scale from 0 to 4 (see Table 5.3). They were then to rank the stability—that is, the extent to which an assumption is likely to remain stable over the planning horizon on a scale of 0 to 4 (see Table 5.4). The results were then tabulated, with each assumption given a number representing the average importance and another

Table 5.3. Critical Assumption Ranking—Importance

Please circle the number that best describes your opinion of the importance of each of the following critical assumptions.

Assumption (number taken from original list of critical assumptions)	Ranking from not important (0) to very important (4)
2. All projects can be compared on an equal, rational basis.	0 1 2 3 4
3. We will stay in geographic and technical areas where we have a competitive advantage—we will explore in areas we know.	0 1 2 3 4
6. The stability of price, cost, and demand for oil and natural gas impacts our ability to profitably add reserves.	0 1 2 3 4
8. Cash flow is the most significant restriction to growth.	0 1 2 3 4
10. Quality people will make a difference to our future success.	0 1 2 3 4
13. The bonus program will impact performance and increase the retention of highly skilled people.	0 1 2 3 4

Table 5.4. Critical Assumption Ranking—Stability

Please circle the number that best describes your opinion of the stability of each of the following critical assumptions.

Assumption (number taken from original list of critical assumptions)	Ranking from not stable (0) to very stable (4)				
2. All projects can be compared on an equal, rational basis.	0	1	2	3	4
3. We will stay in geographic and technical areas where we have a competitive advantage—we will explore in areas we know.	0	1	2	3	4
6. The stability of price, cost, and demand for oil and natural gas impacts our ability to profitably add reserves.	0	1	2	3	4
8. Cash flow is the most significant restriction to growth.	0	1	2	3	4
10. Quality people will make a difference to our future success.	0	1	2	3	4
13. The bonus program will impact performance and increase the retention of highly skilled people.	0	1	2	3	4

number representing the average stability ranking. A table with three columns was set up. The first column listed the six assumptions. (The numbers in parentheses indicate the original number of each assumption on the list of thirteen.) The second column listed their relative importance, and the third their relative stability (Table 5.5). A scatter diagram was then constructed (a four-part matrix), with the horizontal axis measuring importance, the vertical, stability (see Figure 5.1).

The quadrant labeled I contains those assumptions (2) that are somewhat important to the organization, but are either somewhat stable or very stable. These assumptions are not candidates for a lot of tracking. Quadrant II contains those assumptions (3), (10), and (13) that are very important, but are stable or very stable and some attempt should be made to track them. Quadrant III contains the assumptions that are somewhat important but also somewhat unstable: they change rapidly over time but are not very important. Consequently, it is not important to track such assumptions. Quadrant IV contains those assumptions (6) and (8) that are most important and most unstable. They are the candidates for careful tracking because they have a significant impact on the company's CSFs and, ultimately, the Grand Strategy—any changes in these assumptions will change the strategic direction of the company.

In the case of our crude oil and natural gas company, assumptions about the prices of crude oil and natural gas are very important, but they are also very unstable. Consequently, major energy companies devote significant resources to track these assumptions. One of the critical assumptions underlying all three of these CSFs was "The stability of price, cost, and demand for crude oil and natural gas impacts both earnings and cash flow." In addition, there was agreement that the assumption was highly important and very unstable—consequently, information had to be identified that could track this assumption. Some of the information required to track the assumption would be the spot price of crude oil—historical, current, and projected; trend information for demand in energy products; and information on oil tanker fleet movement. Since all of the information required could be obtained from publicly available databases, the company gained a competitive edge because of the astuteness and awareness of the company executives—the way they analyzed the numbers and related them to their operation was what made the difference.

Table 5.5. Critical Assumption Ranking—Importance and Stability

Assumptions	Importance	Stability
1.(6) Stability of price, cost, demand	4	1
2.(2) All projects can be compared	1.5	4
3.(8) Cash flow is most important restriction to growth	3	1
4.(13) Bonus program will impact importance	2.5	2.5
5.(3) Stay in area of competitive advantage	4	3.5
6.(10) Quality people make a difference	4	4

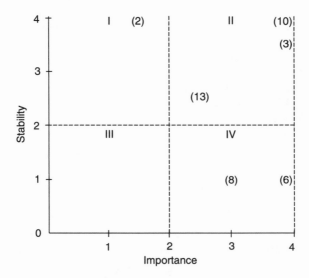

Stability: The extent to which an assumption is likely to remain unchanged over the planning horizon; 4 represents the highest stability.

Importance: The relative importance of any given assumption to the successful attainment of a critical success factor (CSF); 4 represents the highest importance.

Figure 5.1. Assumption Set Evaluation Matrix
© 1993 B. Goldberg and J. G. Sifonis

The executive support system put in place for tracking this assumption gave them the anticipatory capability to make better, more informed decisions, sooner than the competition.

COORDINATING THE INFORMATION COLLECTED

With the completion of the interviews, the first step of the Dynamic Planning Framework, identifying the problem, draws to a close. Now the members of the task force who have been doing the internal analysis will move on to the second step, the search for solutions. In this step the members of the internal analysis task force check the information gathered in the interviews against the survey results and the information collected from documentation in a working session in which they try to uncover discrepancies or determine if they need any additional material.

This is an important part of the preparation for the focus session that will be held with the planning team in order to resolve differences in views that emerge. This session is a necessary prerequisite to the later work that will be done by the members of the task forces and the facilitator in order to develop the position paper (Activity 4.0).

The position paper will be a summary document folding together the organization's internal picture of what it does for a living, how it does it, why it does it the way it does, highlighting its strengths and weaknesses, with information obtained from the external analysis about the competition—principally, what are they doing and how well are they doing it. The position paper will serve as the information base that will be used by the planning team members to determine the options that make the most sense for the company to explore (Activity 5.0) in its search for solutions.

PART II

SEARCHING FOR SOLUTIONS

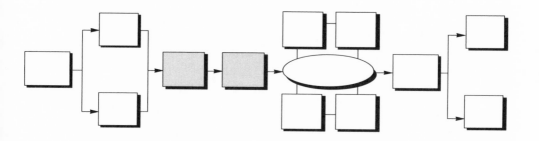

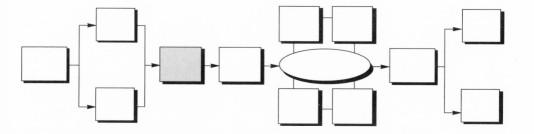

CHAPTER 6

DEVELOPING THE POSITION PAPER

The greatest and noblest pleasure which we have in this world is to discover new truths, and the next is to shake off old prejudices.

Frederick the Great

In order to succeed, a business must know what it is and what it can do; it must learn its own strengths and weaknesses; and it must be sure that it is not fooling itself about any of these. The last two chapters, which covered Activities 2.0 and 3.0 of the Dynamic Planning Framework, were preliminary steps on the road to finding the truth about your business. The goal of Chapter 4 was to help the business understand where it fits into the world, and the goal of Chapter 5 was to help the business's leaders understand the essential nature of the business—what it does and how and why it does it.

This chapter describes Activity 4.0, the initial activity of the second step of the Dynamic Planning Framework, the search for solutions. It will explain some techniques for examining the information collected in the two concurrent steps of the Framework that have just been completed and for formalizing that information in a position paper. Theoretically, the position paper could cover enormous amounts of material, including detailed analyses of information ranging from financial data to organizational history. But realistically, at a minimum, it must pull together for the planning team basic information about what the business is, what it could be, and how it compares to similar businesses.

It is important to remember that we are working within a Framework, not a methodology. The process involved in formulating the position paper will vary depending on the size and complexity of the business, the skills and involvement of the members of the planning team, and the size and membership of the task forces doing the internal and external analyses. In some cases, the planning team is involved in every step; in others, the team delegates much of the work to subordinates who are named to serve on the task forces. We are taking a middle ground here, showing how this activity would be handled in an organization sizable enough for the planning team to be able to appoint two task forces, independent enough to work on their own a great deal of the time, to do much of the preliminary work. Based upon our experiences in numerous assignments, the Framework is applicable in virtually any for-profit organization. However, differences in business scope, scale, and culture may require adjustments with respect to the actual processes used to successfully implement the Framework in a given business environment.

Usually, the examinations of the material gathered in the internal and external analyses take place in working sessions of the task force that sometimes also include members of the planning team. The objectives of these sessions is to try to reconcile any discrepancies in the information collected and to discuss any gaps between the internal views of the business held by the executives and the actual place of the business vis a vis the world outside.

READING FROM THE SAME PAGE

The first step on the road to developing the position paper is to review and confirm the internal view of the firm held by senior managers based upon the information collected from them by the task force charged with the internal analysis. The primary objective of this review of executive insights is to ensure that all members of the group are reading from the same page; that is, to see that everyone involved has the same understanding of the strategic direction of the business and what has to be done to make the journey.

In many cases, after the individual executive interviews are aggregated and analyzed, a high degree of consistency will be found in the executive interview responses covering the goals; critical success factors (CSFs); problems with obtaining information; the organization's strengths and, to a lesser degree, its weaknesses; the strengths and weaknesses of its current competitors; and the existing market and where it is going over time. The information that will usually create discussion—and sometimes dissension—is senior managers' underlying assumptions about their own business, the competition, and the external environment. Indeed, one striking finding in almost every assessment of internal interviews is how divergent the critical assumptions held by executives are, and not only within the same company but often within the same division and functional area. (This problem was examined in some detail in Chapter 5 in the explanations of CSFs and critical assumptions.) The reason is that most executives have very rarely, if ever, discussed their assumptions about the business or the environment with other members of executive management.

This problem of inconsistency is more than the task force can or should handle on its own. That is why, once the task force has collected the information from documents, surveys, and interviews, and analyzed it in a number of working sessions, it must call together the members of the planning team and, in a focus session conducted by the facilitator, have them resolve as many of the differences among their views as possible before turning to the preparation of the position paper. This cannot be done during the interview phase, because it is only when the separate views of senior managers are aggregated that the degree of differences between their views becomes clear.

For example, in the case of a banking client in the late 1980s, there were differing views among senior management as to whether it was a conventional bank, offering traditional banking products and services, such as checking, savings, loans, and certificates of deposit, or whether it was a financial services institution, offering such additional services as investment portfolio management and worldwide credit and investment services. This difference of views, with respect to the business, would lead to a dramatically different set of business and information technology (IT) strategies and the need for different business structures and different sets of organizational skills. (Today, it is almost impossible to find a bank that hasn't, to some extent, become a financial institution.) Discussing these different views with the executives, who were also planning team members, and getting them to agree on a common set of planning elements were necessary to achieve internal consistency.

The participation of the planning team members at this point, especially if they have delegated much of the work to task forces, is critical to the project. If members do not bother to attend, the project might as well be abandoned. Unless they face these differences in opinion between themselves and others in their organization—and explore and resolve them—there will be little buy-in to Dynamic Planning. The major problem in bringing these differences to the surface is that these discussions can feel threatening. The sessions force the planning team members to begin to think about the real nature of their business—and where they fit in, how their fellow executives perceive the business, and what the business may be able to achieve. Changes that have taken place in the business that make their talents seem less appropriate than they once were may emerge and have to be faced. Difficult as this is, however, it is better than the alternative—a business that fails. In most instances, realizing the changes that have occurred in the nature of the business leads to new growth, which in turn, presents new opportunities.

If run well, these sessions are also a safe place to put forth ideas, to air grievances, to point to long-standing problems. They also help to clarify the problems facing the organization and uncover differences in understanding about the firm's goals and resolve them so that at a minimum, even if no new directions are taken, all the members of the team, who are part of senior management, will be working toward the same end in the future. The confusion about goals that frequently emerges during these sessions is not a result of a lack of competence or skills or even brilliance, but a result of a lack of communication or more appropriately stated, miscommunication. And the larger the organization, the more likely it is that such misunderstandings will occur.

For example, we did a planning project with an electronics company in the Netherlands that, a few years earlier, had hired a new manager to run a manufacturing division. At the time the manager was hired, the division was pushing as much product out the door as possible because that product was in great demand. The manager was very successful and, as a result, had recently been promoted to run another division. What he did not realize was that the critical success factors for the new division were different. In his first position, the demand was so high that any costs associated with increasing production, such as in this case, adding a second and third shift, could, within reason, be passed along to the consumer. Scheduling and acquiring resources were the dominant critical success factors, not keeping production costs in line or even reducing them.

In the second division, increasing production using the same techniques just did not do the trick. The product the division manufactured was a commodity product, and there were several competitors in the marketplace offering the same or similar products. Price sensitivity was critical. The manager used the same technique for increasing production, which, again, resulted in increasing the product's price; this time, however, the result was a loss of market share.

During a meeting of an internal task force looking at the whole organization for a planning project, it became clear that this division represented a weakness that the company had to deal with. In the course of the meeting, this manager's mistaken understanding emerged. After much discussion, they were able to work through the problem. Once he understood that to succeed he had to increase production without increasing costs, he established a competitive benchmarking program to implement best-in-class manufacturing processes and regained market share by establishing a reputation for being the low-cost producer in the marketplace.

The group not only uncovered the problem but analyzed its cause. What emerged was that the manager had been thrown into the new position with little information besides management's "Do for these guys what you did before." These requisite CSFs were never communicated to him, because senior management assumed that they were obvious. As a result of the realization of what caused the problem, the task force recommended that management put in place a system whereby information meetings are held with all new managers and with all managers taking over major new responsibilities to review the division or department's goals and critical success factors.

DEVELOPING THE BASELINE, OR FINDING OUT WHERE YOU ARE

To return to the process of developing a position paper, once a consensus about the nature of the organization is reached, the task forces involved in the internal and external analyses go back to work. They have been communicating with each other throughout the information-gathering process, and in response to questions and requests for information they have been enriching their knowledge of the business and its place in the world. At this point, they have a great deal of information about changes in the competitive environment that might affect the business—for example, the industrial sector CSFs and assumptions, competitors' strengths and weaknesses, industry drivers, and trends. In addition, they have collected information about senior management's views of the business's goals, CSFs, and assumptions. Now it is time for the members of the two task forces to weigh and measure the information each has collected.

BRIDGING GAPS—AND NOTING UNBRIDGEABLE CHASMS

The gap analysis is a structured evaluation of the stated views of where senior management thinks the firm is with respect to its competitors, and the reality of where it is according to the external audit. Management is often surprisingly blind to the real strengths and weaknesses of the competition, especially to the strengths. One of the ways to expose this misreading is to compare the CSFs of the business with the generic CSFs of the competition. In most instances, the CSFs of the industry will be captured in the derived CSFs of senior management. For example, there are a number of generic fast food industry CSFs—standardization of products, brand image, speed of service, location, quality and availability of raw materials, and price. If the business's CSFs do not include those CSFs, they should be reexamined. Although the business may have more and very specific CSFs—the list should include a subset of the generic, and thus the competitor, CSFs.

The assumption set of senior management needs to be weighed against the information gleaned from the Environmental Analysis. As with the CSFs, the business will, more than likely, have more specific assumptions than the assumptions derived from that analysis. The important point, however, is to discern if we have dramatically different assumptions or beliefs from our competitors. If the differences turn out to be dramatic, then the gap must be left unresolved by the task force and presented to the planning team in the position paper for resolution.

Using a major car rental company as an example, let's look at the potential problems that gaps in the views held by the senior executives and the findings of the external analysis can cause if they are not resolved. In this example, the analysis of external factors, the industrial sector, and the competition suggested the following major assumption: the size of the workforce would shrink in future years because the generation currently at work had smaller families; fewer workers meant that many people would retire at a later age, thereby impacting the market for travel and leisure. The assumption that the senior management of the car rental company had, however, was that because there were so many workers reaching retirement age in future years the market for travel and leisure would increase. This major difference in assumptions could dramatically impact the company's future direction and, potentially, its ability to compete and survive. Once made aware of this unresolved—and unresolvable—gap, the company decided to establish a formal mechanism to track the information associated with this assumption; for example, tracking employment data by age bracket and checking for changes in immigration law that might add to the pool of available younger workers. For the moment, however, as will be seen in the analysis of the organization-specific vocabulary that follows, it took a middle ground, assuming that the numbers would balance each other.

Decisionmaking without this kind of analysis can have dire consequences. For example, senior managers of a retail convenience store chain believed that the emergence of gas stations providing a limited set of convenience items was not a threat to their core business. Conventional wisdom suggested that a gas station's core business was supplying gasoline, not convenience items. However, the patrons of the gas stations began to pick up many of the small items they would usually buy on nonsupermarket trips at the stores attached to the gas station (they were already parked so it was another added convenience) instead of stopping a second time at the convenience store. (The chain's options for countering this problem will be discussed in detail in the next chapter.)

POSSIBILITIES ANALYSIS: ADDING NEW DIMENSIONS

Another element of the position paper is putting together the future possibilities unearthed by the external task force. These should be very tentative scenarios, derived from the work done in Activity 2.0. In the course of this analysis, as noted in Chapter 4, the external task force members began compiling an organization-specific vocabulary for use in identifying some of the possibilities for the future.[1] Now it is time for the members of both task forces to review the vocabulary lists and see if they can select the words that represent drivers—those few things that are likely to have the greatest impact on their business and their competitors and over which they have little control. For example, as a result of conducting an internal and external analysis of a car rental group in the transportation sector, the following industry-specific vocabulary was derived:

service	location
price	convenience
capital	business renters
fleet age	travel and leisure customers
availability	replacement renters
market share	economy
demographics	information technology
interest rates	vehicle costs

Further discussion resulted in the selection—and removal—from that list of a set of drivers:

demographics
economy
interest rates
vehicle cost

The members of the team then sat down and started making sentences out of the words, using simple business verbs such as

affect   impact   need   demand

to tie the list of nouns together. The result was a list of sentences that could be checked against the task forces members' accumulated knowledge base.

Before going on with this discussion, it is important to clarify the process used in this kind of analysis. Think of these four words

girl   cat   milk   drank

They can be used to form six sentences that follow the rules of grammar:

1. The girl drank the milk.
2. The girl drank the cat.
3. The milk drank the girl.
4. The milk drank the cat.
5. The cat drank the milk.
6. The cat drank the girl.

When you read these sentences, you apply a reality check to them. Although they are all correct sentences in structural terms, you *know* that the girl did not drink the cat, nor did the milk drink anything, nor did the cat drink the girl. That leaves you with two possible sentences. If you had more information, you could probably decide in a given case which was more likely. For example, if someone had told you that the girl had just gone to the house of a friend to take care of her cat, you would probably decide that the likeliest sentence was "The cat drank the milk."

To return to the example of the car rental company: when the task force members reviewed the vocabulary and constructed sentences, they quickly found that they instinctively discarded many of them, leaving a short list. For example, "Fleet age impacts location" was discarded; however, "Location impacts fleet age" is a possible sentence, particularly when the driver "economy" is applied. If the location is one in which there is a severe recession, older cars at a reduced rate may bring in business.

Among the other likely sentences, with a brief explanation of the reasoning behind the acceptance of the validity of each, were:

1. Business renters demand location, convenience, and service. (Price is less important than making a meeting on time in good shape.)

2. Travel and leisure renters demand price. (Since time is less important, they will trade convenience for price.)

3. Location affects market share. (Business renters want car rental locations inside the airport for speed.)

4. Information technology impacts service and price. (Quickly transmitted information allows quicker response to manufacturers spot offers of discounts to rental companies, more responsive movement of fleet between locations, and greater efficiency in record keeping, which cuts operating costs.)

5. The lower the price, all other things being equal, the greater the market share. (Customer loyalty was considered unimportant.)

6. Leisure customers and business renters impact market share. (Replacement renters are a small part of the market.)

Now, the drivers—economy, interest rates, vehicle costs, demographics—will be applied to the information in the sentences. Any sentence can be chosen as a starting point. As the analysis progresses, task force members are likely to pull in other sentences to elaborate. In fact, if others are not pulled in, it is likely the original sentence chosen for analysis will not lead to a useful scenario. Much of this is trial and error. The major value of the process is that it expands the group's thinking about the business in terms of the future. Applying the drivers to sentence 6, the following conclusions can be reached:

Economy: In a bad economy fewer business trips would be made, but more short trips that were made would be by car than plane or train. Alternatively, a booming economy would increase business travel of all kinds. In a bad economy, leisure customers travel less.

Demographics: The population is rapidly aging, and there are likely to be more retirees who vacation more as the population ages. This increase in leisure travelers would thus mitigate some of the problems created by a bad economy.

Interest rates: Increased interest rates help those retirees who have savings, and those are the retirees most likely to travel, but adversely affect those on fixed incomes.

Vehicle costs: Increases in the cost of vehicles whether because manufacturing costs go up or because purchases are mistimed (poor fleet management; that is, the acquisition and disposition of vehicles) cause rental prices to go up; decreases in costs because of proper timing of purchases has the opposite effect.

The task force members now played with those ideas and, given their belief that the economy would be difficult over the next few years (this conclusion was a result of its research and trend watching), decided that since the number of travelers would remain the same, the costs of vehicles would be the major determinant of market share. Then, adding sentence 5, "The lower the price, all other things being equal, the greater the market share," and sentence 4, "Information technology impacts service and price," it concluded that, given this possible future environment, information technology would play a major role in ensuring that the company could hold the line on prices. (The way the company used this information in conjunction with other information it gleaned from its internal and external analyses to develop an information technology strategy is described in Chapter 9.)

The views that emerge from this kind of analysis of the organization-specific vocabulary should be included in the position paper for use during the focus sessions that lead to option generation. Discussing such forecasts in the focus sessions helps the planning team think out of the box. Peter Schwartz, president of Global Business Network, explains that

> The scenario process involves research—skilled hunting and gathering of information. This is practiced both narrowly—to pursue facts needed for a specific scenario—and broadly—to educate yourself, so that you will be able to pose more significant questions. Investigation is not just a useful tool for gathering facts. It hones your ability to perceive.[2]

EXPLORING YOUR DISTINCTIVE COMPETENCIES

Up to this point, we have performed our internal analysis, reconciled the executive insights with our external analysis, and performed a possibilities analysis to derive a set of alternatives for the future. Before the position paper can be drafted and turned over to senior management, a competency assessment—that is, a determination of the business's ability to compete not only in today's environment, but also in possible future environments—must be performed.

The most traditional and easiest technique for assessing your competencies is a SWOT analysis—determining the business's strengths, weaknesses, opportunities, and threats. The rationale for conducting a SWOT analysis at this point is to leverage the knowledge that has been gained in the internal analysis. The first step in a SWOT analysis is to develop a listing of your strengths as a competitor in today's environment—and then, using your derived possibilities or scenarios, to determine if these strengths will be applicable in the future. That is, you must determine whether or not you can leverage your current strengths or if you have to develop new strengths for the future.

A good starting point in determining your strengths is to review the materials about critical success factors and assumptions drawn from the executive insights. It is useful to categorize the strengths and weaknesses by functional area; that is, your marketing strengths, the special skills your executives bring to the table, your information technology capabilities, and your name recognition in the marketplace. At this stage of the process, the discussion of strengths and weaknesses is likely to be realistic: you have a solid understanding not only of your capabilities with respect to other firms in your field, but you also have an understanding of what it will take to compete in the future. What you are doing is listing those resources and skills you can draw on to exploit opportunities that come your way and to minimize threats that appear.

When you look at your weaknesses, you are acknowledging that you have deficiencies that prevent you from performing as well as you should and that must be overcome to avoid failure. Examples of weaknesses could include the length of time required to take a product from the lab to the market, lack of overseas presence, or a failure to leverage your brand recognition with suppliers.

In most cases, only surface weaknesses are admitted. The most delicate issue, and one that is normally either glossed over or merely alluded to, deals with the assessment of the strengths and weaknesses of existing management. This is part of the issue mentioned earlier when discussing the problem of achieving planning team cooperation with the task forces. It is, however, a problem that must be confronted at this stage for Dynamic Planning to succeed to the highest degree possible. Although the Dynamic

Planning process itself encourages a new awareness and openness to change on the part of senior management, it cannot force personality changes. It can, however, be used to find ways to make accommodation possible. For example, say the CEO of a fairly new company is a strong, dynamic leader as well as visionary. As the business begins to grow, key management, people who are excited by companies in a growth stage, people somewhat averse to bureaucracy and boundaries, are hired. These individuals have exactly the skill sets needed to build a business. The problem is that once the business has grown past a certain point, they may lack the skills necessary for managing a large business, or they simply may not want to manage within the structured environment of a large business. The fact that this has happened is often uncovered in the planning process.

If the planning team members face this reality, they can use the information in the option generation phase to place a heavy emphasis on, say, spinning off start-up divisions to develop new products and markets. They can place those managers least comfortable with managing established businesses in charge of the start-ups. They then could bring in or promote from within new managers with more administrative than innovative strengths. Taking such a path allows them to retain the skills of creativity and innovation that were responsible for their original growth, and yet run the original business in such a way that it provides the financial means for future growth and development as well as current profit. In other words, by not ignoring the truth about their own skills, they may be able to leverage those skills into a means of securing the business's long-term future. If the facilitator makes clear the growth potential in honest evaluation, and some form of guarantees about the future are put in place, everyone can benefit.

There is no denying that this issue is difficult to address and discuss objectively with senior management in a focus session. And there are times when an internal facilitator simply cannot get through to senior management on the subject. When there is such an impasse, one of the best courses of action would be to engage a consultant with a change management and human resources background to hold sessions with the planning team and to discuss the problem with the appropriate leaders of the organization to ensure that everyone's concerns and needs are treated fairly. Once the internal issues are dealt with, the next step in the SWOT analysis is to compare your strengths and weaknesses with those of your major competitors. Again, the information about your competitors is not precise—but it represents a starting point or strawman position for the discussion. As stated previously, the intent of these discussions is to obtain a realistic and objective perspective about your competencies. One of the major tasks facing the facilitator in this discussion is to ensure that finger-pointing comments are diffused; the point is to acknowledge the weaknesses of the organization in the context of collective weaknesses, not singular shortcomings of any individual, group, or functional area. In addition, the weaknesses that do surface should not be attributed solely to external forces; for example, "The strength of the dollar has hurt our overseas markets" or "The market is soft because of the recession and no one is buying—see, our competitors are having the same problems."

The same process would apply when discussing opportunities and threats. Again, the facilitator would lead a focus session aimed at surfacing the opportunities and threats not only in today's market, but also in any potential future markets. No matter how rudimentary your view of the future of your industry is, this kind of analysis provides an advantage when opportunities as well as future threats appear.

As with the discussion and admission of weaknesses, most planning team members underestimate threats—primarily future threats. This is a mistake because today's competitors were yesterday's threats; you just didn't notice or pay attention to them as they emerged. For example, returning to our convenience store chain, if you examine the retail convenience store sector, two of the generic CSFs for the sector are number of locations and speed of service. A retail convenience store chain may assume that the notion of speed of service is a core competency, a strength of the business that has been built up over time. Given this assumption, it may also assume that other new entrants into the sector will have a difficult time coming up the learning curve. In addition, location, and more precisely, the need to have a large number of locations, may be a significant barrier to entry. However, if you examine the sector today, it appears that service stations are now in the retail convenience business—they have prime locations, basically on every major intersection in most cities, and they have optimized the notion of convenience. They are no longer a potential threat; they have become active competitors in the retail convenience business (see Chapter 7).

In addition to examining threats that exist today, you should try to identify potential future threats—current suppliers, customers, or possible new entrants. In some instances, businesses may bring customers or suppliers into a SWOT analysis session. Involving customers and suppliers can be extremely beneficial—if the planning team members are open and willing to accept criticism. One of the concerns that will come up is the motive of the customer or supplier—are they being open, or do they have a hidden agenda? If a CSF of the firm is to build partnerships with external stakeholders (because we all have to work together if we are to succeed), then this would be a positive move toward attaining the CSF. If the planning team feels that working closely or sharing information with suppliers or obtaining customer input is not critical to the success of the business, then the perceived value of external stakeholder involvement would be minimal.

You can use a number of techniques to augment the basic SWOT analysis. One that can help is a driving force analysis—selecting and analyzing how best to use the single, most important focus of the business. For example, a business may be product or service driven, technology driven, or market driven. A business should have one driving force—the force that will form the basis upon which it will compete. For example, let's look at a product-driven distribution company (in this case, a company selling computers) that decides that it can gain more opportunities if it maintains a database of all the information it collects about its suppliers and customers, and by analyzing these data, it can add enough value to be able to sell that information to customers in different markets. That would switch it from product driven to service driven (that is, service in the form of information and knowledge rather than selling a product). It now has a different driving force, which requires a new mission statement, different CSFs and assumptions, and new strategies and actions for the company. (The story of this switch is presented in detail in Chapter 10.)

Yet another technique that could be used to supplement and enhance the SWOT analysis is Michael Porter's framework for analyzing competitive forces.[3] It is a way of looking at the various factors that the business should consider when examining its position with respect to (1) new entrants, (2) substitute products or services, (3) customers, and (4) suppliers in terms of the competition it is facing. By mapping the assumptions that were derived and discussed in the focus sessions to determine which of these four areas each assumption falls into, you will develop insights about senior management's focus. For example, if the majority of your assumptions deal with other competitors, but few, if any, deal with the threat of new entrants or substitute products, you will know that you are neglecting an important set of threats and opportunities.

You could also use this kind of analysis to position your business to take advantage of your strengths and find ways to mitigate your weaknesses. For example, based upon a SWOT analysis, your strengths may be your information technology capability and distribution network. In addition, based upon your analysis of the competition and the industrial sector, and the derived scenarios, you may conclude that your strengths can be leveraged to establish a global distribution network. Based upon what you know, although your competitors have comparable strengths in distribution, they have limited information technology capabilities. They would be slow to respond because of the time and costs required to play catch-up. Thus, you have uncovered a significant opportunity.

Another Porter technique that is useful in analyzing what you do well today and how this can be leveraged in the future is to analyze the value chain of the organization. The value chain, which is also a tool in activity-based costing, details all the internal operations of a business and assigns costs to them.[4] By examining the way goods and services move through the organization, you gain insights into your strengths and weaknesses. In addition, you will begin to understand how a change in one aspect of the value chain can impact other relationships in the chain. It is a means of looking at the trees as well as the forest.

The Porter technique can also be used to examine the influence of external stakeholders in the value chain and the impact any changes made to the value chain will have on them. For example, the value chain of a distributor may include generic business functions such as marketing, sales, distribution, and after-sales service. Other aspects of the business may include human resources, finance, legal, information services, and a variety of administrative functions. If you look at the value chain in terms of the information collected and analyzed during the internal evaluation, you may identify ways to leverage strengths and opportunities as well as develop ways to minimize your weaknesses. In this instance, by examining the value chain, you may realize that there is a significant amount of information about customers, markets, and products that you distribute that is literally passing through the value chain untapped. This information may prove to be valuable not only today, but also in terms of a future possibility—that is, selling value-added information: trend information about specific products in various markets (who is buying what, where), information about product performance, what product configurations yield the optimum margins, and what product configurations best support specific customer needs (again, selling capability, not just products).

By examining the value chain in the context of the business's buyers, suppliers, or even competitors, you may be able to find opportunities (both current as well as future) to offer services to the other external players of the business's extended value chain, including your competitors. In some instances, it may be possible to extend the boundaries of the organization electronically, establishing electronic links to a customer's order entry system in order to manufacture and distribute products to the customer on a just-in-time (JIT) basis.

A natural adjunct to value chain analysis is business process redesign (BPR). This technique is used to break down the activities of the generic or core functions of the organization identified by a value chain analysis. By asking what is being done (within each of the core functions) and why the activity is being performed, it is possible to isolate those activities that don't add value or are redundant and, consequently, are candidates for BPR—that is, candidates for rethinking and redesign. For example, in many companies, the same set of activities, under different names, may be performed by different groups in the company or at different locations. "Purchasing" may be the name for the set of activities that the manufacturing department in Peoria uses to buy materials, while the manufacturing department in Tyler, Texas, which produces the same product, may call the same set of activities "procurement." The two locations may have different procedures and different systems for handling these activities, which may in fact be able to be addressed by a common purchasing system, which would enable the company to save money because it could get bulk discounts and the operation can be handled by fewer people.

The discovery of areas for redesign is a value added of the analysis portion of the Dynamic Planning Framework. During the focus session in which the options are generated, the team should decide if there are areas for redesign that would produce substantial savings and incorporate that into their planning for the future. The team should be able to derive that information from a review of the position paper.

PULLING THE PAPER TOGETHER

The time has now come to complete Activity 4.0 by putting all the information collected into a formal document—the position paper—which will serve as the foundation for the planning team's deliberations about the future. There is no set of hard and fast rules on what a position paper should look like. The purpose of the paper is not to present a detailed account of how the information was collected, but rather to summarize the important points of agreement and explain the areas of disagreement. The culture of the organization will dictate the style and format: some organizations present materials in bullet or outline form; others use written documents with diagrams, charts, and figures illustrating extensive narratives.

The position paper should cover all the categories explored during the analyses; that is, it should discuss, at a minimum, the goals, critical success factors, assumptions, strengths, weaknesses, and competencies as well as any other categories the facilitator and the task force members believe would be pertinent to senior management. The paper should highlight those categories whose importance was agreed upon by senior management, but more important, those areas in which agreement could not be reached. The paper should also explain how the agreed-upon goals, CSFs, and all the other categories compare with the teams' findings for the business's competitors. It should then present the information gathered that relates to the structure of the business: governance, managerial talents, information needs, and the business's assets, including information technology (that is, what it has in the way of hardware and software as well as the level of computer literacy of its personnel). The paper should also explain what the task forces believe the future holds in terms of the industrial sector and direct competitors, based on their observations of the external world and their analysis of the industry-specific vocabulary they collected. As a conclusion, the paper should discuss the problems the task forces believe the company faces as well as the concerns it has about the possible negative impact of trends in the outside world as well as the implications of these trends for the future direction and success of the business.

The point is that the position paper should provide the planning team with the information it needs, in addition to its own knowledge and expertise, to explore the current state of the organization as it really is. It should force the members of the team to see the true state of the business from a broad perspective, bringing the team to an understanding that cuts across turf, privilege, and function, exposing the business to its true self.

CONCLUSION

Once the position paper is ready, the members of the planning team and the facilitator will meet in an extensive focus session, for which the paper will serve as an agenda, exploring the options that are available to help move the organization forward. The planning team, in other words, will use the information in the position paper as a basis for generating the options available to the organization if it decides to be a player in the future. This activity (5.0), which is explored in the next chapter, forces the firm to make sure it examines all the paths to the future so that it can choose the path that is best—and not end up bemoaning the path not taken.

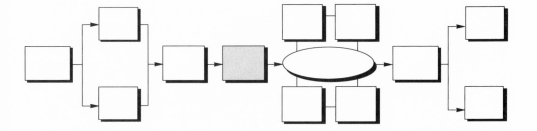

CHAPTER 7

GENERATING OPTIONS

Two roads diverged in a wood, and I —
I took the one less travelled by,
And that has made all the difference.

Robert Frost

Those living in totalitarian nations or prisons say that the lack of control over their lives is the worst aspect of their existence. They have little or no say over what will happen to them day to day and few options for the future. Yet how many of us, and how many corporations with no such restrictions, never take control, never examine what it is we want for the future, never sit down and decide how to apply our skills, talents, and resources? The point of Dynamic Planning is to look ahead, decide what the future may hold for your firm, examine what role you can play in achieving that future, and then choose the path that will mean the greatest success.

The position paper developed in the last chapter will serve here as the starting point for generating those options for the future that seem most reasonable. The paper, developed in Activity 4.0 of the Dynamic Planning Framework, becomes the agenda-setter for meetings at which the planning team will, first, focus on determining the possibilities that seem most viable for the organization to pursue. Once the team pulls together a list of options, the focus session turns to a preliminary analysis of those highest on the list, evaluating the risks they pose in terms of their cost, time, value to the business, and types of personnel needed and available. The result of the evaluation should be a set of three to five business options that everyone agrees make some sense—at least on the surface—for the business to consider pursuing. These meetings, or focus sessions, comprise Activity 5.0, generating options, the final part of the second step in the Framework, the search for solutions. (Once this second step of the Framework is completed, another process is used to look at the effects of the options on the strategic and operational aspects of the business. Going through this process, as we shall see, often brings to light additional options based on the combination of the options being tested with the information technology already available.)

INTERNALIZING THE TRUTH

At this stage, the members of the planning team need to review the position paper, discuss it, internalize it, and decide what business options can be derived from it for the future. The planning team must decide what the organization can do to ensure at least its survival, and at best, to find ways to change and grow.

It is often difficult, however, for senior managers to accept the information in the position paper. Even if they know that the time has come to change the business to ensure its continued success, they must overcome their own perceptions of the value of various paths taken in the past (paths they may have chosen); they must accept the possibility that what will be best in the future may limit their advancement in the firm (and perhaps change the nature of their jobs); they must give up precious time to work on planning for the long term (when they believe they should be spending their time working toward enhancing quarterly profits both to meet shareholder and board demands and to ensure successful performance reviews or greater profit shares).[1] And, of course, there are those who do not understand why the business, which is doing well, should change at all. Although they recognize that emerging external factors may hurt the company at some time in the future, they do not believe that it is possible to really predict the nature of those changes. These, and any number of other forms of resistance, which range from loyalty to the intent of the company's founders to a failure to understand that the market for a product is dying, also make long-range planning difficult.

Many will argue that the fact that senior managers were visionary enough to even support the concept of Dynamic Planning shows that they will not be resistant to whatever suggestions for change might emerge. Unfortunately, this is far from true. What all too often happens is that those managers who must accept the changes, having realized that the company's leaders are endorsing the process, give lip service to the concept, but subtly, and often subconsciously, do everything they can to undermine it. Managers just can't attend a session on that day, or the next, or the next week; or they attend, but their secretaries call them away time after time; or they spend the time at the session raising inappropriate issues, grandstanding, or making life unpleasant for everyone else.

LET THE SESSIONS BEGIN

Since this kind of resistance on the part of at least some managers is, in our experience, very likely, the role of the facilitator is often extremely difficult. The facilitator has to keep the meetings focused on the official, business-oriented agenda of the sessions while carefully monitoring the unofficial psychological ploys of the participants. The facilitator may have to change strategies several times during a session, moving from assertive to inquiring to demanding to soothing to provocative, depending on the situation. It is therefore important that the facilitator set strong ground rules and enforce them; for example, insisting upon agreement in the opening minutes that he or she will set time limits on discussion and will have the right to cut off speakers or decide to change topics.

In these intense sessions in which the first group of options are generated, the facilitator works with the planning team members (with advice and additional information from representatives of the internal and external analysis task forces when appropriate) to help them decide in what ways the organization can adapt and change to meet the challenges and opportunities that seem to lie ahead. Much of the value of the focus sessions held at this stage of the Dynamic Planning process is that they begin the process of opening management to the possibilities of and necessity for thinking long term. The sessions also provide the consensus building that is necessary in order to come up with a narrow list of options to work with in the next stage of the Framework. Therefore, the facilitator must see to it that everyone participates and that no members of the team become so unhappy that they refuse to accept the will of the majority and undermine the process.

There are many techniques for leading discussions of what is possible for an organization. The methods used should be different from those that predominate at the organization's usual meetings; using a different format frees people to make suggestions that don't fit the norm. For example, if the usual style at meetings is to ask for an idea and then discuss it and decide on whether it is good before moving on to another idea, a focus session aimed at generating options might be a free-wheeling session in which the facilitator collects ideas and writes them down on large flip charts, but allows no discussion until a given number are collected. The fact that no idea is shot down allows people to speak their minds without feeling that they will be attacked. If the list is assembled rapidly and no attribution listed for the items, then in our experience, people open up more and more as the list grows. This is important, since one goal is to get people to think more broadly about the business, and to speak freely, not just to say what they assume will be noncontroversial.

In pursuit of this goal, the facilitator must ensure that there is as little negative feedback as possible on a personal level. It is also useful to have either the facilitator or someone high in the organization come up with a "far-out" idea or two so that people will feel freer to explore ideas. If run well, this kind of focus session also can become a safe place to put forth ideas, to air grievances, to point to long-standing problems.

REVIEWING THE POSITION PAPER

The position paper should be a springboard to open and honest discussion of the firm and its future. The goal is to pull ideas out of the material presented in the paper, to put together "A" and "B" and arrive at "C," and then to evaluate whether or not, given financial resources, available technology, personnel with appropriate skill sets, current economic conditions, and competitors, each of the "Cs" you arrived at is, at least on the surface, possible. The final choice of which options to pursue will be made after analyzing the few options deemed feasible following a preliminary evaluation by the planning team.

The process for doing this, the third step of the Framework, analyzing the solutions, will be described in detail in the next three chapters. It is important to note here that the process used in this later evaluation, the Strategic Alignment Model, considers information technology an equal partner in the business; doing so changes the usual paradigm of having options wholly generated by the business side of the organization. Because the Alignment Model gives information technology strategy an almost equal role in determining the business's future, it tends to generate additional options that are not possible without technology.

It is also important to keep in mind that since Dynamic Planning is a continual and ongoing process, there will be times when, in revisiting various steps, it will be necessary to do new planning for a portion of the business rather than the business as a whole. Once Dynamic Planning becomes a way of life, it will not, as we will show later in this chapter, be unusual for, say, the information technology organization or the manufacturing division to revisit its planning using the Framework.

In any and all such uses of Dynamic Planning, the normal steps in the Framework apply. The focus sessions begin with a question and answer segment that allows the members of the planning team, whether for the whole organization or a division or functional area, to ask for clarification and explanation of areas that seem unclear or contradictory. The facilitator, who has worked closely with the members of the task forces, is often the one to explain the discrepancies. Once all the issues seem to be resolved (it is normal to have many other questions arise in the course of the session), the facilitator can begin to collect the planning team's initial perception of the options available to the organization given the realities of its operations, its competitors, and the world outside.

The focus sessions are never as cut and dried as this sounds. When you get a group of people together to discuss their futures—and that is exactly what these sessions are about—the sessions tend to take on a life of their own. Every time we conduct one, we find ourselves surprised at the end of the day by the course the discussion took, although the end result is not usually far from what we anticipated. Since flexibility and openness are the goals, the meeting cannot be run in such a way that those qualities are inhibited. At the same time, the sessions must constantly hark back to the hard information contained in the position paper. Each of the options suggested should be tested against the realities set forth in the paper.

OPTION GENERATION IN REAL TIME

The planning assignment for the chain of retail convenience stores mentioned in the last chapter provides a good example of the option generation process. The chain had been built around a service concept that involved numerous locations and seven-day-a-week, twenty-four-hour-a-day service. The goods sold by the store included soft drinks, juices, milk, bread, eggs, a small selection of canned goods, paper goods, and toiletries—those things you need to get as soon as you run out of them (items such as disposable diapers and aspirin) as well as fast foods (frozen and microwavable-in-the-store breakfast and lunch items as well as coffee, donuts, and simple ready-to-eat, prepared items) and newspapers and cigarettes. In addition, it had recently introduced a small-scale video rental operation and the sale of money orders.

The senior managers of the chain, which was based in the Southwest, were looking for ways to grow the business. Although they normally shared the same views about the future of the industry and the competition, some executives had expressed nominal concern about the recent development of gas stations stocking some convenience items in their facilities, turning them into tiny stores. There was also some concern about the reputation of their own stores, which, because they were often fairly deserted late at night, had become the target of robbers. The goal was to find ways to overcome these problems and to expand and grow.

The project involving the selection of future options for the convenience stores was built to conform to the Dynamic Planning Framework, and the task forces assembled and delivered a position paper in short order. The position paper pointed out, for example, that although there were two other major players among convenience stores, they were the market leader and dominated their industrial sector. Among their major strengths were their large number of store locations; name recognition in the marketplace; strong financial position; the ability to develop and rapidly introduce new lines of fast foods (such as frozen burritos that could be purchased and heated in a microwave oven in the store) or innovative services (such as video rentals and money orders); and their emerging information technology capabilities. In fact, their introduction of low-cost video rentals in their convenience stores literally destroyed the local market for video clubs that charged a membership fee. (Since that time, large-scale video rental chains have come to dominate that market.)

The major weaknesses that were highlighted in the position paper were the existing profile of their customer base (primarily eighteen- to thirty-five-year-old blue-collar workers), the number of layers of financial and operational management needed not only to perform the financial accounting activities but also to manage the store operations, and the high turnover rate of store personnel. With respect to major threats, the position paper pointed out that the convenience store market would be saturated in as little as three years, but no more than five years. In addition, the paper also confirmed the fact that gas stations with attached minimarts were not only a significant threat to the traditional notion of a convenience store but also were an existing force in the sector and were likely to become major competitors in an increasingly tough battle for market share. The advantages of the stores attached to the gas stations were location (to accommodate cars they are nearly always located on major intersections); safety (they tended to be in high traffic areas even at night); and additional convenience (you could fill your gas tank while stopping to make a purchase). In addition, even supermarkets had begun to pose a threat to the claim of convenience—they were enhancing their level of service by staying open twenty-four hours a day and adding express lanes for purchases of a small number of items.

The position paper also highlighted the fact that any new fast food product the company developed could be copied and introduced by the competition in less than six weeks. In other words, the threat of substitute products being introduced by the competition in this environment was very high, making it almost impossible to gain anything other than a short-term advantage in the marketplace. The position paper developed by the task forces confirmed the intuition of the planning team members; to ensure continued success in the short term, they could fix existing problems such as safety and operational efficiency, but if they were to continue to grow the business they would have to look for other business options compatible to the convenience store.

One of the key members of the external analysis task force was the manager of strategic planning for the company. He was innovative, had the respect of all members of the planning team, and served as day-to-day liaison among the task forces, the team, and us. As a result, he was able to help the planning team develop and evaluate various business options— and present additional options that we and the task force members believed warranted consideration given our knowledge of the outside world. Among the options we agreed the planning team should consider were the following:

- Increasing the real estate development operation of the business, a natural adjunct to its core business, since it managed the purchase and lease of many of its store sites

- Acquiring competing convenience stores; here, the planning team decided that, given the intensity of the rivalry among and between the owners of the competing chains, it was unlikely that this option would succeed without significant cost and disruption to the existing business

- Encouraging the introduction of additional, related services similar to its entry into video rentals and money orders. (In fact, the money order service was so successful, given the demographics of its customer base, that it had not only created a new market, but in the process was able to use the funds generated from the sale of the money orders to gain additional revenue by placing them in overnight and weekend money market accounts.)

The third option created the most heated debate. During the discussions with the task force members that led up to the position paper, the manager of strategic planning had presented the idea that the future of the company was in the development and delivery of electronic services of some sort. This idea was, in part, based on the forces that seemed to be pushing the sector in new directions according to the external analysis of the task force. It appeared from that analysis that none of its competitors were considering offering any form of electronic services. Since the idea of putting in more information systems and technology to increase operational efficiency and better track customer buying habits seemed likely to be adopted, given the chain's record in this area, and since this was likely to involve electronic ties between stores, it seemed to the manager that there was a tie between the two ideas, although he was unable to be more specific.

In the course of the planning team focus session, the idea was put to discussion and an insight emerged: in addition to its core strengths of understanding the notion of convenience and its ability to develop new products and services, the company had over five thousand store locations across the country. (They were no more than five minutes away from 50 percent of the population in their strongest regions.) By viewing this strength in a different fashion, the planning team developed the concept that the stores could really be viewed as five thousand nodes in an electronic network, if they were "wired" together. In essence, the locations were not only a physical asset that sold convenience store items, but each location could also serve as a node, an electronic entry point, to every other node across the network. This was a radically different view of their asset. Wiring the stores as nodes in a network meant that the company could then develop and deliver a variety of financial services on a national basis. The team developed a list of over thirty-five financial products and services ranging from installing ATMs in the stores that would accept a number of different bank cards to handling money transfers on a national basis. If this option proved viable after further analysis it would literally change what the company did for a living. It would take the next step, the analysis of the options in the Strategic Alignment Model, to determine whether the option was one it could successfully pursue.

The discussions of the options put forth included testing them in terms of the information collected about the outside world as well as the knowledge base of various team members. For example, in discussing the option, "develop the real estate operation" of the chain, the Chief Financial Officer, who was responsible for that part of the operation, pointed out that the current staff was inadequate to the task, that the amount of credit needed to run such an operation would be difficult to establish, and that the reason for the earlier success it had in the area was because the person who had originally been in charge of it had had a great deal of training in zoning policy, but she was no longer with the company. Each option put forth, and the three mentioned were only a fourth of the ones considered worth discussing, was subjected to this kind of scrutiny.

EVALUATING YOUR CHOICES

The result of the focus session should be a narrowing of options to a handful that the planning team agrees justifies further analysis. However, the process of narrowing options often takes on a life of its own. As the team learns to pick the important issues of risk each option raises, the discussions become more pointed and focused. In most cases, a formal criteria for evaluating options should be developed by the facilitator and the members of the task forces. A formal evaluation criteria would not only reduce the time and effort it takes to narrow the list of options, but more important, it would help focus the discussion of the planning team members. The evaluation criteria would include such determinants of risk as:

- Time frame against the competition. If you know whether it is likely to take your competitor six weeks, six months, or six years to duplicate an innovation, you can decide how viable, and valuable, the option is.

◆   Resources needed. If you were to try to take over a competitor, what kind of debt would you incur and how exposed would that leave you to someone trying to take you over?

◆   Ease of implementation. What additional personnel would you need and how many current employees would have to be dismissed? Would you need larger or different facilities?

◆   The state of technological advances. If the technology to allow you to do something faster is available now but the cost is higher than what you would gain, is it still worth purchasing because it is likely that the technology will serve as the base for future technological advances? That is, should you risk investing for the future in this area?

If the team is having difficulty, one method of moving the discussion along is to set up an option/criteria evaluation matrix—similar to the one used for determining the relative importance of critical assumptions in Chapter 5. On one axis of the matrix, list the options the team has generated; on the other axis, list the criteria the team has agreed to use to evaluate each option. For example, resources required, risks, costs, time frame, or any number of factors that the team believes is critical for evaluating each option. The facilitator would then lead the team in filling in each cell of the option/criteria matrix (see Figure 7.1). This provides a convenient mechanism

Criteria	Option 1	Option 2	Option 3	Option 4	Option 5
Resources Required					
Costs					
Risks Implementation Technology Funding					
Value					
Time Frame					
Skill Sets					

Figure 7.1. Option/Criteria Matrix
© 1993 B. Goldberg and J. G. Sifonis

for narrowing the list of options that need further analysis. At the end of the day, however, it is essential that the team agree on no more than three to five options to analyze further. The time needed for the next stage of analysis, the Strategic Alignment Model (Activity 6.0), if properly explained, will help push the team to gather its resolve for decisionmaking.

OPTION GENERATION THE SECOND TIME AROUND

As mentioned earlier, once the business has been through Dynamic Planning, it is easy to apply it to more specific reevaluations; for example, planning for a division or functional area. The materials collected by the task forces serve in these cases as starting points for adding specific, detailed information about the division or functional area. When a large public utility holding company in the Midwest, for example, embarked on a Dynamic Planning project, it decided that, as part of the drive to remain open to constant change, it would keep in place two groups in the future. The first would be a team charged with watching developments that might affect the company in the future (its members would be drawn from the external analysis task force); the second would be a team charged with periodically reviewing the implications of changes going on internally as a result of the planning process already under way (its members would be drawn from the internal analysis task force).

These teams proved to be invaluable, joining together to serve as the task force each time a division or functional area decided to review the way it was doing what it did for a living. These reviews were conducted to accommodate the changes taking place within the organization as a result of the decisions the planning team in charge of overall Dynamic Planning were implementing. The teams, for example, served as the information technology task force responsible for developing an information technology strategy that would be aligned with the new business strategy of the organization.

The situation facing the IT task force was that the holding company had been in existence for over fifty years when a new CEO had come into office. During the initial years of his tenure, this CEO had increased revenues and profitability by acquiring small- to medium-sized power companies across the country. Although the strategy was successful, it did not produce the growth he had envisioned for the company. Therefore, in the early 1990s, he and his management team decided to reexamine their business strategy.

One of the options the holding company evaluated and ultimately elected to implement was the acquisition of nonregulated companies. This was a bold move away from its traditional business strategy of acquiring other public utilities in different geographic regions of the country. It also meant learning how to manage nonregulated businesses—businesses in which there was no guaranteed rate of return because of their geographic monopoly as a public utility. The CEO also held the assumption that not only was IT critical to the success of the company, but also that a change in business strategy meant that it was necessary to look at the implications of these changes on the IT strategy of the company.

This was the point at which the IT task force was chartered to develop a new IT strategy. Leveraging the information gleaned by its members when they served on the internal and external analysis task forces for the overall Dynamic Planning project, the IT task force members, through a cooperative and consensus process, identified a number of options for evaluation. The intent was to examine all viable options that would support the corporate strategy and fit within the assumptions and constraints derived by the task force. For example, one of the critical assumptions of the task force was that the operating companies were to have IT autonomy; that is, the right to have their own processing capabilities if they desired. A number of options were generated:

◆   Establish a centralized processing facility. This option called for all information processing to be performed at one location for all operating companies.

◆   Outsource the IT services. This option called for all processing for the operating companies to be performed by an outside service provider.

◆   Create autonomous, but structured, downsized facilities. This option called for each operating company to have its own IT capabilities. It also required that each adopt downsized or client/server technology; that is, personal computer-based technology and applications as compared to large, mainframe-based technology. In addition, this option required that the same set of applications (the programs that produce usable information) be usable by all operating companies; that is, it must be a structured operating environment. This would significantly reduce costs, provide commonality and sharing of information among and between all operating companies, and still allow each operating company to address its local market needs.

◆   Create autonomous facilities. This option called for each operating company to be given the right to choose whatever technology or applications it felt would be in its own best interests, or it could elect not to have any IT capability. This was the ultimate option in terms of operating company autonomy. However, it would also foster a variety of different technologies across the company and increase costs because there would be no sharing of resources among and between the operating companies.

After conducting preliminary research and discussing the issues, two options were deleted from the list. "Establish a centralized processing facility" was rejected because it meant that an operating company could not have its own processing capabilities and therefore violated the assumption of operating company autonomy. In addition, "outsource the IT services" was rejected because the company would lose control over its information processing resources if it did so. This option also was felt to violate the assumption of operating company autonomy with respect to obtaining its own processing resources.

The other two options were argued and discussed at length. Although the members believed that the option "create autonomous, but structured, downsized facilities" came closer to satisfying the evaluation criteria established by the task force—it was aligned with the business strategy and supported the new strategic direction of the company—both it and the option "create autonomous facilities" were put through the Strategic Alignment Model (Activity 6.0) to examine the implications and feasibility of implementing these options on the structure and operations of the organization.

THE VALUE OF THE PROCESS

At this point, the planning team has developed a thorough—and collective—picture of the organization. They understand its current and future goals. They have a sense of what problems it is likely to face and have come to some agreement on how to deal with those problems. They also should have a sense that there are opportunities that are theirs to seize. If the process has worked well so far, the senior managers of the business should also know one another a little better and certainly should be less likely to miscommunicate in the future. They also should be more aware of the importance of keeping alert to developments in the outside world.

If the fact that the growth they have experienced—that is, intellectual, conceptual growth in terms of how they view the business—has been valuable can be brought home to them, they will also be ripe for the suggestion that they must help their employees do the same. This is the moment at which the idea for a company-wide communication project is born. The organization is entering a new period, one of change for anticipated growth and success, and this should be communicated to the organization through a change management program. (The way such a program is developed is described in detail in Chapter 13.)

The necessity for beginning such communication is driven by the fact that the next step in Dynamic Planning, analyzing the solutions, requires a thorough analysis of the internal working of the organization, including an evaluation of available skill sets. Since nothing that senior management is involved in goes unnoticed for long—and since such an evaluation is particularly threatening to employees not directly involved—not communicating what is going on will lead to anxiety and confusion that will create inaction, the exact opposite of what Dynamic Planning is about.

PART III

ANALYZING THE SOLUTIONS

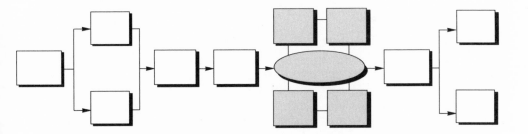

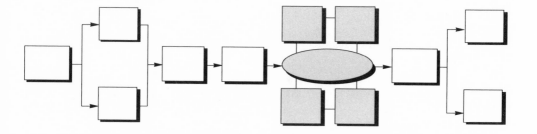

CHAPTER 8

STRATEGIC ALIGNMENT MODELING

A clear-cut definition of structure and strategy and a simplified explana-
tion or theory of the relation of one to the other should make it easier to
comprehend the complex realities involved in the expansion and manage-
ment of the great industrial enterprises. . . .

Alfred D. Chandler, Jr.[1]

T he planning team has selected a limited number of options that, at
least on the surface, make sense for the enterprise's future in terms of
what is happening in the world and the marketplace and in terms of its
own strengths and weaknesses. Now it is time to analyze those options.
The objective of the analysis is to determine which options will provide the
organization with the greatest opportunities. Obviously, each option will
mean changes within the organization, and some options will fit into the
organization better than others do. Moreover, some will generate additional options when examined more thoroughly.

Often, by selecting the option that has the potential to bring the greatest success to your organization—and that may mean choosing the road
less traveled—you may be choosing an option that will cause disruption.
The point is to be able to anticipate the problems various options will create so you can adjust the organization to accommodate them.

THE ANALYTICAL PROCESS

The process used to analyze the options, Activity 6.0, Strategic Alignment
Modeling (Figure 8.1), is the third step of the Dynamic Planning
Framework, the analysis of the solutions. Since Strategic Alignment
Modeling (SAM) requires a deep understanding of the organization, the

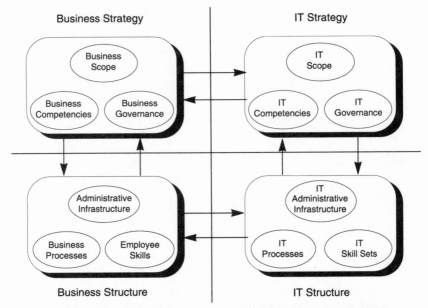

Figure 8.1. The Strategic Alignment Model: Aligning Business and IT Strategy
Source: Adapted from J. C. Henderson and N. Venkatraman, "Strategic Alignment," CISR
Working Paper No. 190, August 1989.

planning team is going to have to apply all the information it gathered in
the internal and external analyses in a different context. This is made possible by the work done in the focus sessions, which helped the planning
team internalize the knowledge it was amassing.

Working out options through SAM requires analyzing the effects of
each option on both the strategy and structure of the business and the
information technology (IT) sides of the organization. SAM makes explicit the relationship between the business strategy and structure (the building blocks of the business side) and the IT strategy and structure (the
building blocks of the IT side).

Strategic Alignment Modeling starts from the premise that every
change made in any one of the four building blocks has an effect on the
other three. SAM shows, for example, that as changes are made in the
business strategy, changes take place in the staffing needs on both the IT
and the business side; as changes are made in the IT structure, the way the
business is managed can change and the services a company offers can be
expanded. If you think of the business and IT strategy and structure as the
anchors of a cat's cradle where you have to adjust the strings evenly every
time you want to change the design, you will have a better picture of the
need to analyze what each move will do so you can make the changes
necessary to restore the alignment before your string gets tied in knots.

EXAMINING THE FOUR BUILDING BLOCKS OF THE ENTERPRISE

Before we can examine the effects of changes in the organization's business or information technology side on each other, it is important to thoroughly understand each. Even though analyzing the blocks requires looking at them concurrently, in this chapter they are presented in a linear fashion in order to ensure understanding of the terms as used in the context of the business and the IT sides of the enterprise. As noted in Figure 8.1, the business strategy building block consists of three interrelated components: business scope, business competencies, and business governance. The business structure building block also has three interrelated components: administrative infrastructure, business processes, and employee skills.

BUSINESS STRATEGY

This box of the model is usually considered the key to an organization, and in the past, it set the strategic direction and all policy. Each division and functional area was controlled by those responsible for the business strategy. Even though this is no longer the case, the components of the business strategy remain the same.

BUSINESS SCOPE

This component determines what products and services the organization offers, who the customers for those products and services are, and what markets they are trying to reach (local, regional, national, multinational, or global). For example, the decisions made about business scope may result in creating an organization that focuses on selling competitively priced commodity products, such as personal computers or software, to computer literate customers in the domestic market (Commodity Products, Inc.).[2] At the other extreme would be decisions about business scope that resulted in the creation of an organization focused on selling only powerful, multimillion-dollar scientific computers anywhere in the world where there were highly sophisticated customers requiring massive computing power (Leading-Edge Technologies, Inc.). There are numerous other areas where such contrasts can be found—for example, L.L. Bean and Giorgio Armani or posters and works of art. These scope-of-business decisions— low end or high end, mass market or exclusive—are interrelated with and impact the choices the organization will make with respect to the other two components of the business strategy: business competencies and business governance.

The information needed to determine the organization's existing scope of business was collected by the internal analysis team in Activity 3.0 through questionnaires and interviews with the planning team members. One of the objectives of collecting and reviewing this information was to ensure that the planning team members not only developed a thorough understanding of, but were in complete agreement about, the enterprise's existing scope of business.

COMPETENCIES

The next component is the organization's core competencies; that is, those distinctive attributes that give the organization the capability to differentiate its products and services from those of its competitors in the marketplace. They are the attributes of an enterprise that make a potential customer select it instead of its competition when deciding to purchase a product or a service. For example, firms such as Nordstrom and Home Depot excel in customer service. They ensure that all customers get what they want with as little effort as possible.[3]

The choices an organization makes with respect to competencies are related to its decisions about its scope of business. Given the scope of business of Commodity Products, it may decide that selling directly to customers through electronic channels as compared to mail order or retail stores is the best way to keep its prices low enough to gain market share. To implement this plan, Commodity Products may decide that its distinctive competency will lie in providing superior ease and speed of electronic order processing and product delivery, thereby differentiating its services in the marketplace. For an organization such as Leading-Edge Technologies, the competencies required for differentiating its products may be superior circuit design, manufacturing, and post-sales customer service.

The information necessary to determine the organization's competencies is also part of the information the internal analysis team collected through the questionnaires and interviews with the planning team members in Activity 3.0, when it ascertained the strengths and weaknesses of the organization and reviewed the findings with the planning team members to ensure agreement. Analyzing the strengths of the organization leads to the identification of distinctive competencies.

GOVERNANCE

The last component of business strategy is governance—the collection of policies or rules that control its actual operation. Governance involves the social, economic, political, and legal ownership choices made by the business. Business governance choices are interrelated with the organization's decisions on business scope and competencies.

Turning again to Commodity Products, the organization may decide to outsource all processes associated with the design and manufacturing functions and focus only on the final assembly and product distribution processes. In this example, the governance choices may include establishing strategic alliances or joint ventures with a number of designers, manufacturers, and suppliers of the components that are needed for assembling the computers. The implications of choosing to form strategic alliances rather than joint ventures are very different from a business governance perspective. In a strategic alliance, the alliance partners may work closely with one another, but there is no direct ownership. The partners work together because they believe that they are receiving some form of benefit from the alliance. In a joint venture, there is a degree of ownership and the risks and rewards are shared between and among the partners. Since the success or failure of one partner may significantly impact the other joint venture partners, there is a clear perception of the need to work together. These represent two significantly different governance choices, one involving questions of governance within a nonstructured, relationship-based setting and the other involving rules of behavior that are mutually agreed upon, contracted, and therefore enforceable.

Now, turning to Leading-Edge Technologies, a different governance choice would be performing all the processes associated with critical functions in-house (such as research and development, design, and manufacturing for all key computer components) and dealing with only a limited number of suppliers and manufacturers for noncritical components on a transaction basis rather than as business partners. In this case, the choices and implications of governance are not as complex as they were for Commodity Products. The organization, for all practical purposes, does not have to rely on outside sources for designing or manufacturing its products. Its success or failure is not dependent on or influenced by other parties, but is based on its own ability to compete in the marketplace.

In considering such questions of governance, it is important to understand the realities of the organizational structure you are working within. Is the organization a group of business units that function autonomously under the umbrella of a holding company? Is it a family-held enterprise where every division is under the direct control of a family member? Is it a virtual company that expands and contracts in response to opportunities in the marketplace on an as-needed basis? Does it have an overarching IT plan that every separate business unit must adhere to? Are the business units, even if they are equivalent in size to some lower-tier Fortune 500 companies, allowed to set their own agendas so long as they bring in a mandated minimum profit? How do you examine and plan for the whole business using Dynamic Planning?

Gaining a deep understanding of the existing rules and attributes of the enterprise—its governance—is essential to exploring the possible ways in which it can be set up administratively. In many instances, the governance choice may be rational given the scope of business and the organization's competencies, but may be impractical to implement given the existing, imbedded rules and culture of the organization. These are all questions that have to be kept in mind when examining the effects of various options during Strategic Alignment Modeling.

The clean lines of theoretical concepts and models are often blurred when examined through the lens of reality. When applying the model, this blurring has to be taken into account and the actual effects of the existing organizational structures and their governance must be recognized. It is all very well and good to note that, for example, a huge corporation has a corporate head of IT; however, that organization may have a culture that allows each division to set its own IT strategy while the business strategy *is* controlled at the corporate level. The corporate head of IT in such a case does not function on the same leadership level as, say, the corporate head of finance. These operational truths should emerge during the internal analysis. So long as those doing Dynamic Planning keep these issues in mind when working with the Strategic Alignment Model, they can avoid stepping on landmines.

BUSINESS STRUCTURE

What we are describing when we talk of the business strategy is what business the organization is in, what makes it different from the competition, and how it conducts its business. These are the things we learned about the organization in the internal analysis. These components not only define the business strategy of the organization, but also drive the other building block—the business structure. Indeed, when we move down into the business structure side, we are turning to how the business strategy is executed: who does what, how they do it, and what skills it takes. These are the three components of business structure—the administrative infrastructure, the businesses processes, and the skills of the people.

ADMINISTRATIVE INFRASTRUCTURE

This component determines the management structure, roles, responsibilities, and authority required to execute the defined business strategy. What we are looking at in operational terms is how the business should be organized to best support the defined business strategy; that is, should it be organized around products or regional markets; should it be decentralized so that the local level has authority to make decisions; or should it be centralized at the corporate level with minimal authority and responsibility delegated to the local level?

In the case of Commodity Products, given its business strategy of keeping costs low, the enterprise may choose to organize around product lines, each of which is managed by a product manager in a single location that handles orders and distribution of that single line nationwide. In this instance, there is no need to establish regional sales and service outlets for any of the organization's product lines. The enterprise may also choose to be a flat organization, in which product line managers have the responsibility and authority to make critical business decisions such as establishing pricing strategies for their products in order to rapidly respond to changes made by competitors.

Given its business strategy, Leading-Edge Technologies may choose to have a hierarchical structure and organize around product lines within geographic areas. For example, the domestic market may be divided into three regions, each headed by a regional manager who reports to the vice president for sales and marketing. Each region may contain a number of branch offices responsible for product marketing, sales, and service—and within each branch, there may be individuals assigned to market, sell, and support specific product lines of the enterprise. Given the hierarchical structure, the branch offices may have little, if any, authority to establish pricing strategies at the local level. All decisions, but more important, the setting of product strategy, would come from the corporate level, from the vice president for sales and marketing.

In the 1990s, companies are beginning to examine the need to develop new ways of operating aimed at increasing their flexibility and competitiveness, many of which will impact the administrative infrastructure. For example, companies are turning to strategic alliances, to partnerships, and to joint ventures to keep costs down. With those decisions come the need to shape new ways of running the organization, with managers having to rely on other companies for various services and components. This may mean, for example, that in the future, a company such as Commodity Products could develop a strategic alliance with a software manufacturer to have many of its products available in retail outlets. This would change the infrastructure of the company dramatically, taking away some of the authority now given managers. This decision, in turn, would create the need to rethink and possibly redefine the role, responsibility, and authority of management.

BUSINESS PROCESSES

Most organizations consist of a number of generic business functions such as research and development, engineering, manufacturing, distribution, sales, finance, and human resources. Each of these business functions, in turn, consists of one or more business processes, each of which involves a number of activities and tasks. These processes each produce some form of output (product or service or information) required by the organization to conduct its business. For example, the business processes within manufacturing may include casting metals, assembly, and painting; in finance, it may include payroll, payables, receivables, and credit checking; in sales, it may include order entry, sales forecasting, and after-sales services; in human resources, it may include recruiting, employee benefits, and management succession planning. (The recruiting process includes activities such as ad development and placement, which, in turn, require such tasks as calling a newspaper to reserve space, approving the invoice from the newspaper when it arrives, and forwarding the invoice to the finance department for payment.)

Here we are looking at how the business processes should be organized to best support the defined business strategy. Sometimes processes normally associated with one area of the business may end up in another as a result of combining processes from different functions (cross-functional integration) to support the defined business strategy and structure. In the case of Commodity Products and Leading-Edge Technologies, the choices already made will affect the process for the handling of credit checks. For example, the order entry clerks working the telephones for Commodity Products are responsible for checking credit (with the assistance of a product manager when a problem arises) during the order-taking process. While talking with the customer, they can access a number of on-line credit-checking services to get credit card authorizations. If approved, the order can be processed immediately, and the customer can receive shipment within twenty-four hours.

In the case of Leading-Edge, the payment process is very different. The finance office is informed of a possible purchase at a point in the sales process where the sales team decides a prospective buyer is turning into a likely buyer. Since they always deal with large companies, the sales force has some sense of the health of the company from the outset. But as the sales cycle goes on, the sales force informs the finance office that a sale is possible, and they do a Dun & Bradstreet (D&B) check on the prospective customer. As the deal solidifies, the finance office becomes heavily involved in the negotiations because of the complex payment structures that are likely to be needed; for example, because it takes time to put the technology Leading-Edge sells in place, the pricing can involve staggered payments on delivery of components through full implementation. Moreover, the customer may need to obtain financing for the purchase.

Thus, the sales function in Commodity Products is responsible for order entry and credit checking, leaving the finance function to handle payment collection; at Leading-Edge, the sales function involves order entry and the finance function is responsible for the credit-checking and payment collection processes. Once the companies determined their business strategies and administrative infrastructures, the processes necessary to support those decisions followed. Although the processes may be improved or redesigned or reengineered through the use of new methods and technologies as time goes on, they will always have to support business choices.

EMPLOYEE SKILLS

The nature of the activities and tasks that comprise the business processes and the way those tasks are assigned determine the skill sets needed by employees. Given a change in the enterprise's business strategy and structure, are new skills required? Do the new skills required for successfully implementing the business strategy and structure conflict with the existing culture or the way it does business? Can current employees be trained to do the new activities, or do new employees have to be recruited?

Again, all of the decisions reached so far will impact the choices of personnel and training. The skill sets needed to carry out the various processes discussed in these examples are very different. Punching a credit card number into a machine and copying an authorization code are obviously less complicated than arranging complex payment and interest schedules over a period of delivery and implementation stages. But within the simpler process there are levels of skills. For example, let's say that Commodity Products wants to offer its customers twenty-four-hour ordering capability. Unfortunately, the community in which its electronic order-processing operation is based does not provide a broad enough base of skilled employees for it to find people to answer questions about the product during the swing or night shifts. To maintain twenty-four-hour service, it must train those who take the orders after 9 P.M. and before 9 A.M. to answer basic questions by referring to a simple question-and-answer list that can be called up on the computer screen and to respond to any questions not on the list with the statement: "You need a special representative to answer that question. Our toll free customer representative line is open between 9 A.M. and 9 P.M." This allows Commodity Products to provide the basic service necessary to meet demand for twenty-four-hour ordering without bringing in more expensive, better-trained personnel to answer the phones after normal hours.

Changes in the organization's business scope or processes usually require new skill sets. Whether a company decides to retrain existing employees or bring in new employees with those skills, the effects are likely to be traumatic. The company that fails to prepare for these changes will find them extremely difficult to make; office politics, resistance, and anxiety will often cause the new processes to look less effective for a considerable time after their initial implementation. The more employees understand the need for these changes, the greater the chance for speedy implementation and the clearer the gains will be from the outset. Today, technology is usually the reason behind the changes taking place; it is a driver of change because it enables new, usually speedier processes to be put in place. But it also brings enormous changes in the kinds of skill sets needed by employees in every area.

THE PERSPECTIVE CHANGES

In looking at the business side as if it were the force behind all decision-making, we are looking at an older paradigm of how enterprises operated. Today, the IT side of the business can affect the business strategy and structure as much as the business side does the IT side. Moreover, the IT side is clearly as complex as the business side, involving numerous decisions that will impact not only what the business does now but what it may do in the future. In addition, the IT side is complicated by the fact that in most instances, the customer for IT is internal and often has little or no choice of supplier (this limited competition is an important factor in the way that IT is perceived).

It is important to understand what the IT side involves. It is composed of intangibles, here in the form of information (on the business side, the intangibles are ideas for products and services) and equipment for making those intangibles useful. A business asset is the combination of, say, the idea of providing a service such as sales combined with a specific product, such as a computer, that will be made or purchased for selling. The IT area deals with an asset (known as data) that when manipulated by hardware and software becomes useful information for the organization.

In the following discussion, the presumption is that the business strategy is driving both the business structure and the IT strategy and structure. This is sometimes the case, but as shall be explored more fully later, it is far from the only case. Later in this chapter, and even more in the two following chapters, variations on this theme will be analyzed.

INFORMATION TECHNOLOGY STRATEGY

In the context of the organization, information technology includes not only computer hardware ranging from personal computers to workstations to mainframes but also the software; that is, the programs (like word processing), the applications (groups of programs that work together to, say, process payrolls), and the systems* (clusters of applications that allow handling enormous amounts of data, such as an airline reservations system). IT also includes imaging systems that use technology to translate

---

* In the IT area, systems not only refers to groups of applications but to a combination of applications and technology meant for a specific purpose.

written documents into computer usable data. In addition, IT refers to the data asset that, when processed by the hardware and software, produces information used to run the business and make decisions. It also includes communications technology such as telephone lines and the technology required to transmit voice as well as data from one point to another, from the office next door to the one halfway across the planet. The list is long and growing, now encompassing virtual reality, holographs, and concepts on the verge of discovery, all of which will be yesterday's technology in a very short time.

The issues revolving around IT strategy include such questions as: What information technology does the organization need to best support its business strategy? Would it benefit from more? If more would be useful, does the company have to significantly enhance its employees' existing skill sets? Can it use its existing information technology to enhance its scope of business or competencies? What role can information technology play in determining how the firm is structured? How can information technology be used to improve business processes? Should the organization enter into a joint venture for developing applications? And if it does, what are the control and ownership issues involved?

The similarity of many of these questions to those that crop up on the business side should not be surprising. After all, as noted in Figure 8.1, the information technology *strategy* building block consists of the same three interrelated components as business strategy: scope, competencies, and governance. The IT *structure* building block also has the same three interrelated components: administrative infrastructure, processes, and skill sets. The first step in understanding the interrelationships and cross effects of these areas is to define, in simple terms, all the parts of the building blocks—and to note similarities between these components and those on the business side.

IT SCOPE

This component is responsible for determining which information technologies would best support what the company does for a living. Scope involves examining the array of available information technologies in the IT marketplace and choosing those that enhance as well as help formulate the company's business strategy. For example, IT scope involves deciding what level of sophistication and range of information technology (that is, client server or mainframes or expert systems or image-processing systems) would provide the company with the best support for the business it is in today and provide a base for it to build on to meet its competition tomorrow.

This component of the IT strategy also involves answering questions such as: Given the level of information technology needed to support the business strategy of the organization, does it make sense to have someone else provide the IT services needed; that is, would it be advisable to out-source some or all of the IT services? Among the other questions addressed in IT scope are: Should the information technology that helps the enterprise do what it does for a living be state-of-the-art technology if none of the business's competitors use advanced technology? Perhaps it should be, if state-of-the-art technology is likely to provide a higher level of customer satisfaction. For example, this would be the case if the technology pur-chase allowed the company to gain greater market share (a gain that would offset its costs in a reasonable period of time) and if it will provide the base for the next technological breakthrough that will inevitably come along. Or should the enterprise choose to be a "fast follower," waiting until a technology has been proven in the marketplace before buying it? Or should it try to be a leader, buying the newest, most innovative technolo-gy in order to attempt to get a jump on its competitors, even at the risk of occasional failure?

These IT choices reflect an organization's business strategy. For exam-ple, Commodity Products may choose to employ low-cost, state-of-the-art client server computer hardware and communications technology. In this case, these scope choices reflect the business strategy's focus on the processes critical to running its business—order and distribution process-ing. On the other hand, Leading-Edge's critical processes are research and development, circuit design, and manufacturing, which are best support-ed by state-of-the-art workstations, supercomputers, and advanced man-ufacturing technology.

The IT side must determine how the business side of the enterprise can be best supported and enhanced through the constant advances being made in technology. To make these decisions, the IT leadership who served on the task forces and planning team need to weigh the information they have been gathering both about the business and its technology against the infor-mation they have been collecting about the outside world, particularly information about the IT capabilities of competitors. They also need to have detailed knowledge of how new technology fits with existing technology. The advantage of the earlier activities in the Dynamic Planning Framework is the accumulated knowledge that can be applied to this kind of decision-making not only by the technologists who now better understand the busi-ness, but by the businesspeople who now have a greater understanding and appreciation of the benefits of technology as a result of working together.

IT COMPETENCIES

This is the part of the equation that allows the enterprise to use the IT choices made to the fullest extent possible. In other words, IT competencies enable an organization to use the information technology it has chosen to differentiate itself in the marketplace. For example, in the case of Leading-

Edge, given its business strategy and its decisions related to IT scope, a critical IT competency may be the capability to rapidly develop programs for the engineers who design its computer circuits. Having this competency may prevent its competitors from getting a substantial jump in terms of the time required to design and incorporate new circuits into the computers they manufacture.

In the case of Commodity Products, its business competency is having a low-cost order-processing system available on a twenty-four-hour basis. This is supported by an IT competency—the ability to develop programs for order processing that are state of the art, user friendly enough for the evening crew to access and enter data at all times, and robust enough to prevent users from crashing the systems. The twenty-four-hour capability is also supported by hardware with enough redundancy that it has failed only once in the company's five years—and then was back on-line in two hours. The result is that when a buyer calls and is ready to purchase, the sale can be completed. In addition, to support a low-cost strategy, Commodity Products chose state-of-the-art client server hardware (which is much less expensive than a mainframe but able to handle the necessary number of transactions for their business) and communications technology.

Once these information technology decisions are made, the rules and standards governing the IT operation must be set so that the technology meets everyone's expectations and delivers what is promised in return for the expenditures made.

IT GOVERNANCE

IT governance is that set of policies an organization puts in place to control ownership decisions, set rules and standards for, and regulate use of its information technology. These policies affect and are affected by decisions about IT scope and competencies. In the case of Commodity Products, one of its IT scope decisions was to establish a national communications network to support its business strategy. It could do this by setting up its own network, forming a joint venture with another firm to share the costs of building the network, or forming a strategic alliance with a company that had a network in place. If it set it up itself, it would own it outright and have complete control—but enormous costs, which would go against the business strategy of keeping costs low. If it chooses to embark on a joint venture, it keeps costs down somewhat—and has a great deal of control. If it forms a strategic alliance, it may have little, if any, ownership of the network and consequently very little control—but very low costs. If it has an IT policy that mandates maintaining tight control, it may have to opt for a somewhat more expensive network.

Another set of IT policies is needed, for example, if a company or division chooses to outsource its IT services. The relationship with the service provider must be codified. And questions of governance become extremely complex in the case of systems such as client server, where governance involves setting rules about access, standards controlling the kinds of programs that can be added to the system, and control as well as ownership of the various components of the system. The complications often result from cultural clashes. For example, putting in place standards governing the kinds of programs that can be added to the system is very hard in a hospital setting, where a knowledgeable community of doctors who do research using computers has a strong power base and a dislike of the rules; it is far easier in a corporate environment run as a command-and-control hierarchy.

The policies governing an organization's IT strategy not only reflect the IT scope and competencies but will impact the IT structure as well. In particular, it will reflect the three components of the IT structure.

INFORMATION TECHNOLOGY STRUCTURE

What we are describing when we refer to the IT strategy is the kind of information technology that will best support what the organization does for a living, how IT will be used to differentiate the organization in the marketplace, and what policies are needed to make it work within the organization. These components not only define the IT strategy of the enterprise, but also drive the other IT building block—the IT structure. In moving down to the IT structure side, we are focusing on how the IT strategy is executed: who is responsible for IT, how what the technology has to do gets done, and what skills it takes to do it. These are the three components of the IT structure—the IT administrative infrastructure, the IT processes, and the IT skill sets.

IT ADMINISTRATIVE INFRASTRUCTURE

As in the business structure, this component determines the management structure, roles, responsibilities, authority, and technical considerations required to execute the defined IT strategy. What we are looking at in operational terms is how, once the IT strategy side formulates the IT scope, competencies, and governance required to support the organization's business needs, the IT administrative infrastructure should be organized. (The issues here, it should be noted, go further, covering the technical choices and decisions associated with implementing the IT strategy; namely, developing architectures for hardware, systems software, applications, data, and communications. Although these issues were dealt with in many of the companies we use as examples, the level of detail involved in this aspect of the alignment model is beyond the scope of this book.)

Other questions that also need to be addressed are: Should the IT resources be centralized at the corporate level with minimal authority and responsibility delegated to the IT leaders of the business units or functional areas to decide what hardware and software should be in place? Or should the IT resources be decentralized, giving the leaders of each business unit or functional area the authority and responsibility for choosing hardware and software as long as they adhere to corporate policies for data use and access and see to it that their purchases are compatible with the equipment already in place? Or should a hybrid structure be established?

In the case of Leading-Edge, given its IT strategy, a decision was made to establish a centralized IT group headed up by the vice president, information technology and services. The vice president, for example, had the responsibility and authority to define the standards for hardware, software, communications, and data; to set the rules related to acquisition of hardware and software; and to set the priorities for the allocation of IT resources to projects. In the case of programs, for example, all business units had to use the same financial programs, they had to run the programs on equipment that was compatible with the existing information technology, and they had to follow the corporate standards for defining and accessing the data used by the program. However, when it came to nonfinancial programs, the business units had the authority to purchase or develop their own programs to meet specific market opportunities as long as they followed the appropriate corporate standards.

These administrative decisions, of course, do not stand alone. They are a result of IT strategies, and they tie in to the IT processes and are a reflection of, and will to a certain extent determine, the IT skills needed in the organization.

IT PROCESSES

IT processes, like business processes, are a set of activities and tasks that enable the organization to conduct its business. For example, IT processes include the development of software systems—the set of activities needed to analyze a business problem, design an IT-based solution, program and test the solution, and develop the user manuals and systems maintenance (the set of activities needed to maintain the system once it is up and running, such as changing tax or FICA rates to comply with federal regulations).

Here we are looking at how the IT processes should be organized to best support the IT strategy. For example, in the case of Leading-Edge, management may choose to form a single group that would be responsible for both software development and maintenance, but create separate teams within that group responsible for building programs for the circuit design engineers and for the manufacturing function. In this case, the same individuals who programmed the applications would also be responsible for their maintenance. For the finance function, since all of the programs were purchased rather than developed in-house, Leading-Edge would have just a maintenance process responsible for updating the programs; for example, to reflect changes in the tax codes.

In the case of Commodity Products, the software development process is in the hands of an extraordinarily talented, very small group. They not only develop fail-safe software systems, but build them in such a way that the maintenance (recoding to add new products on an almost day-to-day basis) is very simple. The result is that Commodity Products' large maintenance staff does not have to be a very experienced group of computer specialists, which keeps costs down.

In order to decide how to organize the processes used by an IT organization to ensure that they are done as efficiently as possible, you must understand them fully. Learning what the processes involve, and then finding ways to combine or reengineer them, has the added benefit of revealing the skills needed to ensure that the investment in IT pays the highest dividends and pinpointing the kinds of education and training programs that need to be put in place.

IT Skill Sets

The nature of the activities and tasks that comprise the IT processes and the way those tasks are assigned determine the skill sets needed by employees. Given the enterprise's IT strategy and structure, are new skills required? (This is a particularly important issue to address because the cost of technology represents only one-third of the technology investment—the rest goes to education and training.) It is also important to decide whether the new skills required will fit the existing culture and if not what can be done to gain acceptance for the change.

These are just some of the questions that will impact the choices of IT personnel and training each company makes. There are many others; for example, one of the skill set issues on the IT side involves computer languages (if Commodity's programs are coded in C++, choosing a programmer who works in Fortran and Basic poses a problem), another is knowledge of an industrial sector (such as transportation or oil exploration) or specific business function (such as order entry), yet another is finding people with a combination of specific, difficult-to-master technical skill (such as circuit design) who also have good communication skills (so they understand the requirements of the engineers).

Changes in the firm's IT scope or processes usually require new skill sets, just as changes in business scope or processes require new skill sets on the business side. Whether a company decides to retrain existing employees or bring in new employees with those skills, the effects are likely to be traumatic. And here, as on the business side, there is a need for managing the changes that will take place.

WHERE DO YOU START?

This explanation of the four building blocks sets forth the basic components of each. However, because we were looking at the blocks in a linear fashion, it appears, as noted earlier, that the only driver is the business strategy. Although it is the usual starting point, it is not the only one. Strategic Alignment Modeling is meant to help you think as much about the effects of your IT strategy and structure on your business strategy and structure as the reverse. SAM looks at the interaction between all the parts of the organization and how changes in any one part affect every other. Since many of these interactions occur simultaneously rather than sequentially, SAM ensures that you do not overlook any of the possible effects that may occur.

SAM clarifies the interaction of the complex elements that go into moving a business ahead in an integrated fashion. By doing so, it ensures that when the business strategy is developed it does not ignore the capabilities the IT side could provide. SAM also ensures that the IT side doesn't acquire technology without a business context because no one has clarified the future strategic direction of the firm.

Examining each option generated as a result of Activity 5.0 in terms of SAM will bring to light its impacts on each of the building blocks of the business. In addition, as the effects of each option are examined, the planning team may discover that if it looks at what follows from implementing an option, it may provide a new possibility, another option that may have been overlooked. Changing something in one block, say, deciding that you want to improve your competency in sales and marketing, may lead to a request to the IT side to find a way to create a single mailing list to make advertising campaigns more efficient.

For example, the IT division may suggest putting in place a system that combines and checks and organizes the lists, and note that the system also makes it possible to include information about total purchases over a certain period of time. In discussions of the new system, the team then realizes that it has a mailing list that could be useful to other companies because it can be broken into specialized lists of, say, those who spend large amounts on a specific product. Those may be the perfect customers for another company, one that sells related products. The company then has a list that can be sold. In the case of Commodity Products, its list of major customers would be of value to a publisher of computer magazines aimed at computer literate consumers who spend a lot of money purchasing the latest hardware and software products. The original option for improving the company's bottom line was to find less expensive, more efficient ways to do its sales and marketing; the outcome of the examination was an enhanced scope of business.

Strategic Alignment Modeling provides a way to look at the effects of strategic decisions on the enterprise. Changes in the business strategy affect the IT strategy and structure. At the same time, changes in business strategy will affect the business structure, and that, in turn, will affect the IT structure. The effects will, in the end, have to fit together. The same is true of changes driven by the IT strategy. They affect the IT structure, which will, in turn, affect the business structure. But changes in IT strategy also change the business strategy, which, in turn, affects the business structure. In other words, the process takes you through all the impacts of each element on the other—a circular but necessary road.

GOING BACK IN

Dynamic Planning is typically done by organizations that are trying to find ways to improve or change what they are doing. As a result, it is important to know all the changes that are under way in the organization, especially multiple changes being made concurrently—and that have perhaps not been fully communicated to every level of the business. Ignorance of cross impacts is a particular problem, since changes often have a subtle ripple effect. It is hard to do alignment modeling without involving many managers; thus, the overall effects of simultaneous and planned future changes can be folded into the examination of a specific change on the organization's alignment.

LOOKING AT THE KEY RELATIONSHIPS

The examination of the options generated looks at their effects from four different perspectives:

+ *Strategy Execution.* Driving off the business strategy, what is the impact of the business strategy on the business and IT structures; that is, given our business strategy and structure, do we need to change the IT structure to better support the organization? What is the impact on the IT administrative structure? Do we have to reorganize the IT processes? What will it mean in terms of employee skills? (See Figure 8.2.)

Business Strategy

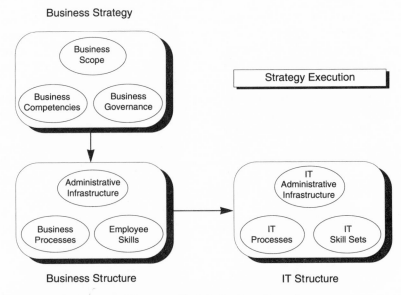

Figure 8.2. Strategic Alignment Model: Strategy Execution
Source: Adapted from J. C. Henderson and N. Venkatraman, "Strategic Alignment," CISR Working Paper No. 190, August 1989.

- *Technology Transformation.* Again, driving off the business strategy, what is the impact of the business strategy on our IT strategy and IT structure; that is, does our business strategy require a different IT strategy? Do we need to enhance or change the scope of IT, do we require new IT competencies, and do we have to reexamine our IT policies? What impact do these changes have on the IT structure: Is our existing IT structure able to support a new IT strategy, or do we have to change the IT administrative structure, IT processes, and IT skill sets? (See Figure 8.3.)

- *Business Transformation.* Driving off the IT strategy, what is the impact of the IT strategy on the business strategy and structure; that is, does our IT strategy enable us to change our scope of business, competencies, and governance? What is the impact of these changes on our business structure? (See Figure 8.4.)

- *Level of Service.* Again, driving off the IT strategy, what is the impact of the IT strategy on the IT and business structures; that is, what changes have to be made to the IT structure in order to make sure it can execute the IT strategy? What will the impact of these changes be on the ability of the IT structure to support its primary internal customer, the business structure? (See Figure 8.5.)

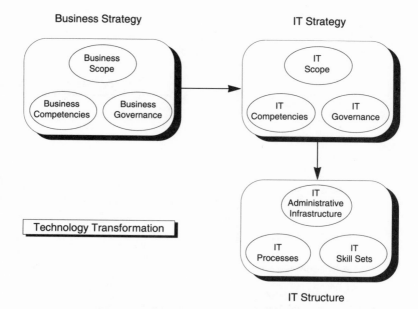

Figure 8.3. Strategic Alignment Model: Technology Transformation
Source: Adapted from J. C. Henderson and N. Venkatraman, "Strategic Alignment," CISR Working Paper No. 190, August 1989.

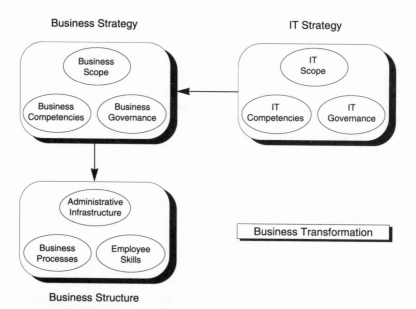

Figure 8.4. Strategic Alignment Model: Business Transformation
Source: Adapted from J. C. Henderson and N. Venkatraman, "Strategic Alignment," CISR Working Paper No. 190, August 1989.

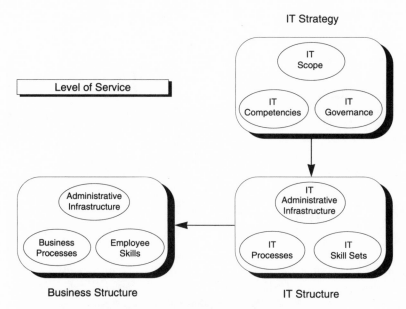

Figure 8.5. Strategic Alignment Model: Level of Service
Source: Adapted from J. C. Henderson and N. Venkatraman, "Strategic Alignment," CISR Working Paper No. 190, August 1989.

The objective of applying SAM is to understand the strategies and actions necessary to make sure that any distortions caused by an option can be corrected. Finding answers to the questions raised through this analysis is the business of the planning team, which must apply everything it has learned about the enterprise to the consideration of the probable effects of each option. This chore may be lightened by looking at examples of how such analyses have been done by others.

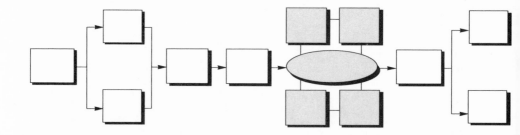

Chapter 9

The Four Questions

Thinking across boundaries, or integrative thinking, is the ultimate entre-preneurial act. . . . Call it holistic thinking. To see problems and oppor-tunities integratively is to see them as wholes related to larger wholes. . . . Blurring the boundaries and challenging the categories permits new pos-sibilities to emerge, like twisting a kaleidoscope to see the endless patterns that can be created from the same set of fragments.

Rosabeth Moss Kanter[1]

The Strategic Alignment Model (SAM) provides the planning team with a formal process for thoroughly examining the options it has generat-ed in order to determine their effects on the organization. In the course of examining the likely consequences of different options, the planning team may, as will be seen below, uncover additional opportunities. Thus, SAM can generate further options—and those also need to be examined to deter-mine their effects on the organization.

Looking at the alignment of a firm is not a simple task, as we saw in the last chapter (and shall see in the more complex examples presented in this and the next chapter, involving actual cases in which SAM was used). The possible permutations of the twelve elements that comprise the strategy and structure blocks are overwhelming if they are looked at individually, with the effects of, say, an option involving a change in business scope examined to determine the change it makes in business competencies and governance, or an option involving a change in business governance being examined for its impact on business scope and competencies. Therefore, the discussions will look at the overall effect of changes in a building block—say, business strategy—on the other three building blocks. Thus, the complexity becomes manageable.

Moreover, because the planning teams narrowed the field of options considerably in their analyses in the earlier part of the Dynamic Planning Framework, the number of possible permutations has also been considerably narrowed. In addition, the drivers of the SAM analysis are usually the strategy blocks; that is, even when an option emerges from an organization's structure (either on the business or information technology side), it must still be analyzed at the strategic level because that is where the decisions that affect strategy are made. For example, an option that is structural and originates in the administrative infrastructure, say, a change in a process suggested by a line manager, must still first be examined at the strategic level to see if it fits within the organization's scope, competencies, and governance—and that, therefore, is where the SAM analysis of that option starts.

The first step in analyzing a given option is to look at its effects on the business strategy (again, the option is likely to initially affect scope, competencies, or governance, but because of the interrelatedness of the components, it will impact the other two components as well, changing the business strategy as a whole). The analysis will then look at the impacts of that change on the business and information technology (IT) structures. It raises questions such as: What do I have in place that can support the new strategy while allowing the business to continue to do what it always has done, and what has to be done in the short term in order to support the new strategy? Tactically, what do I have to do in the next year or two to keep things rolling while finding new ways to support the strategy as effectively and efficiently as possible?

At the same time that the impact of an option on the business strategy is being looked at from that perspective, it must also be examined to see what impacts, if any, it will have on the IT strategy and structure. That is, the first look deals with the short-term impacts and needs involved in *executing the new strategy*; it tells you what it will take to keep your firm running smoothly while adopting the strategy. The second examination has to do with the ways in which you are going to have to *transform your technology* to make the new business strategy effective in the long term; that is, what you have to do to manage the change over time.

The next pair of perspectives starts from the IT strategy side. Here we are looking at the short-term impacts on the *level of service* that result from a change in IT strategy and what has to be provided in the short term to ensure that the business can run smoothly while the IT strategy is being adopted. The second—but remember, concurrent— examination is of the way the *business can be transformed* by the effects of an option on a component of the IT strategy (scope, competencies, and governance) and the impact of that change on the business strategy and structure.

THE QUESTIONS TO ASK ABOUT OPTIONS

Examining the options from these four perspectives is done by finding the answers to a series of questions:

1. What impact does a change in *business strategy* have on the existing *business structure*, and what effect does that have on the *IT structure*?

2. What impact does a change in *business strategy* have on the existing *IT strategy*, and what effect does that have on the *IT structure*?

3. What impact does a change in *IT strategy* have on the existing *IT structure*, and what effect does that have on the *business structure*?

4. What impact does a change in *IT strategy* have on the *business strategy*, and what effect does that have on the *business structure*?

QUESTION 1. WHAT IMPACT DOES A CHANGE IN BUSINESS STRATEGY HAVE ON THE EXISTING BUSINESS STRUCTURE, AND WHAT EFFECT DOES THAT HAVE ON THE IT STRUCTURE?

This question involves examining *strategy execution*, the way in which the business strategy impacts the business and IT structures of the organization (see Figure 8.2). Remember that business strategy decisions affect the way the business operates, its business structure: that is, the administrative infrastructure, the business processes, and the employee skills. These, in turn, have impacts on the IT structure: the IT administrative infrastructure, the IT processes, and the IT skill sets.

A strategy execution alignment exercise allows us to determine the impact of a decision by those responsible for the business strategy on the business structure, particularly the need to redefine the requisite business processes and determine what impact the need for new skill sets will have on the business. The outcome of the alignment may be an adjustment or redefinition of the organization's IT structure. It will show what changes have to occur in the IT structure to support and enable the new business strategy and business structure.

EXAMPLE: SUPPORTING A NEW BANK STRATEGY

Our client, a bank in the Midwest, had just gone through the first two steps of the Dynamic Planning Framework. As a result, it was examining the probable effects of implementing an option generated by the planning team that called for it to switch from being a very tightly controlled centralized bank spanning a large geographic area to a decentralized operation with autonomous business units. The bank was examining this option because it believed it was a way to increase its responsiveness to local market demands. (In this case, the geographic area was divided into a number of regions, each with a president responsible for the local banks in the region.) This change in business strategy would require a major switch in governance, granting the regional presidents and local executives authority that they did not have under the centralized structure. This greater autonomy would result in regional banks that could meet needs that its executives best understood because of their grounding in the economics of the specific region.

Decentralization would mean that each region's president would report to corporate headquarters, but would have a great deal of local control. It also meant that while a basic set of products and services with a common fee structure would be offered across all regions, the regional banks could develop additional products and services for markets in their region and determine their own fee structures for these products and services. However, to maintain a single image, the long-standing corporate Sales-Value-Service Program, an early customer satisfaction quality initiative, would be retained, but customized.

These changes would make demands on the business structure. Each regional bank would have to train or hire more skilled individuals at each management level. The regional bank presidents would be responsible not only for conveying corporate decisions, but making decisions specific to their own branches—and have bottom-line responsibility for those decisions. (They would have to achieve profits on products they developed.) Moreover, the reporting procedures would be more complex, involving the same reports across all common bank operations as well as separate reports about the special services developed by the individual banks— and a combined report would indicate the overall affect on profits of the new services and products.

The regional banks also would be responsible for putting in place a small marketing group that would develop marketing programs to promote their special services. These regional marketing groups would adhere to certain corporate requirements concerning the main bank's image while promoting the new products and services. They also would coordinate advertising plans with the corporate group responsible for promoting both the bank and the common services—and with neighboring regional banks. The coordination would be essential because some of the regions are served by the same newspapers and local television and radio stations.

In order to support these new business structures and processes, changes would be needed in the IT structure. For example, to encourage the individual growth of the regional banks and support a decentralized, empowered structure, the computer systems would have to be decentralized. However, in addition to each region being tied to corporate headquarters for financial reporting, the regional banks would have to be tied to one another to facilitate marketing.

Decentralizing IT would require the business line managers to put in place their own IT groups. Although IT no longer would be the responsibility of the manager of corporate information technology, corporate IT would continue to assist the regional banks with technical problems. In addition, standards for data, telecommunications, policies, and procedures related to managing the IT structure at the regional level would be set by corporate IT.

This decision would have an impact on corporate IT, which would have to be downsized, and the remaining staff (some of whom were hired by the regional banks) would have to be retrained to handle programming and networking personal computers instead of just working with mainframes. Since the reporting structures would demand compatibility, corporate IT would choose corporate-wide technology and applications and develop the required training and education programs, working with the regional IT managers to customize the training needs for each district.

By going through the Alignment Model process before actually implementing the new strategy, the bank was able to identify issues that normally would not surface until the change to decentralization was well under way. By examining the strategy through the lens of the strategy execution perspective, the bank ensured that when it did decide to go with this business option, it not disrupt the operation of the organization while the new strategy was being put in place.

QUESTION 2. WHAT IMPACT DOES A CHANGE IN BUSINESS STRATEGY HAVE ON THE EXISTING IT STRATEGY, AND WHAT EFFECT DOES THAT HAVE ON THE IT STRUCTURE?

This question involves *technology transformation*, the way in which a change in the business strategy impacts the information technology strategy and structure of the organization (see Figure 8.3). This is the other portion of the Strategic Alignment Model process that is driven by the business strategy of the organization. An examination of this perspective shows that as the business strategy is redefined or changed, the existing IT strategy and structure may have to be transformed to enable and support the new business strategy.

This perspective of SAM addresses questions such as: Given the changes in business strategy, is a change in IT scope required and, if so, are different IT competencies required? And what about IT governance? Are policy changes necessary? Then, given the changes in the IT strategy, what is the impact on the investment in existing systems and current IT staff? Is a change in the IT administrative infrastructure (IT organizational structure or hardware or applications) required to support the changes in the IT strategy? Are new IT skill sets required to support the new IT strategy?

EXAMPLE: THIS CAR FOR HIRE

This is the story of a car rental company that decided to implement a new business strategy. The history of this change needs to be reviewed to set the stage for the problems the company faced when it came to determining how it had to change the information technology side of the organization to accommodate its new business strategy. That strategy was working, but it was putting, as we shall see, a strain on the organization. The time had come for the company to transform its information technology side.

This national company based in the Midwest defines its primary business as "the occasional rental of transportation"; that is, it rents cars to individuals to satisfy their business, personal, and leisure needs. The rental agreements, on average, are short term, less than a week in duration. This company is considered a big player in the industry and has a number of distinctive business competencies—the most important and the one that can be best leveraged is its control of local markets. Its major competitors have very centralized operations—consequently, these competitors are less responsive to the changing needs of the local markets in which they compete. Although industry growth is not outstanding, the company has continued to increase its market share primarily at the expense of the competition by focusing on the needs of the local market and by skillful acquisition of rental vehicles.

Indeed, for any car rental company, fleet management—the acquisition, maintenance, and disposition of vehicles—is a critical success factor. The car rental industry purchases several thousand vehicles each year through arrangements with major auto manufacturers. The better a car rental company is at fleet management, the greater its competitive advantage. Since the cost to rent a car from most rental companies is about the same, lower acquisition costs from manufacturers translate into higher profit margins for the car rental company, given that all other costs of conducting business are roughly equal.

Within the past five years, however, this car rental company shifted its strategic direction dramatically—moving from a franchise operation to a corporate-owned and operated structure. This shift was the result of a decision to pursue a new business strategy, one built on a consistent image focused on customer service and expectations, a strategy that would have been difficult to implement under its earlier structure, given the lack of control it had over the service-level provided by independent franchise operators. The questions the company faced were: What would be the impacts of the new business strategy on the existing IT strategy and structure? Could its new business strategy be supported by the existing IT strategy and structure? Could the existing IT strategy and structure provide it with a significant competitive advantage? If the new business strategy necessitated making major changes to the existing IT strategy and structure, should the choices for IT scope be sophisticated, leading-edge technology that would allow the company to leap-frog the competition, or should it be a fast follower, thereby learning from the mistakes of its competitors? Would this require developing or acquiring new IT competencies? Given the choices related to IT strategy, would it have the necessary IT skills to implement the new IT strategy? Would it have to reorganize the IT administrative infrastructure to support the IT strategy? And last, but most important, what would be the risks, costs, and value to the organization given the choices related to IT strategy and structure?

These were the questions we were called in to examine (the company had come to this point through a reexamination that did not include all the steps in the Dynamic Planning Framework). It represented a classic case for the application of the technology transformation perspective of SAM— understanding the impact of changes in business strategy on the existing IT strategy and structure. Before the first site visit, the industrial sector in which the company competed and its competition were studied and analyzed. Once on site, senior managers were interviewed and the existing IT environment was assessed. In other words, we did the work usually done by the planning team in order to gain an understanding of the new strategic direction and the environment in which the company was competing as well as an understanding of its existing IT strategy and structure. The next step was to use that understanding to determine if there was a gap between the existing IT strategy and structure and the requirements for successfully carrying out the new business strategy.

The analysis of the information collected made it clear that the existing IT strategy, developed to support autonomous regional operations, was inadequate. For example, it did not support communications among and between the regional offices and the corporate office. As a result, very little information regarding operational performance was transmitted to the corporate offices. Each region had the discretion to conduct business as it thought best.

The problem was that the current IT structure consisted of a number of mid-range computers that, at best, could be classified as being loosely connected. It was designed to support the business needs of the regions rather than the needs of the business as a whole. In addition, the existing IT strategy and structure were designed to support a firm whose governance and business structure were oriented more toward franchise than corporate operations. And although the existing IT strategy and structure were well-suited to support local markets within a region, they were not designed to support a major core competency—fleet management. (The importance of fleet management to the future of the company was explained in Chapter 6.)

At the time the analysis began, fleet management was being performed well, but its success depended on the efforts of one individual; if anything happened to him, the fleet management function would almost cease to exist. He had a unique set of skills and a prior history and current relationship with the car manufacturers. This relationship allowed him to know when he could cut the best deals. In addition, he had the experience and insight to anticipate the need for fleets across the various regions. If a system that would readily provide information about fleet availability and needs on an organization-wide basis could be developed, the process could be systematized, allowing others to manage fleet almost as well as he did.

Based upon all this information, we concluded that a new IT strategy and structure was needed to support the new business strategy. This new IT strategy would replace the loosely connected mid-range computers with a combination of mainframe and powerful intelligent workstations connected by local-area as well as wide-area networks. This strategy provided the company with the best of both worlds—the capability to support local markets and the ability to coordinate, control, and integrate information from a corporate perspective. Understanding the business strategy provided the context for the new IT strategy. The company, for example, now had available the information needed for fleet management across the enterprise as well as the capability to collect and analyze customer information for enhanced regional marketing and sales programs.

These changes in IT strategy had an impact on the existing IT structure—the IT administrative infrastructure, IT processes, and IT skill sets. For example, new facilities had to be acquired to house the new mainframe and the new, higher-speed communications network that was required to support the intelligent workstations that replaced the mid-range systems in the various remote locations. The company also had to retrain many of its IT personnel to work on the new mainframe as well as hire additional personnel who had expertise in developing software on intelligent workstations. In addition, the IT administrative structure had to be reorganized to better support an organization-wide computing environment as compared to autonomous, regional operations.

Again, these are just a few of the major implications of a dramatic shift in the business strategy of the company on the IT strategy and structure. What the SAM process does is allow us to view the dynamics of change in a more holistic fashion.

QUESTION 3. WHAT IMPACT DOES A CHANGE IN IT STRATEGY HAVE ON THE EXISTING IT STRUCTURE, AND WHAT EFFECT DOES THAT HAVE ON THE BUSINESS STRUCTURE?

This question involves the level of service provided by the IT side of the organization to the business structure (see Figure 8.4). In other words, given our IT strategy, how do we ensure that the IT structure provides the business structure with the *level of services* it needs to conduct its business—and how much IT can the business structure deal with now and what would it take to raise that level?

Here we are dealing with the alignment of the organization's IT strategy with its IT and business structures. The alignment process involves determining how a new IT strategy and structure are put in place and adopted, examining their impact on the business structure, and determining the level of service required to support the business structure.

In essence, we are viewing the IT structure as a business within the business. The IT structure must provide levels of service in the form of new products (usually hardware and software) and training in the use of those products to its internal customer—those who operate the business.

EXAMPLE: TELECOMMUNICATIONS

Because of deregulation as a result of the court-mandated split-up of AT&T, a regional telecommunications company (RTC) that was no longer a part of the AT&T family decided to turn to personal computer (PC) technology on a massive scale in order to adapt to the more competitive environment in which it found itself. Working with this RTC, our first step was guiding senior managers through the process of defining their goals, critical success factors (CSFs), and critical assumptions now that they were a separate organization. (These activities would normally involve the planning team and would be performed by the internal analysis task force.) The managers had to think about their business in new terms, as a standalone company, in order to understand what they would have to do to succeed in the new and different business environment that was emerging. Not only were there competing long distance carriers but, even within their service area, there were now competitors selling all forms of telecommunications equipment and services.

One of the critical success factors defined during the rethinking process was: "Reducing the costs associated with service delivery in their area by 10 percent per year, each year, for the next three years." They decided on this CSF in order to meet future competition—or preempt it.

If they were to achieve this, they would have to start by developing a new set of critical assumptions—the fundamental, underlying set of beliefs about the competition and the industry that govern business decision-making. After considerable discussion and analysis, the senior managers derived a major set of assumptions related to future competitors: "Our major competitors are likely to enter with more advanced IT than we have in place, which would allow them to deliver a wider variety of services and provide services at less cost than we can: this means they would be able to gain major market share by reducing prices."

Another critical assumption was: "Somewhere over the next decade, many smaller companies formed in the wake of the AT&T breakup will disappear through mergers, failures, or acquisitions. As a result, there are likely to be few, perhaps only two, such major competitors. Our competition, however, will at that point probably include some of the other regional telecommunication companies created at the same time we were. Our competitors will focus their marketing and sales efforts on price and the fact that the consumer now has an alternative."

Their analysis of the implications of these new critical assumptions led them to conclude that one of the major levers for reducing the cost of service delivery could be the adoption of more advanced information technology throughout the organization. The decision was based on their belief that improving the work flow or redesigning the business processes would increase efficiency and, consequently, productivity. However, they felt that, over the long term, these efforts alone would not be sufficient. As the volume of work increased, more people would have to be hired, which would, in turn, increase the cost of service. Without technology, the relationship between volume and cost was linear—a relationship they could not afford in the future. Technology could affect how they redesigned the way they did business and would improve employee efficiency by automating many time-consuming manual functions such as account reconciliation and credit checks; this would increase productivity and thus lower the cost of service delivery, allowing the company a chance to compete.

The senior managers on both the business and IT side accepted the need to adopt and implement PC technology at the financial and related levels of the company.

Using the Strategic Alignment Model as a framework, we examined the impact of the decision to turn to intensive use of information technology (that is, our information technology strategy) by large numbers of employees. To do this, we had to evaluate the effects of this change on the RTC's IT structure. One of the more obvious effects would be the impact of this change on the existing IT architecture, which was predominantly mainframe driven with terminals directly attached for accessing but not processing data (by today's standards, it was a very primitive system).

Management carefully evaluated the network in place to determine if it could sustain the addition of a large number of PCs connected to each other on local networks that controlled access to the mainframe. Since the system in place did not connect all levels of the organization, it quickly became clear that a new architecture—that is, a network capable of handling the large number of PCs—was necessary. The next step was to choose an appropriate implementation plan. The decision regarding the selection of an implementation plan had to take into consideration three major factors: time, risk, and expense.

A decision to start with a pilot site, in one of the major cities in the RTC's service area, and then evaluate the results prior to a full-scale implementation would delay implementation by six months and incur evaluation costs. However, the risks associated with the project would be reduced by observing the problems that occurred at the pilot site and discovering ways to avoid them during the wholesale implementation. On the other hand, if all the PCs were brought in at one time, there would be a significant risk that the potential problems would so stretch the IT resources that the difficulties would seem overwhelming and the project would be abandoned by business users. But if it worked, there would be a significant time advantage in terms of positioning the company to beat the competition.

The decision made was to implement the new technology location by location. Despite the enormous number of compatible PCs purchased—for example, there were several hundred in the accounting division alone—which all had to be attached to local-area networks that permitted the individual PCs to communicate between and among themselves as well as with the mainframe, implementation did not prove a particularly difficult process. Predictably, the process ran more smoothly at each new location because of the increased experience of those doing the implementation. The obvious beneficiary, with the smoothest implementation, was the last location to receive the equipment.

Another key IT structure issue involved the skill sets within the IT organization. Was there sufficient personnel trained in PC technology to support such a massive implementation? In practice, the step-by-step phase-in ensured that enough skilled personnel were available because IT personnel did not have to cover every location at the same time, and moreover, their skills were strengthened each time they brought a location on-line. Part of the rationale for a phase-in program was to ensure that current IT personnel, who were primarily expert in mainframe computer systems, could be retrained and brought up to speed as more and more networked PCs came into use.

Another IT issue was: "What kind of policies and procedures are needed for the acquisition and control of the technology?" Should standards for data and the type of PC and associated software the users could purchase be set by corporate IT, or should a variety of PC choices be offered as long as all equipment would be compatible? If a central point is established for placement and coordination of PC orders from the various groups and business units, the company could negotiate with vendors for volume discounts that would result in significant savings across the company. However, this may be viewed as dictating to some groups who may desire to order their own PCs, without corporate direction, as the need arises. If a standard is established for data, software, and the PC vendor, it will be easier to institutionalize a common set of procedures and standards that would allow anyone to go to any location and virtually have no learning curve time in utilizing the system. If a variety of PCs are authorized, as long as they conform to a set of industry standards, is there a risk of incompatibility, over time, if the major vendors change their standards and the others don't follow suit?

These were some of the implications driven by the newly defined IT strategy, which was, in fact, driven by the business strategy as dictated by the new conditions in the industrial sector. As it turned out, several IT strategy decisions were made: the corporate IT function established the policies and procedures related to the acquisition and control of the technology—one vendor of choice was selected to supply PCs for the company through a master purchase agreement administered by the corporate office; standards were established for data definitions (that is, a common definition for customer, invoice, etc.), training, education, and the types of software that would be used.

Referring to the Strategic Alignment Model, the RTC also had to examine the impact of the IT structure on the business structure—the people who used the system. Changing the IT strategy had implications on the level of service the IT structure had to provide to users as well as the expected level of service desired by users. The choices made by the IT managers had a significant impact on the users' capability to absorb or institutionalize the technology and ultimately on the chances for successful implementation.

As noted earlier, the critical success factor the RTC was trying to achieve was the reduction of costs to the consumer in its service area over the next three years. Achieving this CSF was highly dependent on the level of training and the level of support, or service, users received. If the IT structure has sufficient, dedicated resources for implementation, training, and education, those on the business side of the organization are much more likely to adopt and, literally, institutionalize the new technology.

In this case, the users, for the most part, started out almost computer illiterate. Consequently, they not only required extensive training and education, but also, at least in the early stages of implementation, a lot of handholding. The IT organization had to have the skills to address the training and education issues, as well as be available to assist the users. Fortunately, the company had enough resources to divert to the implementation of the PCs without significantly impacting the ongoing business structure. In addition, there was enough advanced planning to ensure that there was a dedicated set of IT personnel trained on the new technology. Much to the credit of executive management, they realized that this was a major under-taking—the cost of the technology was only one element in the total cost of adopting PC technology. The major cost element would be in training, edu-cation, and support. Given this reality, they planned accordingly—they were in this for the long haul, not just an immediate short-term impact.

As users become more proficient and more sophisticated, they will, in turn, probably demand a higher level of service from the IT side. In the case of the RTC, in the initial six months of the implementation, the pro-ductivity of the PC users increased measurably. They were able to process more work in a shorter time and with fewer errors than they ever had before. During the next six-month interval, the users became increasingly more effective—they were not only doing things right, but they were doing more of the right things. The next six-month interval was the most fasci-nating: the users became computer literate and sophisticated. They began to redesign their jobs—in essence, they performed their own business process redesign; they did more analysis and less routine processing, lit-erally redefining their positions.

At the end of an eighteen-month study conducted to understand the implications of institutionalizing PC technology, over 90 percent of the study group was still using the technology. This retention rate was attrib-utable to the level of education, training, and support provided by the IT organization and other help groups initiated by the users. At the end of the day, they not only reduced the cost of service and, over time, the price to the consumer, but they enhanced the work environment. People viewed what they did for a living as a career, not a job.

QUESTION 4. WHAT IMPACT DOES A CHANGE IN IT STRATEGY HAVE ON THE BUSINESS STRATEGY, AND WHAT EFFECT DOES THAT CHANGE HAVE ON THE BUSINESS STRUCTURE?

This question involves *business transformation*, the way in which the IT strategy impacts the business strategy and structure of the organization (see Figure 8.5). Business transformation examines the impact of an option on the IT strategy, revealing the ways in which a change in IT strategy can end up redefining or enhancing the organization's scope of business, its distinctive competencies, or its governance. In addition, business trans-formation deals with the impact of the changes in the business strategy on the business structure.

Examples of business transformation through IT are the most complex to describe, since there are rarely clear-cut cases in which a single IT option redefines or enhances the organization's business strategy. Moreover, opportunities for business transformation are more likely to occur in those industries or industrial sectors that are information intensive. The results of examining the impact of options on the business transformation perspective of the Strategic Alignment Model are most likely, for example, to be the development of new information-based products or services for existing markets, delivering existing products or services to new markets that could be potentially opened through IT, and/or delivering new products and services to new markets. In these cases, changes in IT strategy have an impact on the business scope of the organization, which may force changes in its competencies or governance. And as we have seen, these in turn have an impact on the components of business structure.

EXAMPLE: FROM KNOWLEDGE GATHERER TO KNOWLEDGE SOURCE

While working with a South African company whose business was research, development, and implementation of advanced technologies for profit, we had the opportunity to use the *business transformation* perspective of SAM. Prior work with the client using SAM for strategy execution, technology transformation, and level of service literally paved the way for examining business transformation. One of the more significant results was the development of a new information technology strategy that called for the implementation of leading-edge information technology, relational database software, and the adoption of the concept of data as a corporate asset. Ultimately, the IT strategy would lead to a business transformation.

Earlier projects had provided the client with an understanding of the model and the process—and the information necessary to understand and analyze the data assets within the company (information about markets, customers, products, and processes); their distinctive competencies; and a detailed understanding of the administrative infrastructure, business processes, and skill sets. Business transformation is as much based on insight and creativity as a formal process.

The information and knowledge gleaned from understanding the business led to a number of insights: the business units collected an amazing amount of information about their markets and customers; they also collected an enormous amount of information about the economic and technological factors that drive a number of industrial sectors that they serve (for example, they have fourteen business units that do directed research for industries as diverse as production technology to forestry); and they have access to a large number of public databases from which they can extract data on business and technology trends. However, until they went through the strategy execution and technology transformation portions of SAM, senior managers did not realize the extent of the data they had accumulated. (Each business unit collected data for its own purposes and was unaware of what the other business units were doing.)

Given the breadth of their experience and expertise in a number of industries, their distinctive competencies (of the 4200 employees, 2600 had advanced level degrees), their global reputation, and their excellent R&D infrastructure, they were able to use information technology to enhance the scope of their business. They could combine existing information, add their expertise, and sell knowledge—about processes or technology, or about markets and market trends. They were able to position themselves to be in the business of selling value-added information-based products and services. Based upon market research done as a part of the business transformation examination, senior management estimated that the market for these types of information-based products and services would be several billion dollars a year by the late 1990s. The business transformation perspective of the Strategic Alignment Model identified an opportunity for the company to use IT to leverage its existing distinctive competencies and information assets to position itself as a potential leader in what may become a very lucrative global market.

Remember, though, that the business transformation perspective of the Strategic Alignment Model not only deals with the changes in the scope of business and the other elements of business strategy, but also examines the impact of a change in the business strategy on the business structure of the company. Although the future looks very rosy from a business strategy perspective, when the probable impact of a change in business strategy on the business structure is examined, a potential problem becomes evident.

As currently structured, the business unit responsible for selling specialized consulting services is also responsible for developing the IT strategy. In addition, it is responsible for the hardware and communications components of the IT structure—that is, its architecture. But it has no responsibility or authority for applications or the IT processes associated with developing and maintaining the applications. In other words, the responsibility for the IT structure is divided between two managers who are in different business units, a situation that is not only highly unusual but also irrational. There should be one unit and one individual responsible for both the IT strategy and the IT structure. In addition, the dual role of developing the IT strategy, controlling the architecture while having profit and loss responsibility, leaves something to be desired in terms of trying to serve two masters—an external market as well as an internal market. Under these circumstances, the consequences of having two individuals making decisions that impact each other could be devastating. It takes complete cooperation and trust among and between the individuals, working as true partners, with a common, shared vision, to make success likely.

To complicate matters even more, the business unit that has the responsibility for the new line of business (selling information-based products and services), which, incidentally, is distinct from the other business units, must now deal with two business units and two individuals to obtain the IT resources needed to build and run this business. In essence, any decision to implement a new product or service or adopt a new technology has to be mediated among and between three individuals. If the new business is to succeed, the business and IT structures have to be changed, and the issue of control over the resources needed to pursue a market has to be resolved.

Clearly, the problems they face require another walk through the Strategic Alignment Model. This is not unusual. As noted before, the examination of options through the model often generates new options—and these have to be examined much as the original options are.

CAVEATS

Each of the four key relationships examined through the Strategic Alignment Model has major effects on other areas. When the layers of change are overlaid, one on the other, the various conflicts that can be created because of a failure to develop these areas in an integrated way become clear. For example, what happens when the business strategy managers decide to expand an area of the business that requires a greater level of service from the IT side at the same time that the IT strategists see a new service that IT can provide the business structure? The strategists on both sides can end up overwhelming the employees of the organization with rapidly expanding demands. The effects on the employees of the changes made may not be understood by either set of strategists; each side sees only the human resources costs of the changes *they* themselves instituted.

It is also important to remember when applying the Strategic Alignment Model that every area looked at is not necessarily in need of adjustment. For example, a company may have a business strategy in place that will, if successfully carried out, make it a leader now and in the long term. Or a company may have in place an IT strategy that will enable it to remain on the cutting edge because the IT leadership was extraordinarily far-sighted.

CONCLUSION

Each of the examples examined here looked at a single question. When an organization is engaged in Dynamic Planning, it tests its options against each of the perspectives and then examines the additional options generated in much the same way. Unless the four perspectives fit together, the business will not be able to function smoothly; anyone viewing them will think they are seeing them through a kaleidoscope rather than a clear lens. An example of a company that worked through all four questions follows in the next chapter.

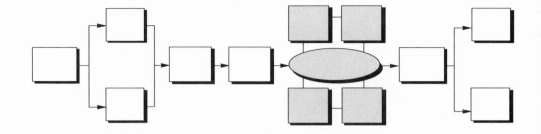

CHAPTER 10

SAM: A THREE-DIMENSIONAL APPROACH

The general who wins a battle makes many calculations in his temple
before the battle is fought. The general who loses a battle makes but few
calculations beforehand. Thus, do many calculations lead to victory. . . .

Sun Tzu, *The Art of War*

The four perspectives used in Strategic Alignment Modeling are normally applied to a single organization; however, each time an organization is looked at from the four points of view, one tends to be more
interesting than the others. In the last chapter, the example for each perspective was chosen because it conveyed the clearest, yet often the most
complex, view of that perspective. But it was a static example; that is, it
showed how the company would choose an option given its effect on,
say, technology transformation. It did not look at the other perspectives,
and it did not explore the further options that the first change would
make possible.

The following example shows how to apply the Strategic Alignment
Model (SAM) in a more comprehensive way, and it makes the point that
with Dynamic Planning it is always essential to keep the longer term firm-
ly in mind. Dynamic Planning is not about making a change in the business
to improve it at a single moment in time; it is about making a journey
through time and planning ways to accommodate future changes, which
will build on earlier ones. SAM is the third step in Dynamic Planning, the
analysis of the solutions developed through Activity 5.0, generating the
options. After this, the organization begins to put the solutions in place,
first by determining its Grand Strategy (Activity 7.0), which is based on the
options selected earlier through SAM. But remember that the options may
be put in place in a series of stages in order to maintain the firm's alignment and ability to conduct its current business.

MOVING AHEAD IN STAGES

What we are discussing here is a nontraditional view of Strategic Alignment Modeling. In the classic version, SAM was an analysis of an organization at a specific moment. What has become clear in working with companies that are engaged in Dynamic Planning is that a new dimension—time—must added to the model, making it three-dimensional (see Figure 10.1). Options are examined for their current effects on each perspective. Once the changes that will take place in each of the boxes is understood, a more complex option, which might have been discarded given the business as it was, may become possible in the business as it is after the first changes are implemented, and so on. The problem is, as noted in the headnote to Chapter 2, "Too often the planning process reflects what organizations know how to do rather than what they should do."

As might be expected, this approach, which is somewhat like playing three-dimensional chess, is not one that has been applied in a multitude of cases, but a few of those examples will be explored here and in the next chapters. What becomes clearer as the examples are delved into is that Strategic Alignment Modeling used over time is similar to staged planning in development economics.[1] In simple terms, staged development is a logical program for growth over time. It is the opposite of haphazard national development in which a ruler invests foreign aid in a huge manufacturing plant built in a remote area because there are ores nearby— and a shiny new plant is a symbol of progress. Unfortunately, there are no skilled workers in the vicinity and no infrastructure to support it. And attracting foreign management is impossible because of the primitive environment. In the meantime, the country is importing food to ease famine because of a lack of irrigation.

In staged development, the foreign aid is first used to build road and irrigation systems to help the peasants become farmers who are able to grow enough food using modern methods to be able sell excess capacity to neighboring countries. The money that is brought into the country is then invested in transportation systems (now that you have roads on which to transport the materials for building, say, railroads) and schools (with newer farming techniques and more profits, children can be freed for schooling). Once the railroad is available for transport of the materials, the country moves to the next stage: mining the ores and getting them to market, thus bringing more capital into the country. And then comes the time to build the manufacturing plant, when there are roads, a moderately educated workforce, and acceptable living standards to attract management.

Planning in this kind of rational manner precludes jumping on the buzzword of the moment—and prevents Strategic Alignment Modeling from

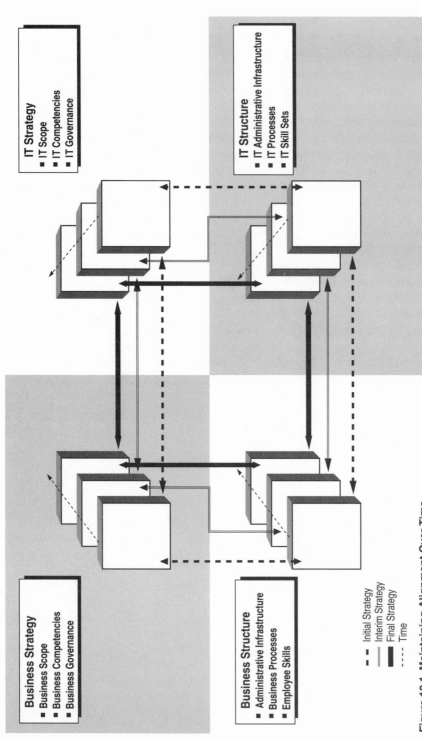

IT Strategy
■ IT Scope
■ IT Competencies
■ IT Governance

IT Structure
■ IT Administrative Infrastructure
■ IT Processes
■ IT Skill Sets

Business Strategy
■ Business Scope
■ Business Competencies
■ Business Governance

Business Structure
■ Administrative Infrastructure
■ Business Processes
■ Employee Skills

-- -- Initial Strategy
── Interim Strategy
━━ Final Strategy
---- Time

Figure 10.1. Maintaining Alignment Over Time
© 1993 B. Goldberg and J. G. Sifonis

becoming just another buzzword. SAM, when a part of the Dynamic Planning Framework, is a model that can help an organization think holistically. It brings the greatest rewards in the context of Dynamic Planning. In the example that follows, a company starts with a long-term vision and uses Strategic Alignment Modeling to determine which options to put in place—and in what sequence—in order to achieve that vision. In other words, it looks at how each option would affect each of the cornerstones of the business. Then it looks at the business as it would probably look with that option in place to evaluate a subsequent option. Then, once again determining what the business would look like with this change, it evaluates the effects of yet another option. The goal is to determine which options will, when put in place at a given stage, fulfill the vision.

In examining the original options generated by the planning team, sometimes it becomes clear that an option that would disrupt the current culture will be possible once another option is in place, and the firm has reached a new stage of development.

EXAMPLE: FINDING THE RIGHT CHANNEL

A personal computer (PC) hardware and software distributor used SAM to help it decide what changes it should make to continue to increase market share and eventually to achieve its long-term goal of controlling the market. The client company acted as an intermediary between PC and software vendors, distributors, stores, and end users. It was located in the Southwest, had a small central organization, several hundred million dollars a year in gross revenues, and was growing in excess of 25 percent per year.

At the time the Strategic Alignment Model was applied, the company not only bought PCs and software from a number of vendors and then sold them directly to any interested retail computer store, business, and individual; it also was a franchisor and owner of some of the many retail computer stores that sold such products. It was one player in a highly complex distribution channel (see Figure 10.2).

The problem it faced was that it was in the middle of this channel and could, as things stood, be bypassed by the vendors and other competing distributors as well as by its own franchises and retail stores. For example, a franchise could bypass the company when purchasing equipment by going to other distributors or directly to the vendors. Furthermore, the vendors from whom the company bought equipment could sell directly to the same stores and end users the company was currently serving. In addition, competing distributors were now selling directly to the clients' franchises as well as end users.

The long-term vision of the company's leadership was to leverage the transaction data flowing through the channel. They believed that they

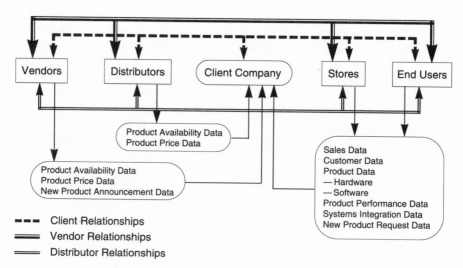

Figure 10.2. Current Channel Member Relationships

could use this information to develop value-added information about the various channel members' products, markets, and customers, information that would be extremely valuable to the channel members. Consequently, by having the capability to collect and package this information faster and better than its competitors, the company had to make the other members of the channel see that they had more to gain by working with them than by bypassing them. The task was to find a way to use information technology (IT) to exert more control over the other players in the channel, thereby enhancing its relationship with the various channel members (see Figure 10.3).

The highly marketable information about the other players and products had been stored in the organization's computers in the course of its normal business operations over the past few years. What was missing was the technology to aggregate the information about specific products and markets, about groups of products (that is, information about hardware, printers, or wordprocessing packages, irrespective of vendor), and about trends in the market. Since the company had also become an integrator of products (hardware and software), it was beginning to collect information about systems integration problems and the solutions to those problems. All of this was valuable information that could be useful to the various members of the channel.

Clearly, the best course for our client was to find ways to enhance its existing databases to position itself to fill the role of being an information provider, market creator, and market organizer for all members in the channel (see Figure 10.4). As an information provider, it could sell information about product performance or market trends to vendors, distributors, or stores. As a market creator, it has product and market information that it could use to create markets for newer and more sophisticated hardware platforms and software applications. As a market organizer, it could coordinate the roles of integrator, information provider, and market creator to position itself as an orchestrator of the market by wielding its information resources to provide the right products and services to customers in specific markets. Distribution of PC technology would then become a secondary, but nonetheless, necessary business for keeping in touch with what was happening in the field—the problems, trends, and players in the market.

Two distinct things now had to happen. First, examining the strategy execution element of SAM, we had to determine the impact of each stage of the business strategy (the options in sequence) on the business and IT structures, and second, we had to examine another element of SAM—technology transformation. Both of these elements are driven by the impact of the business strategy. Technology transformation involves defining an IT strategy to support the strategic direction of the company—the journey from information provider to market creator to market organizer.

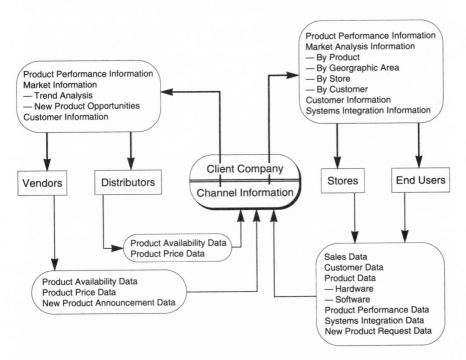

Figure 10.3. Enhanced Channel Member Relationships
© 1993 B. Goldberg and J. G. Sifonis

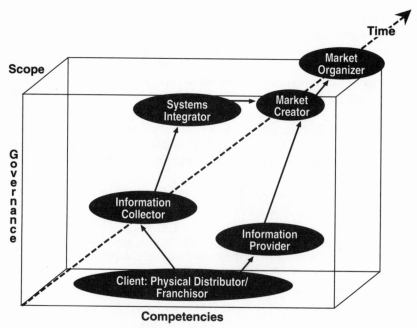

Figure 10.4. Strategic Direction of the Enterprise
© 1993 B. Goldberg and J. G. Sifonis

STRATEGY EXECUTION

First, strategy execution: in order to find a way to push products through
the channel faster, thus keeping all the players in the channel satisfied
with what the company offers (products and information), service quality
had to be improved. The first step was to develop a means to fulfill orders
quickly. After analyzing the problem, the decision was made that integrated logistics—tying orders to inventory to warehouse to credit check to
physical delivery—was the tool that would meet the goal of the first step
of the business strategy. Integration meant redesigning the fulfillment system to eliminate bottlenecks, reducing the time from order to delivery.
This required significant changes in the business structure of the company—namely, the business processes.

Processes that were previously performed by a specific functional area
were now shared by a number of functional areas across the company.
For example, in the past, an order taken by the order entry clerk was sent
to the financial area for credit check and approval. The order was then
sent back to a sales clerk who put it back into the order entry system,
which forwarded it to the warehouse.

The business processes were redesigned so that, as orders came in, a credit check was performed through the order entry system and, if approved,

sent directly to inventory and distribution. The company established process owners who were responsible, in this case, for taking orders, performing credit checks, and recording and transmitting orders to other process owners who were responsible for delivering the products.

From an IT structure perspective, the implications of redesigning the business processes meant that the existing mainframe had to be upgraded. The technology had to provide enhanced availability, greater reliability, and increased time sensitivity for transaction processing. (Executing orders in a timely manner had become a major objective.) In addition, the existing distribution system software had to be significantly modernized to deal with an integrated flow of transactions and information from order entry to delivery. All other components of IT structure—primarily the management of the IT processes and the required skill sets to accomplish integrated logistics—remained virtually the same.

The strategy execution element of SAM helped the client identify needed changes in the business structure and address the support required from the IT structure for the next twelve to eighteen months. However, given the strategic direction of the business, the company proceeded with the next perspective—using the acquired knowledge derived in the strategy execution—to go through the technology transformation perspective of SAM.

TECHNOLOGY TRANSFORMATION

The knowledge gained during strategy execution helped us identify and answer a number of critical questions related to the impact of the business strategy on the information technology strategy. For example: Do we have to significantly augment the scope or types of information technology currently in place in order to support the new strategic direction? Do we need to have a different set of IT-distinctive competencies in order to develop systems more rapidly or implement more sophisticated systems? Do we need a new form of IT governance—instead of going it alone, do we partner with our customers and other distributors, since we will be implementing EDI (electronic data interchange) technology? And what are the implications on our existing IT structure if we adopt or modify our existing IT strategy? Will we need different hardware and software; will we need different skill sets; and will we need to change the way we organize and manage the IT processes? The answers to these questions formed the foundation for the strategic direction of the company for the next three to five years—technology transformation begins where strategy execution leaves off, looking at the longer term.

The technology transformation perspective of SAM allows senior management, including the IT executives, the opportunity to position the IT function for the future—understanding the business strategy and its impact allows the company to put in place the most appropriate IT strategy and structure to enable and support the business's strategic direction over time.

The business knowledge gained from implementing the strategy execution element of SAM made it significantly easier for the IT executives to make strategic choices that would provide a framework for the future. These choices enable the transition of the business through the various states: information provider; market creator; and, ultimately, market organizer. The IT strategic choices included adopting a dispersed computing strategy—that is, a mainframe computer supporting intelligent workstations that are networked to the various locations. This would enable the company to capture general information about customers, products, and services, at the same time providing channel members with a way to maintain location-specific information, giving them a better database for use in the local marketplace.

Another strategic choice was to use only state-of-the-art technology—the company decided not to be on the "bleeding edge" of technology. This choice would reduce the overall investment in mainframe technology but still provide the necessary processing power to support the various locations. The IT executives made a strategic decision to adopt computer-assisted software engineering technology for all future application development, giving the company the capability to develop applications more rapidly while reducing the total cost of development over time. The IT executives also decided to partner with the various stores, vendors, as well as competitors, to develop the network and standards for the implementation of EDI. This was a critical strategic choice, since existing standards were not only confusing, but incompatible. Without such a partnering arrangement, enforcing standardization would be impossible.

The choices made in developing the IT strategy had a significant impact on the IT structure. The IT executives had to decide upon a common intelligent workstation for use at the various locations. Since the current staff had to support the mainframe environment, additional staff—with intelligent workstation experience and a broad background in developing communications programs in a complex environment—was needed to support the strategic direction of the business. And finally, the management processes of the IT function had to change. A more formal method for developing applications had to be adopted both within the IT development and maintenance processes as well as with the business users of the company. The new business direction and its impact on the IT administrative infrastructure and processes had become more complex—requests for new applications or for additional reports could no longer be done on an informal basis. There had to be more planning and business analysis before a system could be developed.

The choices made as a result of the technology transformation effort enabled the IT executives to organize the IT area in such a way that it could put in place the necessary technology, applications, and skill sets to make the business more competitive in the current as well as in future environments. The strategic choices the IT executives made would not have been possible without a thorough understanding of the strategic direction of the organization and an understanding of the implications of this direction on the IT strategy and structure.

LEVEL OF SERVICE

The third perspective of SAM executed was level of service. This examination was made concurrently with the technology transformation effort. (Remember: multiple views of SAM can be executed concurrently.) Strategy execution had led to the redesign of the business processes of the company. So, as we performed technology transformation, we identified the impact of the business strategy on the IT strategy and structure—since strategy execution and technology transformation are both driven from the anchor of business strategy. Now, using the IT strategy as the anchor, we can examine the level of service and business transformation perspectives, both of which have an impact on the business structure.

The level of service analysis identified two critical items that had to be addressed if the business strategy were to be implemented: adoption and acceptance of a formal methodology for developing new systems, and defining the role of the IT organization in redesigning the business processes of the company.

Since the company had a history and culture that fostered entrepreneurship, informality, and an avoidance of any form of bureaucracy, establishing a formal process for developing new systems was viewed by business management as being countercultural. They saw no need to go through a process that required formal definition of the requirements for a new system, any cost benefit analysis, or any involvement of the business users of the new system in the analysis and design processes of systems development. The idea of formal project management—that is, holding individuals accountable and responsible for delivery dates or problem resolution—was antithetical to the existing culture. But informality, while acceptable in a start-up environment, borders on disaster when a company is growing 25 percent per year and rapidly approaching $1 billion in revenue. Conducting business at this level becomes more complex and requires structure and rationalization.

Given the culture of the company, the IT executives proposed building a framework rather than a methodology. A requirement of a methodology is that all the rules, procedures, and techniques have to be followed at all times—a requirement that was too rigid for this company. By comparison, a framework is a series of activities or tasks that have to be followed, but not all of the rules apply at all times—they vary based upon the type of problem that has to be addressed. A framework is more flexible than a methodology. The concept of a framework addressed the concerns of the business users, yet provided a starting point for introducing the concepts of structured systems development and project management that could be phased in over the next three to five years. This approach was acceptable from both an IT and business structure perspective.

The other major problem we faced was determining the role that the IT organization would play in redesigning the business processes of the company. The business processes were owned by the managers responsible for the operations. Yet automating what was currently in place or, in some cases, upgrading the current level of technology would not achieve integrated logistics. On the other hand, the IT organization couldn't effectively redesign the business processes on its own initiative. The business and IT structures had to form a partnership in order to complete the task of business process redesign.

After several discussions, the partnership concept was adopted in the form of task forces comprised of process owners and IT personnel. They would use the new framework as a means to redefine the business processes. This would accomplish a number of objectives: provide the means to introduce the framework and begin the process of adopting a more formal approach to process redesign throughout the company. The task force concept would help to build the partnership between the business and IT structures, and it would be a means for the IT personnel to get deeply involved with the business while identifying to non-IT personnel what could be done with IT. It would also help each party to think out of the box—to try innovative ways of looking at the business. In addition, it would provide the opportunity for the IT personnel to identify the necessary levels of training and education that would be required to implement and support the process owners—that is, provide the necessary level of service to the business users.

The process chosen—task forces, ownership, partnership—would also work to establish buy-in and loyalty among employees. By empowering them and having them play a part in implementing the process, you help ensure that the process works. You are also less likely to lose people you spend time and effort training, and you are, through the inevitable power of word of mouth, likely to find it easier to recruit people with good skill sets more easily in the future.

BUSINESS TRANSFORMATION

The last perspective of SAM we executed was business transformation—identifying how the information technology strategy can impact the business strategy of the firm. The information and knowledge obtained by

executing the other perspectives of SAM helped us identify opportunities
to enhance the business scope of the company. As the company moves
toward the various future states of information provider, market creator,
and market organizer (that is, exercising control over the various market
segments), the choices made in developing the IT strategy create a foundation upon which a variety of potential new products and services could
be developed. The IT strategy and structure, primarily the emphasis on
viewing information as an asset, and the skill sets put in place created a
synergistic effect that, combined with innovative thinking, made it possible to identify a number of new opportunities. For example, the network
could be expanded to provide electronic mail and eventually video conferencing services to subscribers who were not business affiliates of the
company. The skill sets necessary to respond to customer inquiries, in conjunction with the network, could lead to providing telemarketing services
for companies that were unrelated to the organization's core business. The
information and knowledge gained in dealing with the various store locations brought the company significant expertise in identifying market
trends. This expertise could be used to develop a consulting service that
could be provided to locations that needed marketing expertise.

The implementation of these new product and service offerings would
take place as the company implemented its business strategy over the next
three to five years. However, there is an additional factor. The implementation of the IT strategy will develop a technology foundation and
personnel who will be computer literate and have access to a realm of customer, product, and service information. Although we identified new
opportunities, we did not capture them all: there will always be someone
in the company who will, by looking around and seeing the company and
what it does in a broader context, find a new opportunity by using the IT
foundation as a lever for his or her imagination.

APPLYING SAM TO YOUR ORGANIZATION

Once the theory underlying Strategic Alignment Modeling is clear, the
planning team can evaluate the company to see if all the parts are in alignment. If you think of the diagrams of the four elements (see Figures 8.2-8.5)
as transparent and overlay them one on the other, you see that every piece
of the business affects and is affected by the others. Now try to mentally
apply the diagrams to your business. When you are done, mentally overlay them. The way the transparencies fit, how tightly the pieces mesh, will
let you know where and whether you face problems.

Now look at the effects of an option on each of the four elements of
your business. Determine what changes it will make on each area. Then
start exploring another option, one that will move you further ahead. See

what effects it will have on your current structure, and then try to determine how it would work if the first option examined had been put in place. Often, the changes needed when working from the already changed organization will cost less and the probable disruption will appear to be less. The team can then try adding a third option—or often what happens is that by exploring the company in its most changed state, new options are visualized by the team. It is at that stage that you have a dynamic organization ready to face whatever the next bend in the road brings. You have a sense of the future and are ready to develop an overarching Grand Strategy to get there.

PART IV

PUTTING THE SOLUTIONS IN PLACE

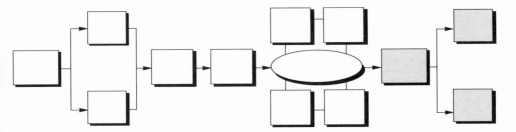

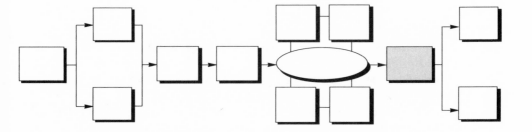

CHAPTER 11

THE GRAND STRATEGY

What follows, then, is the route map of an exploration. The quest begins
in a series of encounters with . . . dynamic forces . . . and it ends . . . at
the level of grand strategy, the level of final results.

Edward Luttwak[1]

A nd here we are at the level of final results. You have completed the first three steps of the Dynamic Planning Framework, and you have analyzed and reanalyzed your organization to determine what it does, how it does it, and what it might do differently or what it might do that it has not done before. Now is the time to pull everything together. This is where you take all that information and turn it into something that will make a difference, that will change your company, that will make it stronger and better. If that sounds too good to be true, it is because what you have actually reached is the point at which you can decide what you need to do to make sure you are prepared to adapt and adapt again as you reach for an ever changing future.

It is time to put in place a process to help keep you aimed in the right direction because, if you remember the dimension of time and staged development, accomplishing the goal of the moment is just a step on the road to victory. This is the time to develop your Grand Strategy, Activity 7.0, the first of the three activities that comprise the fourth and final step of this walk through the Framework, putting the solutions in place.

The Grand Strategy is a combination of three elements: vision, mission, and enterprise plan. The first, the vision of the long-term future, is developed from the information you gathered when you looked at the world around you and the directions in which it seemed to be moving. The second, the mission, is what you believe your company can do to be a player in that world and how the options for the next stage of your development (chosen through Strategic Alignment Modeling) can help it get there. Now that you fully understand your company, a review of your current mission statement is in order. The third, your enterprise plan, is the detailed plan you must now develop for carrying out the mission.

In this chapter, we will review each of these elements of the Grand Strategy and then show them at work in an example. The example involves a small, start-up enterprise we created as a composite from our experiences in helping a number of such companies with various activities in the Framework. (Small companies rarely address all the activities involved in Dynamic Planning in an orderly sequence.) Only in the next chapter do we go into an extensive examination of Dynamic Planning in a organization at the other end of the spectrum—international, enormous, and involved in national economic, political, and social issues as well as internal relationships on many levels. Taken together, these examples clearly demonstrate what the Dynamic Planning Framework brings to the table.

ARTICULATING THE VISION

What do we mean by the vision? Is it an idealist's dream of what the world should be without regard to the realities of life? Or is it the creation of an individual anchored in his or her life experiences and knowledge? Or is it a future view of the world in which the company is but one of many players? Defining vision is similar to defining strategy—we all believe we know what it is, but there is little agreement on how to define it. In Dynamic Planning, vision is the view of what things will be like in the future, given the direction the sector you play in is moving; it is a view beyond tomorrow held by those who are leaders in the company.

There are a number of qualifiers: (1) The vision need not, indeed probably should not, be specific to the firm. (2) A vision held by one leader is not enough: to be successful, it must be a shared vision. (Indeed, even if it is the vision of the head of the enterprise or a unit within it, it must be accepted by others in the organization.) (3) The time frame for the vision must not be so far into the future that no progress toward it will be visible for at least five years, yet it must be far enough ahead that the vision can act as a guiding force.

Visionaries tend to be people who see beyond a specific advance in any one area; they are able to put together advances in a number of fields and extrapolate a general tendency that incorporates those advances and takes them a step further. For example, today many communications companies—across electronic media, publishing, telecommunications—envision a world of interactive wireless communications and information of all types, a world in which there is little paper, where television networks are unimportant, libraries are electronic, everyone is connected to a database, and virtual reality is reality. The day when that is all achieved probably will not arrive before the next century, but it will come. The true business visionaries are not going to turn their companies around overnight. Instead, the visionary book publisher begins to produce books on cassettes and sets up a division to produce on-line reference materials. When what the publisher thinks will happen begins to happen (when the risk-takers and entrepreneurs who are willing to invest in breakthroughs have paved the way), that publishing company will be a fast follower. And because it has money for marketing from its continued, successful business ventures, it will grab a significant market share. These results come from corporate leaders who lead by vision.

But organizations have to encourage visionaries on all levels; in fact, the best of all possible worlds is to have visionary leaders throughout an organization with a culture that believes new is probably better. The Dynamic Planning Framework, by opening people to the developments taking place, by instilling a belief in the importance of looking at developments in the outside world, helps bring this kind of mindset to an organization.

One of the best examples of this kind of culture is 3M, an organization that encourages innovation. Those at 3M believe that the world is always looking for a new and better mousetrap. Nothing is too small to warrant attempts to improve it: this is not surprising in a company that developed self-adhering notepads—a far from earth-shattering innovation—by combining the properties of two common items to create a product that is easy to use and remove without causing damage. Today, Post-its have taken over the world. Steve Jobs and Steve Wozniak, on the other hand, are examples of visionary leaders; they built a company based on the idea of putting the power of computing into everyone's hands. The result was Apple computers—especially the Macintosh—and the birth of the personal, affordable computer and a giant step on the road to the Information Age. The point is that visions come in many forms. And the company that encourages visionaries is the most likely to be a competitor tomorrow.

DERIVING THE MISSION STATEMENT

The second element of the Grand Strategy is the mission statement.[2] At the time most companies undertake Dynamic Planning, they already have a mission statement or credo or statement of purpose in place. It is often something that has been around from the time of the enterprise's founding. When examined carefully, it often reveals many of the components of the enterprise's business strategy; it helps explain why the company does what it does the way it does it. Now, however, the planning team's awareness of the possibilities for growth and its decisions about the paths for the future will bring changes in the business strategy. It is important to make

those changes part of the mission statement. Even if much of the statement remains the same, any enhancements made to it should be used to
communicate the fact that the organization is undergoing change.

Revisiting the mission statement should be done in a fairly formal
manner. By reviewing all the elements in it, the team is given an opportunity to see how what it learned to date fits the organization. It is important that the team keep in mind the culture of the organization when
analyzing and possibly making changes to the mission statement. These
statements inevitably vary in tone and style. (For examples, see Figures
11.1-11.3, notable mission statements of multinational as well as domestic companies.)

REVIEWING THE CURRENT STATEMENT

The review process should start with a thorough discussion of the current
statement. Because mission statements are carefully crafted documents, it
is important to analyze the purpose of each phrase. When the statement is
examined in this manner, it will become clear that it sets forth most, if not
all, of the following characteristics of the enterprise:

- Its underlying values and philosophy

- Its customers and markets

- Its products or services

- Its stakeholders

- Its core technologies

- Its public image

- Its economic goals

SURFACING ISSUES THE MISSION STATEMENT MUST ADDRESS

The facilitator and the planning team must carefully examine the current
mission statement to identify those items that should be changed. Each
item needs to be discussed and understood in terms of both its surface
and underlying meaning. During this exercise certain words will be heard
repeatedly—these should be noted by the facilitator.

In helping the information technology division of a major multinational oil company shape its mission statement, for example, the word *responsive* kept reappearing during discussions. When asked why the word did

Gerber Products Company
Corporate Mission

The human, physical and financial resources of Gerber Products Company are dedicated toward:

◇ Establishing Gerber as the premier brand on food, clothing and care items for children from birth through age three.

◇ Giving our customers and consumers what they want all the time, every time, on time.

◇ Continuously pursuing improvements in all phases of our business.

◇ Seeking intelligent risks that will build shareholder value.

◇ Providing long-term shareholders with superior returns.

◇ Creating opportunities for all associates to achieve their full potential.

◇ Maintaining the Gerber heritage as the authority in the field of infant and child nutrition and care.

Figure 11.1. Gerber Products Company Corporate Mission

Texaco's Guiding Principles And Objectives

The principles and objectives which guide Texaco in doing the best possible job of finding and producing increasing quantities of oil and natural gas, refining superior products, transporting and marketing products efficiently and economically, and further improving its operations and products through continuing research, are:

To deliver to customers only products of proven high quality at fair prices and to serve them in such a manner as to earn their continuing respect, confidence, and loyalty, both before and after sale.

To be financially sound and responsible; pay a fair return to shareholders for the use of their capital; maintain a record of productivity and profits which will enable the company to attract new capital, and continue to grow and expand its earning power; and, through inspired leadership and effective teamwork, strive to be the most highly respected company in industry.

To maintain a high level of employee morale through fostering, by example, an atmosphere of hard work; recognize dignity of the individual by treating every person in the company with respect and courtesy; provide opportunities for employees to develop and advance to the utmost of their capabilities; encourage and carefully consider all suggestions from employees and, if not acceptable, explain reasons why to employees; pay compensation which compares favorably with others in the industry; and provide safe and efficient places in which to work.

To obey all laws, be a good corporate citizen, and willingly assume our share of the responsibilities in communities where we operate both at home and abroad; conduct our affairs in a capable and friendly manner so that every one who comes in contact with us will find it pleasant to do business with us; observe the highest moral and ethical standards in carrying on our business; and keep our organization a fine example of the American system of freedom and opportunity.

To maintain free and open channels for the mutual exchange of information between management, stockholders, employees, retailers, customers, and others having a proper interest in the affairs of the company; work constructively toward securing public understanding and acceptance of the company's policies and performance; defend the company against unwarranted and unjustified criticism and attack; support industry efforts to resolve mutual problems in the area of public affairs; cooperate in other activities undertaken for the benefit of the industry as a whole, where these activities do not involve competitive or operating matters or infringe upon the company's right to independent action.

Figure 11.2. Texaco's Guiding Principles and Objectives

Our Credo

We believe our first responsibility is to the doctors, nurses and patients,
to mothers and fathers and all others who use our products and services.
In meeting their needs everything we do must be of high quality.
We must constantly strive to reduce our costs
in order to maintain reasonable prices.
Customers' orders must be serviced promptly and accurately.
Our suppliers and distributors must have an opportunity
to make a fair profit.

We are responsible to our employees,
the men and women who work with us throughout the world.
Everyone must be considered as an individual.
We must respect their dignity and recognize their merit.
They must have a sense of security in their jobs.
Compensation must be fair and adequate,
and working conditions clean, orderly and safe.
We must be mindful of ways to help our employees fulfill
their family responsibilities.
Employees must feel free to make suggestions and complaints.
There must be equal opportunity for employment, development
and advancement for those qualified.
We must provide competent management,
and their actions must be just and ethical.

We are responsible to the communities in which we live and work
and to the world community as well.
We must be good citizens — support good works and charities
and bear our fair share of taxes.
We must encourage civic improvements and better health and education.
We must maintain in good order
the property we are privileged to use,
protecting the environment and natural resources.

Our final responsibility is to our stockholders.
Business must make a sound profit.
We must experiment with new ideas.
Research must be carried on, innovative programs developed
and mistakes paid for.
New equipment must be purchased, new facilities provided
and new products launched.
Reserves must be created to provide for adverse times.
When we operate according to these principles,
the stockholders should realize a fair return.

Johnson & Johnson

Figure 11.3. Johnson & Johnson Credo

not appear in the draft of the statement, the group explained that it had used the word *flexible* in the draft instead. But as the discussion continued, the word *responsive* kept being used. When pushed to compare *responsiveness* with *flexibility*, it became evident that the group really did not use the words interchangeably.

The word *responsive* was the group's way of answering charges that the IT division did not provide customers with what they wanted on a timely basis. The word *timely*, however, did not surface until that focus session, when it became clear that the group resented what it saw as unfair complaints about the length of time it took them to respond to customer needs. After further discussion, the group agreed that a mechanism to bring the issue of timeliness to the surface was important; as a result, the phrase *in a timely fashion* was added to the statement.

CREATING THE NEW STATEMENT

The facilitator becomes important when conflicts emerge as a statement that is part of the organization's culture is torn apart. Then, when the statement has been analyzed and the team has been helped to arrive at a consensus on what should be changed and added, a few members of the team should be selected to prepare a draft. The team as a whole cannot write the final version. The wisdom of our nation's Founding Fathers in writing the Declaration of Independence should be a model of the proper process. Although the debate over the contents of the Declaration was conducted among more than two dozen participants, they elected a committee of three to do the writing—and two of the three, Benjamin Franklin and John Adams, decided that the third, Thomas Jefferson, should prepare the draft. Thus was born one of the most memorable documents in modern history.

The debate should be over substance, not over phrasing. The Thomas Jefferson of your enterprise is most likely to be found in the marketing, communications, or public relations department. The member of the planning team from that area is, therefore, the most likely candidate. Once a draft is prepared, argued over and refined by the team, and then redrafted, it must be introduced to the enterprise.

ACHIEVING BUY-IN

It is not enough to create a new mission statement; it also has to be accepted. Those involved in developing the credo should truly believe it, for they must sell it throughout the enterprise. If senior management develops a mission that is nothing more than rhetoric, the organization will not achieve its stated goals. Even when senior management is clearly committed, everyone will not buy into it immediately; indeed, it may take some time for everyone to assimilate the new view or modify their current mindsets.

THE FINAL STEP: THE ENTERPRISE PLAN

The third element of the Grand Strategy is the enterprise plan, the roadmap for achieving the mission. The enterprise plan is the sum total of the goals, critical success factors (CSFs), critical assumptions, tactics, and action items of the organization. In Chapter 5, as part of the internal analysis that comprises Activity 3.0 of the Dynamic Planning Framework,^{SM} the goals, CSFs, and critical assumptions held by those responsible for managing the organization were brought to the surface and examined in order to gain an understanding of the organization as it existed at the start of the Dynamic Planning Process. Now that you have chosen a new option, you must once again discuss your goals and see how the new option expands or changes them; then you must review the critical success factors to see how any changes in your goals will affect them, and finally you have to once again check the critical assumptions you are making to ensure their validity given the changes in the organization CSFs.

This review is necessary for the development of the tactics and action items that you will put in place to achieve the new mission. These items—the mission statement, goals, CSFs, critical assumptions, tactics, and action items—can be seen as a hierarchy of information necessary to develop your enterprise plan properly (see Figure 11.4).

TACTICS: THE ART OF SETTING DIRECTIONS

Tactics are a broad articulation of the necessary steps to attain the defined CSFs. For example, if a CSF is "Recruiting and retaining skilled, motivated, and innovative personnel," the defined tactics to attain the CSF might include the following: "Develop an innovative college recruitment program; enhance the performance evaluation process to reward innovative thinking; and create an image of being 'the place' to work in our industry." These are tactics the organization must put in place to attain the CSF; they are not detailed tasks or actions that have a definitive time frame for implementation, nor at this point are budget and resource allocations in place. (As noted earlier, budgeting and planning are treated as synonymous—the budget is the plan. Using the prior year's budget as a basis for extrapolating this year's budget, however, may lead to missing opportunities for the enterprise. If, instead, planning and budgeting are treated as separate processes done in conjunction with each other, opportunities for innovation and growth can be pursued.)

The entire planning team should participate in the development of tactics to support the organization's CSFs. Although not all members will be involved in all phases, the vice presidents of marketing, distribution, and information services may all have contributions to make. The advantage of

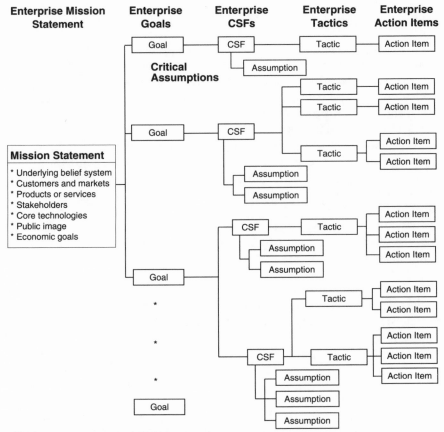

Figure 11.4. Hierarchy of Enterprise Plan Elements
© 1993 B. Goldberg and J. G. Sifonis

the whole group participating is that it helps people think out of the box—
they have the opportunity to think about problems from many different
perspectives.

As was the case with the organization's goals and CSFs, the whole planning team must also buy in on the tactics. Without this consensus, the
team members will each narrowly implement the tactics they are responsible for instead of acting in the interests of the firm as a whole; the results
in such cases will be a misuse of resources, at best, and divisiveness within the firm, at worst. Any lack of consistency in the implementation of the
tactics will result in mixed messages being sent throughout the firm.

There are a number of rules of thumb that can be applied to developing
tactics. For example, for each CSF, there should be at least one—but seldom
more than seven—defined tactics. In many cases, a defined tactic may, in
fact, support the attainment of more than one CSF, something that is often

overlooked as the team is developing tactics. This is a problem when the team members are, literally, so engrossed with the task at hand (developing tactics for specific CSFs) that they lose sight of what others are doing. It is only when the team completes the hierarchy that similarities in meaning, contradictions in tactics, or overlap will become apparent.

Once the tactics have been developed and aligned with the appropriate CSFs, the planning team should perform a reality check to ensure that none of the tactics being put in place are in conflict. For example, tactics for reducing manufacturing costs would involve integrating the research and development (R&D), engineering, and manufacturing processes to redesign the way products are developed—business process reengineering. However, this may mean reducing personnel due to increased efficiencies from the redesigned business processes. This tactic may appear to be in conflict with the tactics defined for recruiting and retaining personnel, a tactic put in place as part of the drive to improve quality. How do we handle the tactic of reducing personnel as a result of redesigning business processes while pursuing tactics to recruit and retain quality, competent personnel, which requires a reputation for being a stable company that provides at least some job security? This seeming conflict will have to be resolved by the planning team before the tactics, and subsequent action items, are developed and made public throughout the organization.

In the case of a heavy equipment manufacturer in the Midwest, the team realized that the company had the right number of people, but not enough of the right skill sets to achieve its enterprise plan. Because the team saw the problem, it recommended the following human resources tactic: "Establish a company sponsored training program to 'reengineer' individuals whose jobs have been displaced." Working through all the different tactics at the same time, and seeing how they meshed, brought a number of concrete benefits—less disruption of personnel and a lower cost for attaining the right workforce (retraining during the period of business process redesign kept the workforce at needed levels and saved such costs as outplacement and unemployment benefits as well as the costs of recruitment). On a less tangible level, it made future recruiting easier because the company enhanced its reputation as a good employer and created enormous loyalty and goodwill on the part of those retrained.

Now that you know what constitutes a tactic, you have to learn how to translate what is really a statement of direction into action items for implementation.

ACTION ITEMS: GETTING DOWN TO BUSINESS

In order to successfully implement a tactic, you have to break it down into action items—specific tasks or goals that must be achieved by individuals, groups, or departments within the company. Every tactic calls for at least one action item, and in most cases, several action items. For example, the CSF "Recruiting and retaining skilled, motivated, and innovative personnel" had three defined tactics. Examining the tactic "Develop an innovative college recruitment program" will explain what is meant by action items and show how they can have an impact on various levels of the company.

The action items associated with this tactic would be the following:

◆ Within the next two weeks, the vice presidents of human resources, R&D, engineering, and information technology will form a task force to identify and develop new recruiting incentives such as signing bonuses for high-potential recruits, full tuition reimbursement with time off to attend graduate school, and fast-track management programs for technically oriented individuals.

◆ Within four weeks, the task force will identify and contact the college placement offices of the five key colleges targeted for recruitment.

◆ Within the next three months, new recruiting brochures and company promotional materials will be developed and distributed to college placement directors. Senior management of the respective functional areas will work with the college placement directors to identify high-potential recruits to discuss possible employment opportunities prior to the normal recruiting cycle.

For most companies, while the action items are usually defined, developed, and executed by the owner or owners of the tactic, they will probably involve operating management and operating personnel as well, for they are the ones who are most likely to be assigned the job of executing the defined tasks. When action items become the goals of this layer of management, they, in turn, develop their own set of CSFs, tactics, and action items.

Specific individuals should be given ownership of action items along with estimated time frames, resources (budget, personnel), and performance measurement criteria. Be careful to ensure that the measures are realistic, especially if your business is developing action items for which you have no previous experience; for example, establishing a foreign distributorship when, in fact, you have never done business abroad. In this instance, establishing performance metrics is extremely difficult, because you have nothing to measure against (how do you know how much time is needed when it comes to all the paperwork necessary to operate in a foreign country); however, establishing a reporting mechanism will significantly enhance your ability to adjust your procedures dynamically in response to the progress being made.

These types of monitoring mechanisms help you avoid catastrophic errors by ensuring that if forward progress isn't being made, steps are taken to get back on track. It is also a means to isolate those things that senior management should be concerned about—in lieu of reviewing all performance measures. Monitoring and control are critical for adjusting to significant unanticipated changes that impact the execution of action items and, ultimately, the successful implementation of the enterprise plan.

Waiting for the Starting Bell

Everything is now in place to begin to move toward the future. The new road has been chosen and all the gear packed. Your organization is ready to move ahead. The big question is: How well will those who have to do the moving respond? Ensuring cooperation from everyone in the company is the next step that will have to be taken. Without that, the best plans are likely to fail. Implementation requires, as will be seen in Chapter 13, change management. But before we get there, here is the first example of the Dynamic Planning Framework in action—the activities are not done in order, nor done formally, but they are done.

Example: Fit & Hearty

Fit & Hearty, a fast food health chain, is a composite of several service-type enterprises we have analyzed in the course of a variety of consulting assignments. The Fit & Hearty story will indicate the way the various steps fit, albeit somewhat loosely, into the Dynamic Planning Framework.

A Business by Default

Some years ago, when fast food chains had first established themselves as look-alike franchises, easily recognizable by their double arches or striped buckets, one of the men who had started a business selling restaurant supplies (trays, napkins, packets of condiments) to them had a fatal heart attack. His three children—a son pursuing a business degree at Harvard, a daughter studying dance and physical education at Berkeley, and a younger son just accepted at MIT to pursue his interest in computer science—were suddenly faced with the problem of finding a way to meet their tuition payments.

Their mother, who had kept the books for the business, did not believe she could fill her husband's shoes. She sold the family's interest in the business to his partner, who arranged to pay her out over a number of years. While this provided them with enough money to live on, it could not be stretched to cover tuition.

The daughter, who had a part-time job in a health food restaurant near Berkeley, had often heard students lament the fact that the kind of food the restaurant served was not available near campus. She also knew that despite their limited budgets, many students managed to find a way to eat at the restaurant for a change of pace from the starchy, bland meals served in the campus cafeteria. After the spring semester was over, she went home and discussed an idea she had with the family. "What I want to do," she explained, "is sell healthy, modestly priced food out of a cart near the campus at lunchtime and in mid-afternoon. I think I can make more money that way than if I put in more hours in the restaurant, and I think I'll spend less time doing it, which means I'll have more time to study." She asked the other family members to provide her with enough money to buy a cart, a car, and the inventory that she would need to set up a business.

They agreed, and by the time the summer session began, she had set up her basic business. Parked near the school, with a city permit in hand, she offered a variety of salads, fruit cups, pita bread sandwiches, and fruit drinks. Careful to select only the freshest ingredients from local gardeners, she soon had a steady clientele. At the end of the summer, she had made enough money to cover tuition for the next semester, and she had managed to carry her course load easily.

Seeing how well the little business had done, the family decided to expand the operation by plunging their savings into two more carts, which her brothers would run at MIT and Harvard. Over the next couple of weeks, they analyzed the Berkeley experience in the context of the kinds of fresh products that would be available on the East Coast, as well as differences in climate and attitudes. After agreeing to make one item (a hearty tomato-based vegetable soup) a coast-to-coast standard to feel connected though so far apart, they developed for each region small and simple menus that were healthy, satisfying, and affordable.

Perhaps it was their location—college campuses in which the findings on heart disease, healthy diets, and the virtues of exercise were accepted well before they became national trends—that made their little business a success. The demographics were also a plus: when they needed extra help to meet the demands of their customers at lunchtime, they could easily get students to work for them part time, for low wages and a free meal. At the end of the year, they decided to expand their operation a bit, acquiring additional carts.

But they did not go much further until a couple of years later, when the sister, recently married and planning to attend graduate school in the Midwest, was asked by one of her Berkeley workers if he could continue to run the cart. That was when the idea of a franchise operation was born. Not only did the business in Berkeley continue, but a friend who had worked for her from the beginning and was also graduating was offered the opportunity to purchase a franchise near the University of Chicago—

the idea of the elder brother, who now had his Harvard MBA. The franchisee would be given the menus, provided with a list of suppliers and a line of credit, a place to park the equipment when it was not in use, and all the necessary permits to run the operation. The elder brother went to Chicago and made all the arrangements, including laying the groundwork for additional franchises if business seemed to warrant it. A company named Fit & Hearty was born.

Since the children saw the business as a sideline, all they did at this point was arrange additional franchise operations as requested or as warranted by revenues in a particularly good market. The brother with the MBA was too busy being an investment banker in the late 1970s to pay much attention to a business that brought him occasional small checks. The sister and her husband were too busy studying. The younger brother was too busy doing research for a computer company in the field of artificial intelligence.

Almost without their realizing it, however, the operation was growing— moving from college town to college town as students who worked in one location went on to graduate school in another. When the nation experienced an economic downturn in 1982–83, the sister and her husband, faced with few professional opportunities due to the cuts in arts funding, paid more attention to Fit & Hearty. They expanded their operation to a small storefront offering mostly takeout and a few self-service tables.

The store did so well that it, along with the franchises, began to overwhelm them with paperwork. They asked their brother, the computer expert, for advice on how to keep the books, organize information about suppliers, and correlate the data from their franchises. The brother was able to rig together various pieces of computer equipment, creating a fairly sophisticated system at a fraction of the usual cost, and customize a series of programs for it that allowed greater efficiency than they could have achieved using packaged software.

As the economy picked up, the family decided to expand Fit & Hearty into other areas of the country with both carts and storefront operations. Their timing was again right; it was a decade of increasing health consciousness. As the decade drew to a close, the next economic downturn hit. This time the pressures turned out to be different. The business the older brother worked for was in trouble, and profits from Fit & Hearty were falling because there were fewer new investors in the Fit & Hearty franchises. Then suddenly, to their surprise, a large food services company offered to buy them out.

ORGANIZING RESOURCES

They held a family council to examine their options. They could sell out, but the younger siblings somehow felt it would be a betrayal of something that linked them to their father's memory. Besides, the money being offered was not enough to make them want to abandon what were, in essence, good jobs that they enjoyed. The older brother argued that they either had to go public, getting enough investors to keep the operation growing, or buy him out. But he added that he could wait for a while; in return, they were to take the business seriously—in other words, analyze the business. He wanted to know what Fit & Hearty was, what it could become, and, if it had potential, how it could be turned into a real business, a money-making enterprise that would produce long-term value for the family. To answer these questions, he said, the family needed to develop a business strategy.

He explained that a critical step in developing a business strategy was to draw up a mission statement because, to quote Peter Drucker, "only a clear definition of the mission and purpose of the organization makes possible clear and realistic business goals." He said that they really could no longer continue doing things the way they were just because the business was successful, and told them to keep in mind something else Drucker had said:

> Success always obsoletes the very behavior that achieved it, always creates new realities, and always new and different problems. . . . The management that does not ask, "What is our mission?" when the company is successful is, in effect, smug, lazy, and arrogant. It will not be long before success will turn into failure.[3]

INTERNAL ANALYSIS

As a first step in doing what their brother had asked, the sister, her younger brother, and her husband sat down to see where they were in terms of having a mission statement. Working from some sample statements they had collected, and remembering the sister's original explanation of what she wanted to do to earn money for tuition, they were able to sum up the informal, unwritten mission of Fit & Hearty:

> Sell healthy, filling, inexpensive food at convenient campus locations for profit. Provide fair compensation to employees. Provide high-quality, fresh products to customers at reasonable prices.

The next step was to figure out what to add to the statement to meet the business-oriented requirements of their brother:

> Increase current profitability and provide long-term value to the family.

In other words, they had to develop a mission statement that would guide them in expanding the business in a systematic way in the future. To date,

Fit & Hearty had grown in a haphazard fashion—by reacting to requests to buy franchises (that is, a cart, a line of credit, permits, and menus) instead of proactively searching for new locations and marketing the franchises. The process of developing the statement was to prove far more difficult than they had anticipated. Working from the list of elements in a mission statement, they have to address a number of questions:

* How do we maintain our commitment to quality products as we get larger?

* How do we translate and embed our family philosophy and values into the business?

* Is our market only college campuses? Are our customers only college students? Do we want to enlarge our scope of business to include a broader set of markets and customers, such as off-campus locations in major metropolitan areas targeting health-conscious customers?

* Do we have to broaden our product line to include food that matches Fit & Hearty's image but appeals to a wider range of customers?

* Do we want shareholders in Fit & Hearty, or do we want to keep the company family held?

* What is our obligation to the communities in which we do business? What are our economic and ethical obligations to our employees? What are our obligations to our customers in terms of providing products that meet their expectations?

* Do we want technology to play a role in delivering our products? Can we use technology to expand our business?

* How can we strengthen our image as a health food provider? How can we change our image from that of a sidewalk vendor to a fast food vendor?

* What level of revenue and net income should we strive to achieve? How fast should we grow each year?

Again proceeding with the internal analysis process (Chapter 5), Fit & Hearty identified a set of goals: increase profitability; increase revenues; maintain family control; protect the environment in which we live and work; deliver high-quality, inexpensive products; and increase personal income. At this point there is one attribute that is missing—quantification.

The goals are not precise with respect to time frame, nor are there numeric figures to use to monitor and evaluate progress; this is not an uncommon problem during an initial definition of many of the elements of the plan.

After considerable discussion, they produced the following list of critical success factors for achieving their goals: adding new locations, finding new ways to satisfy customers, maintaining strong community relationships, hiring and training employees to do things efficiently and well, finding suppliers and developing solid relationships with them; keeping prices competitive with other fast food prices, developing a recognizable image, developing new products, keeping overhead down; ensuring consistency of products and services, making enough extra money to reinvest for growth, and maintaining good sales and financial information.

Although the family members developed a good set of CSFs, they did not meet all of the CSF criteria discussed in Chapter 5, nor did they go into them in enough detail. For example, time frames are not mentioned, nor are the CSFs quantified. Although this is a good starter list, the family will have to augment the CSFs as they go through the planning process.

As a next step, the family members participated in generating the set of critical assumptions based upon a key question: Why is the CSF critical? The assumptions the family developed were for the CSFs that dealt with suppliers, new locations, and information: *our produce suppliers our are business partners*—without good suppliers, we cannot survive and grow; *new locations are key to increasing our revenue*—there is a market for health fast food and we have no competitors; and *tracking sales and cost information will help us manage the business better (revenues and cost) and help us manage more stores in the future.*

Now it is time to see how the CSFs and assumptions translate into tactics. Using the selected CSFs for supplier and location, the tactics the family developed for each of these CSFs were: guarantee minimum purchase agreements to suppliers for the right of first refusal on ingredient purchases, and focus on acquiring ingredients from organically grown produce suppliers. For location, the tactics were: increase storefront locations near competing fast food and restaurant sites, and expand storefronts in upscale markets. Although the tactics are valid and would support the mission and enterprise plan of the company, they may have to be revised as the family members conduct the external analysis. The action items based on these tactics can now be defined:

- For the supplier tactic:
  – Within one week, develop the criteria for choosing key suppliers.
  – Within two weeks, identify ten potential suppliers in each of the markets in which we operate.

- For the location tactic:
  - Within four weeks, conduct a market survey to identify locations in upscale neighborhoods with health club facilities.
  - Within two months, select the target markets and determine the economics of carts versus storefronts in the selected markets.

The family has now done all the internal analysis needed to prepare a hierarchy of enterprise plan elements (see Figure 11.5). As with the other elements of the enterprise plan, these may also have to be revised as the family takes the next steps toward preparing for tomorrow.

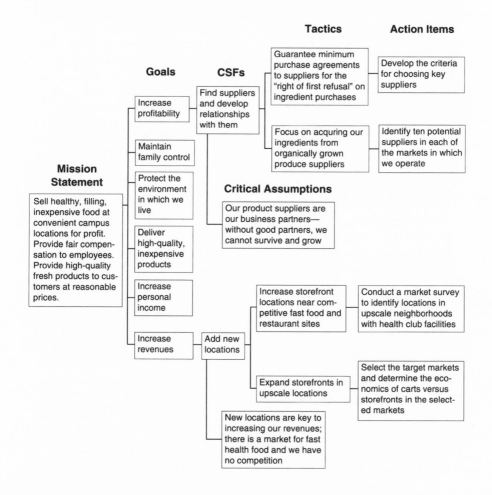

Figure 11.5. Fit & Hearty^{SM} Enterprise Plan Elements
© 1993 B. Goldberg and J. G. Sifonis

EXTERNAL ANALYSIS

A few weeks later, the elder brother met with his sister, her husband, and their mother (the younger brother was at a computer convention) to do some further analysis of the business. He thought it was time for them to determine what possibilities they could see. The brother, who had studied business management, played the role of facilitator. He explained that he had done extensive research on the fast food industry, learning all he could about the competitions' strengths and weaknesses, and thought he had a good sense of where the industry was headed.

He began by asking them each to express what they believed to be possibilities for the business—no matter how outlandish they might sound. After all, the objective of the exercise was to examine alternatives. As each family member gave his or her views of the future, the brother noted them, and also noted the words used to check against the vocabulary he had built up when he was doing his homework on the industry. The six key points made were:

1. The sister's husband started by mentioning that he had heard that a bowling alley chain was looking for restaurants and snack bars to open franchises in their alleys and wondered if it made sense for them because sports types like healthy food.

2. The mother suggested that their soups were so good they should try to get a company like Campbell to sell them for Fit & Hearty.

3. The sister said she liked the idea of trying to get into food courts in malls because she always watched what she ate after trying on clothes.

4. Her husband said that while it might seem far out, he thought they should think about a cookbook or recipes or something like that.

5. The elder brother suggested that they should investigate starting an upscale restaurant, catering to those who would pay more for quality and service—two attributes that he suggested would be key to the success of such a restaurant.

6. After quietly listening and thinking about the business for a while, the sister had another suggestion—"Why don't we just stick to our knitting and keep doing what has made us successful, but more of it?"

PREPARING THE POSITION PAPER AND GENERATING THE OPTIONS

At this point, the elder brother told them that when he matched the words they were using with those he kept hearing from people he spoke to in the industry, the key words were: *service, cost, quality, location, convenience, image, ambiance, low-cholesterol* or *healthy, regional,* and *variety*—a new word recently emerging. He thought, therefore, that the industry as a whole was going to have to make some changes, moving toward more individualized franchises with greater variety in the kinds of foods they served. That, he explained, was why he was suggesting upscale. He said that, however, since he did not want to impose his views on them, they should now turn to an analysis of the ideas—the possibilities—in terms of what they believed to be their distinctive competencies or core strengths. The following are the highlights of the analysis:

1. The bowling alley idea was quickly dismissed: bowling is not a health-oriented sport, but more a social occasion; moreover, they did not want to get into selling liquor in any form, a necessity for any food enterprise operating in a bowling alley.

2. The idea of selling their soups to a company like Campbell was quickly eliminated: they would not have control to guarantee quality even if a company with its own strong name would buy the idea. The brother pointed out, however, that some sort of frozen product sold locally might be something they could look into in the future, if they held onto the business and increased their name recognition.

3. They then turned to a discussion of food courts in malls. Given Fit & Hearty's competencies—quality products and customer service— they thought they could compete with the chains currently in these locations. The idea seemed reasonable.

4. The elder brother said the only problem with a cookbook was it would probably provide only a few thousand dollars and maybe some publicity and had little to do with the need to expand the business.

5. The sister said that going upscale went against everything she believed in. The mother said that an upscale restaurant would make it hard to maintain the stark white, easily scrubbable look that marked their storefront restaurants. She added that while ambiance might be the coming thing for the larger established chains she did not believe it would work for them at this stage when they had to focus on image.

6. The family quickly agreed that more of the same would not work, given the uncertain state of the economy. The elder brother also pointed out that the Fit & Hearty concept was being overtaken and that they really had to either expand to gain recognition or give up.

At that point, the elder brother said that he thought they had made some progress. He asked that they meet again in a couple of weeks, with the younger brother present, to make some hard choices. He said he would further investigate the two most likely possibilities in the meantime.

STRATEGIC ALIGNMENT MODELING

When the family met again, the younger brother, a specialist in information technology, was present. As he listened to the discussion, he grew increasingly impatient. Finally, he interrupted: "You all know more about where we should go in terms of food services, but you're missing something. We have a lot of technology and a lot of information that we capture with it. Our ordering system for supplies, for example. How often have we helped out one of the farmers we buy from by calling a restaurant and offering them a 'buy' on some item our supplier has too much of?"

The family discussed the possibility of being the electronic link between their suppliers and small enterprises. They made some calls and found that a number of restaurants, diners, and coffee shops were very willing to discuss the possibility of Fit & Hearty doing their purchasing. The idea for a new business was born. The purchasing effort would be built on the computer and telecommunications technology already in place for handling orders from the storefronts and carts through the Fit & Hearty home office. It could now also be used for distribution to a network of suppliers for overnight delivery and for billing and payments.

The brother-in-law lit up in the course of the discussion. "You fax recipes back and forth also, don't you, and calorie counts?" The older brother said, "Yes, but . . ." The mother interrupted his protest: "Of course, and people are always asking for them so we have copies around. We could do something to get names and do that book you mentioned." As the discussion continued, the idea was considerably changed and refined. It was agreed that they would try placing discount coupons in local papers that could be redeemed for 10 percent off the price of a meal. The condition was that those turning in the coupons would provide names and addresses in return for which they would also get a recipe. Fit & Hearty would then do a mailing to those who redeemed the coupons, asking if they were interested in subscribing to a newsletter. Even if that didn't work out, they would still have a good customer list of health-conscious individuals—a mailing list that they could sell to direct marketing firms.

The additional benefit of the purchasing arrangement was that they could now obtain better prices because they would have the advantage of scale and, of course, the purchasing arrangements would provide extra income for expansion of the core business. In addition, they decided to increase the number of storefront operations by operating in a few selected malls. The greater presence would increase name recognition, making it easier to acquire clients for the purchasing division and perhaps help launch the newsletter. With these new business ideas to act on, they were ready to construct a final mission statement for the new Fit & Hearty.

BUILDING A GRAND STRATEGY

At this point they realized that what they really were trying to do, in addition to making a profit, was bring healthier food to those on limited budgets. They were determined to make it easy for those who could not eat out in expensive restaurants to eat healthily. And they believed that more and more scientific proof of the benefits of the kind of diet they were promoting would change people's eating habits. They envisioned a future in which the Fit & Hearty menu was as acceptable as a burger and french fries.

Given that vision of the future, they turned to drafting a mission statement:

FIT & HEARTY
OUR MISSION

Our mission is to help people to live healthier lives in an era when time is scarce and eating outside the home is a necessity as well as a social experience. We will strive in every way to build a lasting reputation as a provider of high-value, quality products and services to our customers.

We want to ensure that our organization reflects our belief that honesty, integrity, and loyalty to all those we serve and are responsible to—our customers, our franchisees, our suppliers, our distributors, our employees, and the communities in which we work and live—are our most important legacy.

And just as honesty, integrity, and loyalty are the foundation of our business—excellent service and quality are the cornerstones of our operation.

We believe our first responsibility is to our customers:

We will strive to provide high-quality, fresh food products in a clean, pleasing environment at a reasonable price. We will provide superior service while constantly striving to reduce costs.

For our food product business customers, we will strive to provide superior purchasing services that will bring them the freshest possible produce at the lowest possible cost through the use of advanced information and communication technologies.

We are determined to be good citizens—encouraging civic improvement, supporting health and education initiatives, protecting the environment in which we all live, maintaining the property we are privileged to use in good order, and paying our fair share of taxes.

We have set high economic goals for our business; we will double our sales volume before 1995 and achieve a 10 percent profit. Achieving these goals will enable the business to grow and prosper and provide growth opportunities for all employees.

The third element of the Grand Strategy was the spelling out of the new goals—the purchasing agreement and the newsletter. The family began the process of figuring out the tactics and actions associated with each in a somewhat more formal way than they had begun any other part of the business. Fit & Hearty was on the road to becoming a true corporation.

ONWARD—TO THE SAME PROBLEMS MAGNIFIED

The voyage undertaken by Fit & Hearty was a fairly simple one, not designed in terms of the Dynamic Planning Framework, but instinctively incorporating many of its elements. Because it was such a young company, the work on many of the activities was concurrent or out of formal sequence, but the pieces were all there. The analysis the family did is likely to put Fit & Hearty on a solid footing for a time. However, the more successful it becomes, and the larger it grows, the more likely it is that the process will need to be repeated in a more formal manner. In a few years, if the stated goals have been met, or even exceeded, the business will be ready to take the next steps to ensure continued growth—or to change again. Sometimes, however, enterprises cannot follow such a leisurely and orderly development—unanticipated outside events can intervene, forcing change and reevaluation.

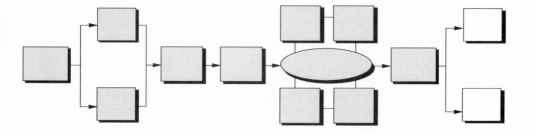

CHAPTER 12

DYNAMIC PLANNING IN ACTION

The ability to learn faster than competitors may be or become the only
sustainable competitive advantage in a rapidly changing world.

Arie de Geus, French strategist

A t the other end of the spectrum from Fit & Hearty are large, established organizations that want to change because of the changes they see taking place all around them or the changes they are undergoing. They are worried about losing market share to a competitor that takes advantage of a new development or provides better customer service or lower prices or new products, or they are facing a takeover or a merger or privatization. The Dynamic Planning Framework offers these organizations an opportunity to manage the change they are facing effectively, for the short and the long term, by helping them become organizations that deal well with, and even anticipate, change.

The organization described in the example below was a good candidate for Dynamic Planning because it had recently been privatized and was trying to do what it already did better and faster now that it faced a bottom line; it also was determined to prepare for a future that involved ever-increasing competition. It is also a good example of how the Dynamic Planning Framework works, particularly when treated as the flexible tool that it is rather than as a methodology.[1] This example also reveals the strength of the Framework as a tool for promoting change.

As the case unfolds, notice that all the steps of the Dynamic Planning Framework, beginning with internal announcements that the company is committed to taking this forward-looking approach, promote openness, learning, and change. The holistic approach is the key to achieving buy-in to new processes, technologies, and structures by employees, whose knowledge, ability, and commitment are the cornerstones of organizational effectiveness.

EXAMPLE: FROM TRANSPORTATION TO TRANSFORMATION

This example is based on an assignment for an enormous, newly privatized company employing 165,000 people in a nationwide transportation business. The company is located in South Africa, a nation with one of the highest per capita incomes in Africa, but a nation in the midst of a major social and political transition, exacerbated by the global economic recession. The problems it faces include dealing with the effects of a national inflation rate approaching 17 percent and unemployment rates of over 70 percent in some areas. In addition, strict foreign exchange control regulations and the lack of skilled labor (although the labor pool is enormous, skilled workers are in short supply because of the nature of the educational system) prevent the country from attracting much-needed foreign investment.

Our assignment was to help the organization develop an integrated information technology (IT) and business strategy that would lead to improvements in its current performance and at the same time prepare it for new directions. The project was complicated by the history, location, size, and scope of business, particularly when looked at in the context of the four dimensions we have been examining throughout the book—economic, social, political, and technological.

BACKGROUND INFORMATION

For several decades after its inception, the company was a government body under the direction and governance of the country's Ministry of Transportation. Historically, it was a state agency; therefore, its operational focus was on controlling its budget rather than on profitability—and it had no competitors. The annual planning process was, in reality, a budgeting process in which the prior year's budget was reviewed and updated for the next budget year, always keeping in mind inflation. Employment was for life, and the prevailing culture was that of a social institution intended to provide employment, even if that adversely affected the services it provided. At its peak, the company employed over 265,000 people.

The company was vertically integrated, doing everything in the transport area from running an international airline to repairing locomotives to building bridges to running its own laundry services. Moreover, it had five divisions, four subsidiaries, five business units, and nine service centers operating under the corporate (that is, government) umbrella. The individual units were aggregated into groups, each under a group vice president (GVP). Although most of the operating unit aggregations were logical, for example, all units responsible for rail operations were the responsibility of a GVP for rail, and the units responsible for port operations were under a GVP for ports, smaller units, such as housing and food services, were artificially aggregated under a GVP. The GVPs of the various units comprised the Management Board, which was chaired by the Managing Director—the equivalent of a Chairman of the Board\Chief Executive Officer; the Board's purpose was to discuss policy and procedural issues. The Managing Director alone reported outside—to the Ministry of Transportation—for budget approval and to seek advice and counsel prior to making *any* major decisions, especially those that could have a potential impact on the social and political environment.

The business structure was Byzantine, still reflecting the bureaucratic style typical of government agencies. The organizational structure was very hierarchical; there was almost no sharing of skilled resources among and between the various units, and decisions were rule based. If there wasn't a rule or regulation to address the issue, no action was taken; the issue was, according to a member of the company, "forgotten to death" in the bureaucratic maze.

The structure of the IT function was almost as Byzantine as the business structure. There were really two IT functions within the company: one was established to support the unique requirements of the national airline, and the other supported everything else in the company (the business units were a captive internal market, since they were not empowered to develop independent IT functions).

Although both functions reported to the same GVP, they were autonomous, sharing few resources, either technical or human. The IT function of the airlines was state of the art; it had a global perspective, very advanced IT skill sets, airline business expertise, and a strategy that was linked to the airline's business strategy. The group vice president devoted a significant portion of his time to the airline's business operations and IT function but dealt with the other units' IT functions on an operational rather than a strategic basis.

The IT function of the airline had a formal, overarching information technology strategy because it had to adjust as the airline constantly changed the way it did things (its business strategy) to compete and interface with other airlines on a global basis. The business strategy of the rest of the company was static, since it did not face similar challenges. Consequently, all the IT function that supported the other businesses had to do was provide the computing resources to support them in the most efficient and effective manner possible. To accomplish this, the director of the IT function had developed an implied IT strategy—utilization of a single vendor's technology offerings to fulfill all the company's computing and telecommunications needs. The rationale for this decision was that it allowed for economies of scale and scope while still providing all needed services to users. It also provided a means to unilaterally impose IT standards across all of the operating units.

The IT function was a classic glass house operation—that is, the users could not influence the level of service the IT function provided or the way it performed. User requests for services or new applications were submitted to the central site and IT personnel responded—if and when they had time. Since there was no free-market competition, the user community *perceived* the mentality and management philosophy of the IT function as providing the users what the IT function thought was best for them, not what they really wanted.

Indeed, the IT group acted very like a utility company, providing a certain generic level of service to all customers. Yet the IT function of the company as a whole, like that of the airline, was truly state of the art. Standards were in place for data, networks, and application development, and the technology was the most advanced available. The computing center was best in class when compared to the IT functions of other major companies in the country. However, unlike its counterparts in the airline's IT unit, the general IT group just didn't have the competencies necessary to analyze business problems and develop applications that would support diverse business needs. As a result, the applications they developed did not meet the business requirements of the users, and the projects were late and over budget. As one senior executive stated: "They do a good job of delivering the wrong answer at the right price."

MOVING INTO A COMPETITIVE WORLD

In the early 1990s, life changed dramatically for the company. The national social and political transitions taking place led to a decision to privatize the company—and to deregulate a number of businesses. Competition in air and ground transport was introduced into what was formerly a protected marketplace. Suddenly, the company not only had to make a profit, but it had to do so in a nonregulated market. Unfortunately, many of the business managers literally could not discern the difference between cash flow and profitability. Not only had the rules of the game changed, but they were playing an entirely different game—survival of the fittest.

Fortunately, the Managing Director of the company was an extremely talented individual. He was politically well connected, had an excellent sense of internal politics, understood the concept of free-market competition, and, above all, was a visionary. His vision was to transform the company from being a provider of transportation services to being a logistics company. Ultimately, the company would add value to its customers by providing services based upon the *information content* of the inventory it was transporting rather than just providing value based on the *physical* transportation of the inventory. For example, instead of arranging for the movement of a container from one point to another, the vision was to not only arrange for the transportation of the container, but also for financing the purchase of its contents, stocking the inventory at the customer's site, and electronically matching buyers and suppliers for the inventory. The intent was to add value for the customer at as many points as possible by being both their physical and electronic intermediary. The Managing Director's vision added a vastly different dimension to the company's historical notion of being merely a provider of transportation services. But most important in terms of the planning for this future, he believed that IT would be the mechanism for achieving his vision.

At the same time the company was undergoing privatization, a senior manager for information engineering was hired by the director of the IT function. His role was to manage the implementation of a new technical concept aimed at addressing user complaints that the IT function could not deliver applications on time or within budget. This was a break with the tradition of promoting from within the company, but the needed expertise in information engineering just wasn't available internally.

The outsider's background had given him an understanding of the world of business that simply did not exist among the IT managers who had risen from the ranks of the company. He had the ability to speak two languages, business and IT, which allowed him to demystify the world of IT for senior executives. He could explain how companies could use information technology to enhance their existing scope of business and deliver information-based products and services. He also had the skills needed to gain access to strategic thinkers at the most senior ranks of an organization.

Since he was unaware of the company's unwritten rule about staying within one's functional area, he began building relationships outside his group. He did this as part of a personal campaign aimed at communicating the fundamentals of IT to senior management, so they would take IT into account in setting their strategy. As a result, a few months later, he and a group of thinkers from the other key business units informally began exploring possible approaches that would allow IT to be used to support the Managing Director's vision of the company as a logistics organization. (The Managing Director had set up the group to start thinking about the business strategies necessary to implement his vision.)

Then, while visiting the United States with other managers in the company, the senior IT manager convinced them to meet with some noted academics in the field of technology, specifically to introduce the managers to the idea that information technology could be used to integrate a company's internal business units electronically and to integrate those with external organizations such as suppliers and customers. What they learned made it clear that the problems the company faced were bigger, more complex, and more difficult than originally thought. The managers began to understand that any strategies they developed had to be integrated, not just linked together.[2]

The conversations with those they met, especially the introduction of the Strategic Alignment Model (SAM), made the group aware that the company would be able to move into the future only if the IT managers understood the company's business strategy along with the underlying assumptions that went into its creation. They realized the next step was convincing their business colleagues of the value of sharing information with those in IT, and even more difficult, getting them involved with and committed to the process, not only in terms of funding a project but, more important, in terms of their time.

Taking the First Step

With the help of the company's auditors, who made a similar suggestion, the IT group managed to convince the Managing Director and other key senior executives, primarily the members of the Management Board, that the company needed an overarching IT strategy. The information engineering manager was appointed Manager, Information Technology Strategy (ITS manager), and was put in charge of developing the company's IT strategy. One of the first steps he took was to get approval to put in place an Information Technology Steering Committee (ITSC) comprised of a dozen or so key executives from the business units, including the director of the IT function. The purpose of the ITSC was to "develop an Information Technology Strategy that would be aligned with, and supportive of, the company's vision and strategic intent, without being unduly influenced by current opinions, changing attitudes, or individual prejudices." Another goal was to ensure that its members would be so involved in the planning project that they would buy into its recommendations, which would be critical to the eventual implementation of the strategy.

Numerous formal presentations and countless informal meetings were held with committee members as well as other members of senior management, aimed at raising their comfort level with the idea of a comprehensive strategy. Once that process was well under way, the next step was to find a methodology or framework that would help them deal with the complex set of issues involved in creating a strategy for so large an organization. It was at this stage that our formal association with the client began.

The new ITS manager and a colleague returned to the United States to meet with us and with the academics who had been at that first meeting. After a great deal of discussion of various approaches to the problem over the course of a week, the idea of using Dynamic Planning,[3] with an emphasis on Strategic Alignment Modeling to develop the IT strategy, emerged as the best course to follow. The ITS manager had been explaining SAM to the group ever since the first meeting in the United States. During the week of discussions, the literature on SAM was reviewed,[4] and case histories of successful Strategic Alignment and Dynamic Planning recounted. In the end, everyone agreed that the Framework would ensure that the strategy chosen would fit with the business strategy of the moment— and the long-term strategy aimed at realizing the director's vision.

Once in South Africa, these ideas were presented and accepted, and the formal assignment began. Because we were all somewhat unsure about how ready a company that had just undergone a major change in culture was to adapt to yet another change, we all agreed that it would be advisable to do the project in three phases over an eighteen-month period. Phase I would include performing the internal and external analysis and developing the position paper. Phase II would involve generating the options, checking them through SAM, and creating the Grand Strategy. And Phase III would be the execution of the remaining activities of the Dynamic Planning Framework—implementing the integrated business and IT strategy and putting in place monitoring and evaluation mechanisms (see Figure 12.1). A phased approach is preferable in such a large project because it provides the opportunity to use the information gained in the early analysis to modify the tasks and techniques of the later parts of the Framework.

PHASE I: THE PROJECT BEGINS

The first activity is the organization of resources. In this case, it meant obtaining the appropriate people with the right skill sets to take part in the project and perform the necessary detailed planning for the entire project. The second and third activities of the Framework deal with learning as much as possible about the company and the world, especially the industrial sector, in which it competes. In fact, all three of the activities were begun almost concurrently.

One of the first steps was arranging for us to visit some of the company's major transportation facilities. We went on a tour designed to give us a better understanding of the size and complexity of the operation. We rode the overnight passenger train to one of the country's major commercial ports, took a tugboat tour of the port facilities in the morning, then flew from the commercial port to a port that specialized in handling bulk commodities, and returned to the corporate headquarters that evening. The next day, we visited the largest train-marshaling yard in the country and toured the parcel-handling facility (basically the facility is equivalent to a Federal Express or UPS hub for the collection and distribution of parcels to over seven thousand locations throughout the country). Going from one vast area to another, all on transportation the company provided, gave us a sense of the complexity—and national importance—of the company.

While on this tour, we met with and interviewed several of the senior executives of the operating units, including those who were part of a small

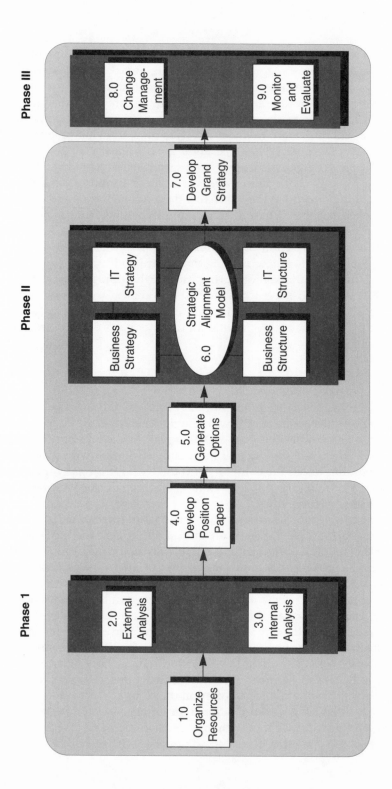

Phase 1

Phase II

Phase III

Figure 12.1. Dynamic Planning Framework:^{SM} **A Phased Approach**
© 1993 B. Goldberg and J. G. Sifonis

division that was already involved in logistics, to get a better understanding of the operational aspects of the individual business units. In addition, a number of presentations were made by other key business units such as telecommunications, information technology, and container shipment. The trip also provided an opportunity for us to meet many of the members of the ITSC and most of the senior management.

Organizing the Resources

Next, we worked with the ITSC team to prepare the detailed task plan that would guide the rest of the project, identified a core group of individuals from the business units who would work with us during the course of the project (the larger the group, the easier it would be to transfer the knowledge from the team to the company), and modified the *specific* tasks of the Framework to accommodate the unique environment of the company. The team then proceeded to develop the questionnaires and other survey instruments that would be required for completing the first step of Dynamic Planning.

Internal Analysis

Given the scope and complexity of the company, after some discussion, the team agreed that three dozen was probably the *minimum* number of interviews that would have to be conducted to gain a comprehensive understanding of the business and the issues facing the company. After an examination of the organizational structures and discussions with the ITSC, thirty-five major players from the top one thousand managers and executives within the key business units were selected for the interviews.

Although scheduling those interviews proved difficult, it was a minor problem compared to the reluctance of many of the participants to take part. Even though they knew the Managing Director formally endorsed the project and urged full cooperation, not everyone bought-in. For example, many of the interviewees were still trying to comprehend the transition to a competitive environment. From their perspective, planning was a waste of time: they had to worry about their bottom line today, not about tomorrow's strategic intent. In addition, they didn't fully understand the world of IT and were uncomfortable discussing what they *perceived* to be the subject of the interviews—IT-related issues. This was a topic they usually delegated to lower-level managers.

The team spent a lot of time explaining the need to integrate business and IT strategy, pointing out that doing so takes an understanding of the business. This helped reassure many of the interviewees that the interviews would focus on business rather than IT issues and that the interview process was business rather than technology driven. In some cases, where this approach did not work or where the potential participants really were under tremendous time pressure because of their difficulty working in a profitmaking, competitive environment for the first time, the team resorted to strongly emphasizing the Managing Director's support for and involvement in the project.

EXTERNAL ANALYSIS

At the same time that the interviews were being arranged, a decision was made about the best way to conduct the external analysis, which in Dynamic Planning is usually done by a task force. Here, over the years, many of the company's executives had made site visits to transportation companies in Europe and the United States. As a result of the relationships they developed during these visits, they had good competitive information and insights into what other companies were doing. In addition, their internal strategic planning group had extensive information about the social, economic, and political trends in the country and the region. They also tracked a variety of economic factors on a global basis.

They did not, however, have competitive information about international trends among companies that provided integrated logistics services. Since this was too complex an assignment to give them at such a difficult time, the competitive analysis of world-class, global, integrated carriers—companies that utilize multiple modes of transportation in an integrated fashion to deliver goods to customers—was contracted out. These companies provide their customers with all the necessary integration services along the logistics chain to move inventory from one point to another. (The Managing Director's vision was broader than that of today's logistics companies—for example, providing all physical as well as electronic integration services through one company.)

INTERNAL ANALYSIS

It is time to return to the ongoing process of the internal analysis. The executive interviews were designed to elicit responses from the interviewees along the various dimensions of the Strategic Alignment Model. The objective was to gain an understanding of the company's vision, scope of business, competencies, business structure, skill sets, culture, the role of IT, and the critical processes of the business. Here we followed the usual Dynamic Planning Framework format of involving all team members in the executive interview process; the interviews were done by two-member teams, one team member working from the questionnaire and the other taking notes and asking secondary, clarifying questions. Structuring the interviews in this manner gave each of the team members a better perspective of the business.

In the end, many of the interviewees were comfortable enough to use the interviews as an opportunity to ask questions related to the Dynamic Planning Framework concepts and IT issues. As a result, they gained a better understanding of the relevance of discussing business strategy and structure as a context for developing the IT strategy, and they also had a chance to voice their concerns about the future direction of the organization. The process thus began to lay the groundwork for the changes that were likely to result from the project.

Once the interviews were completed and all of the responses compiled, the analysis of the interview notes was begun. One of the first steps in the analysis process was searching for common themes or patterns in the response. For example, each interviewee was asked to define "logistics," "time and place utility," and "synergy with autonomy" (concepts that were articulated by the Managing Director as being critical to the success of the company as it made the transition from providing transportation services to providing logistics services). The analysis of the interviews produced thirty-five unique definitions for these terms. This lack of common definition made it clear that the Managing Director's vision had not been widely communicated. The danger was that if it were not clarified and its implications spelled out, each unit would establish its own strategic and operational plans according to its own interpretation. Moreover, this kind of diversity in responses presents problems in analysis.

When common themes are evident—in this case, some questions had thirty-five identical answers—the analysis is far easier. For example, in addition to the common belief by users that, as noted earlier, the IT function is focused on technology for the sake of technology rather than providing the users with the technological capability to address their business problems and that the IT function of the national airlines is superior to the IT function supporting the other business units, some of the other perceptions of the IT function were:

- It does not solve business problems and the IT group tends to dictate to and control the users rather than facilitate deriving solutions with the users.

- The existing information systems and the IT function are constraints to achieving the vision and strategic intent of the company.

- It does not provide value for money with respect to the costs associated with developing business applications.

Negative responses such as these on the part of senior management are not unusual. However, almost every interviewee stated that the IT function operates the IT infrastructure efficiently; indeed, further probing indicated that the IT group is perceived to be the low-cost provider of these services when compared with other companies in the country. The problem is that the users did not think the efficiency and low cost brought them the business applications they needed. (For example, in a major oil company for whom we performed Dynamic Planning, all fifty-one executives interviewed stated that the IT function was not responsive to the needs of the user community and that the information the IT function provided was neither timely nor accurate. Upon further investigation, in this case and many others, the complaint is usually found to be more a result of perception and lack of communication than fact, something IT executives need to keep in mind.)

In addition to the IT observations mentioned above, there were a number of business-related findings:

◆   The existing culture does not foster the sharing of highly skilled personnel or personnel with unique expertise among and between business units.

◆   Business units are more focused on internal rather than external competition; they don't understand the emerging external marketplace.

◆   There is no sense of urgency within the business units about becoming more competitive; in fact, many of the business managers continue to act as though the company is still a regulated monopoly.

◆   There are no companywide rules of the game; each business unit operates by its own set of rules, which often results in actions that are not only detrimental to the company, but also confusing to the external marketplace.

◆   The existing business structure is a constraint to achieving the strategic vision of the company.

◆   There are no mechanisms in place to reward cooperative behavior among and between the business units.

FINDING SOLUTIONS

These observations and the information collected by the internal strategic planning group as well as those of the organization hired to study logistics companies now have to be analyzed against one another; once that is done, the position paper will have to be prepared and options for the future generated. This second step of the Framework should result in the generation of a number of options that could help set the direction for the structure of the business and the IT function of the company over the next few years—and open the company to the changes that will have to take place quickly as well as to those that will undoubtedly take place in the future.

CHALLENGE AND ANSWER: THE WORK OF FOCUS GROUPS

The usual activity that helps the team generate a position paper is focus sessions. Here, the equivalent was the discussion sessions with the ITSC over the findings that emerged from the team's evaluations of the internal and external analysis. (Prior to the analysis, the information collected about logistics firms was analyzed and aggregated with all the other information the team had collected.)

The discussion covered the observations and findings as well as possible next steps given those findings. In the end, the members of the ITSC agreed with the information the team presented. The ITSC members were gaining a better grasp of the work the project team was doing and of the concepts underlying the Dynamic Planning Framework—principally that the development of an IT strategy cannot be, nor should it be, separated from the business strategy and operations of the company. They also were becoming more aware of the problems that the company faced in trying to move ahead. The overall resistance to change and the inability to understand the first set of changes—to a competitive environment—would clearly hinder progress.

PREPARING THE POSITION PAPER

The team then reanalyzed the information gathered in both the external and internal analyses, each member taking turns playing devil's advocate to ensure that the findings were fully defendable. Their major findings were summarized for inclusion in the position paper:

♦   One of the more interesting findings was confirmation of what the team members thought was a critical trend in technology—a general shift taking place from single-vendor, central mainframe environments to multiple-vendor, highly distributed computing environments. In this case, the organization doing the competitor survey had found that successful competitors were dispersing their computing resources and computing capability to the business users. In essence, they were placing the responsibility for computing into the hands of the people who have to deal with their customers at the local level.

♦   Another critical trend was the growth of the notion that information technology is a critical success factor (CSFs) for competitiveness in the marketplace. A critical assumption associated with this CSF is that without IT, a company cannot remain competitive and, further, remaining competitive requires increasing investments in IT.

◆   Another interesting assumption that surfaced was that the customer base expects integrated carriers to have sophisticated information technology. In general, the pervasive use of information technology in today's business environment, in conjunction with the rise in computer literacy within the general population, has lead to an increasingly high expectation level among customers (both business as well as individuals) when it comes to an organization's IT capability.

◆   Yet another important finding was that training is a key element in the implementation of information technology initiatives. Yet all too often, training of user personnel within an organization either is neglected or only token education and training is provided (users are taught only the basics of how to use the system). The result is that users don't know enough to explore possible ways to use the systems to do their jobs effectively as well as efficiently.

◆   And finally, one of the most important findings was that cultural changes are one of the most significant issues when implementing information technology initiatives. New IT usually involves major changes not only in how individuals do their jobs, but also impacts the content of their jobs.

At this point it was necessary to remind the team to keep in mind the Managing Director's belief that his vision required synergy with autonomy, especially the impact of that belief for future discussions of governance. In this case, the problem was so complex and the experience base of most of the participants so limited—remember that most people had worked for the company all their adult lives—that it was necessary to push the team in certain directions. (When a company is this large and complex and so many internal political issues are involved, outside leaders can help to ensure that political maneuvering does not prevent reaching conclusions.) It took six weeks to pull together the findings of the team, prepare the position paper, and prepare presentations to the ITSC and the Management Board.

The findings from Phase I were accepted by the Management Board after careful examination and discussion. Then the Managing Director directed the team to proceed with Phase II of the engagement—developing an integrated business and IT strategy that would support the company's vision. At this point we evaluated the progress to date and decided that the next activity, generating the options, would have to be handled in a slower, multistage fashion. It was clear that the need to develop an IT strategy that would work with a changing business strategy and accommodate changes in technology and skill sets over time would add complexity to the usual problems at this stage.

PHASE II: THE COMPLEXITY INCREASES

This phase began with an exploration and examination of the findings in the position paper, weighing and measuring the insights against the vision in order to develop options that would help the company realize the vision. The discussion focused on directions IT could take and examples of paths other organizations were pursuing.

The team accepted that, by the turn of the century, the company could integrate the various modes of transportation it provided to function as a total source for its customers on a global basis; that is, it would sell the integration of movement, services, and knowledge that encapsulate the inventory. Pursuing this train of thought further, it became clear that the *physical* product (that is, the inventory) will become less important relative to the *information* about the inventory and the companies sending and receiving it. Therefore, the IT strategy and structure will play an increasingly important role in the company.

To create a company that could become a logistics company but was at the moment a transportation company and, moreover, had synergy with autonomy (the Managing Director's clear mandate) meant—in broad terms—moving in four interrelated directions at once:

1. Empower IT decisionmaking at the business unit level.

2. Establish a companywide technology infrastructure.

3. Establish companywide IT standards.

4. Coordinate business and IT strategies.

Since each of these directions would have very different affects on the company, depending on how each was implemented, each had to be evaluated:

1. Empower IT decisionmaking at the business unit level. The team thought that the business units should be empowered with the *responsibility* to identify and leverage information technology and systems for their own business as well as the *authority* to decide how best to design, develop, and implement the required system. This would allow the business units to have all the resources (marketing, human resources,

operations, etc.) within their direct control so that appropriate trade-offs in resource allocations could be made among and between them to meet competitive challenges. Further, from an information technology point of view, the business unit would be in a position to respond quickly and flexibly to the changing requirements of the marketplace. The degree of empowerment, however, had to be decided since that would have major effects on every aspect of the organization.

2. Establish a companywide technology infrastructure. The team thought that there would be great value in developing an integrated information technology infrastructure—involving hardware, software, and communication functionality—that would be managed as one set of resources that would serve all business units of the company. This would create a companywide, state-of-the-art infrastructure with far greater functionality than the individual technologies established by any single business unit, while allowing the units to systematically assess a variety of options to leverage information technology capabilities for business purposes. This would also ensure that there was a companywide mechanism to assess which information technologies (from among the vast set) should be part of this infrastructure.

3. Establish companywide IT standards. Given the strategic requirement of the company to be a flexible network of autonomous business units, the team thought it would be advisable for all information technology and systems to be based on a standard definition of data, a common set of core IT processes, and a culture of sharing information within the company. Companywide standards would ensure that the data definitions across the various business units would be uniform. Establishing standards for IT processes would allow greater transferability of skilled personnel across business units, but more important, business opportunities involving multimodal transport (for example, logistics services) could be facilitated with greater ease and quickness. Further, such standards would reduce the likelihood that the autonomous business units would drift away from one another while facilitating the movement of the company toward a flexible network of autonomous business units.

4. Coordinate business and IT strategies. Given the importance of IT to the company's strategic vision, it was critical that the required degree of coordination be systematically managed rather than left to chance. The team thought that a coordinating body should be established at the corporate level to continuously oversee the alignment of the business strategies and structures with the information technology strategies and structures.

These possible directions were interrelated—changes in one impacted the other three. For example, if the business units are given total autonomy to make any IT decisions they feel are in their best interests, the concept of an integrated infrastructure would not be viable; and it would be impossible to establish standards. Moreover, the concept of coordinating the business and IT strategies would collapse, since each business unit would be totally responsible for its own actions—the notion of synergy with autonomy would be lost. If more focus was placed on infrastructure or standards or coordination, the other three components would be adversely affected. To achieve the necessary checks and balances, these directions cannot be viewed in isolation; they have to be viewed holistically.

After careful consideration of the four directions to be taken, the Management Board accepted them—with the qualification that they be considered recommendations and each recommendation be checked to see what options they had for implementing it and how the implementation would impact the company.

ANALYZING THE SOLUTIONS

Determining the options for each of these directions for managing IT, now officially classified as board recommendations, presented a number of problems. It was clear that they each could not—for reasons of time—be examined against all the perspectives of the Strategic Alignment Model (see Figures 8.2 to 8.5). Moreover, two of the perspectives did not need thorough examination given the current state of the company's technology—business transformation (for which they weren't ready) or level of service (which was not an issue at the moment, since service was consistently assessed as efficient).

A necessary examination, however, was the strategy execution perspective. The first step in the company's transition from a public transportation utility to a logistics company was, according to the Managing Director's reading of the material presented to him by his strategy team and the team working on Dynamic Planning, to construct a business structure comprised of autonomous business entities; the problem was that the existing IT structure was ill equipped to support autonomous business units. The strategy execution perspective, however, would not adequately address the transition to a logistics company—that would require the technology transformation perspective. But the technology transformation perspective alone would not address the problems of the existing IT structure and the requirement to support autonomous business units today.

The answer was to pay simultaneous attention to both perspectives—strategy execution and technology transformation. Applying both perspectives concurrently would enable the company to develop an IT strategy that would support its transition from transportation to logistics as well as the transition of its business structure from autonomous business units to business units that worked together in a cooperative manner, but would still be autonomous. This was the only way to achieve synergy with autonomy.

The team members thus set out to use the Strategic Alignment Model to evaluate the *options* derived from the recommendations. They then would analyze the impact of the options chosen on the other parts of the organization and then develop an IT strategy that would be practical, logical, address the resources and culture of the company, and most important, have the support and buy-in of management at all levels.

USING THE STRATEGIC ALIGNMENT MODEL

The team spent a great deal of effort deciding how to structure the examination of the options through the Strategic Alignment Model. For example, in order to meet the objective of bringing more people into the planning process, the participants would be chosen to involve as many different constituencies from across the company as possible. Therefore, two dozen influential senior business managers (the number of individuals at the management level now involved was still less than 5 percent) were selected to participate in structured workshops that would examine the various options for implementing each of the recommendations. Senior managers' participation in developing the options would, it was believed, make them part of the process of developing—and thus understanding and accepting—the IT strategy. Indeed, the team members believed that if the workshops were successful, these managers would be the change agents for communicating the IT strategy within their business units.

The objectives of the first workshop were to develop options for each recommendation, evaluate the options, and arrive at a preliminary prioritization of options. To accomplish this, the participants were divided into two groups, each with responsibility for examining two recommendations—one technical and one organizational. Project team members were assigned to each group to facilitate the process, but they weren't allowed to assume a leadership role nor to make recommendations or comment on the options chosen by the task group—the work product had to be developed by the participants.

EXAMINING AN OPTION

The first recommendation examined was *Empower IT decisionmaking at the business unit level*. This was one of the most complicated to deal with because there are varying degrees of empowerment and because this recommendation was the key to the other three (see Figure 12.2). With the advent of privatization and the emphasis the Managing Director placed on

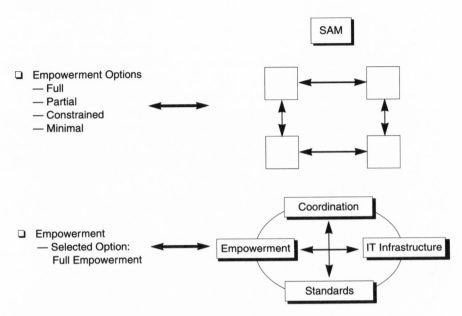

Figure 12.2. Analyzing Options: Empowerment
© 1993 B. Goldberg and J. G. Sifonis

autonomy, the heads of the business units now had control over all business functions related to conducting business, including IT. In other words, they now had control over their business strategy and structure and were going through the process of defining how they should control their units' IT strategy and structure. The problem was that IT was the one business function they had almost no direct experience with, and now they would be responsible and accountable for it, which would mean they had to deal with the issue of IT as part of any business case they made for new services or products.

Thus, the first step was deciding what degree of empowerment is appropriate for a given set of conditions. For example, should the business units own and manage the IT infrastructure (hardware and communications technology), or should they establish and empower a service provider business unit with the responsibility for managing the infrastructure on their behalf? Should the business units have the responsibility for all aspects of building their own applications, or should they perform only those activities such as planning and analysis that require knowledge of the business and outsource the less knowledge intensive activities such as design and building of the application? Under empowerment, even if the business units elected to establish a service provider or outsource certain application development activities, they would be accountable for results.

Once the members of the group had a clear and shared understanding of empowerment, from both a business and IT perspective, they began the process of generating options for empowerment. After deliberating the advantages and disadvantages of each of the options, given their implications for the other parts of the organization, they focused on four, ranging from full empowerment (the business units would have all of the resources—hardware, communications, personnel—to support their business) to minimal empowerment (the business units would only acquire those resources that would be required to support the critical processes of the business).

After discussing the four options, full empowerment was the option chosen: it would fully support the notion of autonomy and give all responsibility for IT decisions to the business units (they could now make choices that were in the best interest of their business). The primary advantage of full empowerment is that it provides the business units with flexibility and control over resource allocation. It also removes the possibility of having alibis for nonperformance—a critical factor if the business units were to compete in a competitive market.

Once each team had selected an option, those options had to be assessed in terms of their impacts on each of the others, since the final recommendations had to be interrelated. At this point in the process, there was enough agreement among those in the workshop that the discussions they had had regarding the recommendations for empowerment, infrastructure, and standards involved just fine-tuning.

The only significant exception was the coordination recommendation, since its options involved governance and structure—key issues in any organization. As proposed by the team responsible for the coordination recommendation, the objectives were to align the business and IT strategies of each business unit with the corporate business and IT strategies, coordinate the IT initiatives of the newly empowered business units, and coordinate strategic investments in IT. Its intended role was to coordinate, not make decisions. However, the participants were concerned that without an appropriate set of checks and balances, the coordinating body, over time, could change from being a coordinator of IT policy to a dictator of IT policy—just as it had been when IT was the central service provider. On the one hand, without some mechanism in place to ensure that coordination occurred, the coordinating body would be a paper tiger. On the other hand, if the coordinating body had too much authority, the fears of the participants would be realized. The critical issue was thus meshing the full empowerment option chosen with the coordination option to ensure that there was an appropriate balance between empowerment and coordination in order to achieve synergy with autonomy.

Once this process was gone through for each of the four recommendations, each set of options generated by each recommendation was checked against the others. The process, which was in each case similar to that described above, took a while to complete. Only when each option had been examined both in terms of the Strategic Alignment Model and checked against the other recommendations as well (see Figure 12.2) were the results of the examination packaged and presented to the Management Board for discussion and approval. What emerged in the discussion was that the workshop process had not only resulted in the choice of an option—full empowerment—but had served as a first step to implementation of the solution because the managers had discussed what was happening with so many others in the company, spreading information and enthusiasm.

PHASE III: FROM GRAND STRATEGY TO PUTTING THE SOLUTION IN PLACE

Although the presentation went well, the Managing Director and the Management Board did not grant immediate approval to begin Phase III—implementation of the recommendations presented by the team. Instead, he assigned the project team to put in place an interim strategy to carry the company forward until the recommendations related to the coordinating body could be put in place. It was a holding action, necessary because of economic and political problems within the nation.

Two months later, approval to move ahead was granted. The recommendations of the team were accepted, and along with that decision came a decision to put in place a new group vice president for information technology and systems. The GVP would report to the Managing Director and among his other duties was responsibility for the strategic IT issues of the company—for example, coordinating the various IT initiatives of each business unit and managing the strategic IT investments for the company. There were no *operational* responsibilities associated with this position—that would be the purview of the business unit's IT manager. Conversely, the business unit IT managers weren't responsible for the company's strategic issues—that was the purview of the GVP. It was a total reversal of the historic role.

GRAND STRATEGY

Developing a Grand Strategy involved formalizing the decisions made in the form of an enhanced mission statement for the next fiscal year. The company specifically limited the statement's time frame to make clear that further changes were likely. The enterprise plan was reworked to aggregate the individual unit's business plans, especially to consolidate the multiple initiatives in IT that now had to be coordinated. Several of the critical action steps the project team developed for implementing the IT strategy were put in place, and work began on formalizing many of the processes for developing and integrating each business unit's business and IT strategy with the corporate business and IT strategy—a formidable task given the differences among and between the business units' lines of business and role of IT.

CHANGE MANAGEMENT, TRAINING, AND MEASUREMENT

At that point, a Skills and Management Development Program was put in place to ensure that the competencies required by the company to compete in the world of integrated logistics would be acquired, and a Change Management and Communications Program, a key part of any implementation process, was developed. This part of the process will be ongoing, changing as the company moves, by degrees, from a transportation to a logistics company.

LESSONS LEARNED

Although the difficult political climate continues to keep external competitors from setting up operations in the country, the company is continuing to keep that eventuality in mind. And the Managing Director plans to continue to move the company along the road to becoming a logistics provider. In the meantime, the work under way is heavily focused on ensuring that the processes put in place to deal with empowerment and coordination are internalized and that cooperative behavior becomes a way of life, not just words. We believe that they will succeed because Dynamic Planning has helped to change the bureaucratic mindset, and because the new mindset includes employee enthusiasm and optimism about the future of the company.

The most important lessons we learned were, first, that the flexibility of the Framework is its greatest strength—and the hardest part to adhere to (with all our training, the instinctive drive to do things the way you have done them in the past and the way that has brought satisfactory results is hard to overcome). The second, and most rewarding personally, was the confirmation of our belief that Dynamic Planning is a solid tool in change management, which is the activity in the Framework examined in the next chapter.

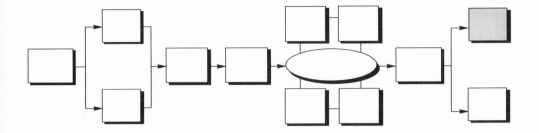

CHAPTER 13

MANAGING THE CHANGE TO A DYNAMIC ORGANIZATION

It must be remembered that there is nothing more difficult to plan, more doubtful of success, nor more dangerous to manage, than the creation of a new system. For the initiator has the enmity of all who would profit by the preservation of the institutions and merely lukewarm defenders in those who would gain by the new one.

Machiavelli

Now that you have determined your Grand Strategy, it is time to see to it that the enterprise does what is necessary to make the changes that will move it in the direction chosen. Knowing where you are going is only half the battle. Putting the solutions in place, the final step in the Dynamic Planning Framework, requires three activities. The first—determining the vision, the mission, and the enterprise plan—has been completed; you know what your Grand Strategy is. The one we are dealing with here is the second—implementing the Grand Strategy: making it clear to everyone in the enterprise what is happening, getting them to accept the vision, and helping them learn the new skills and methods that are necessary to make the enterprise plan effective. This is Activity 8.0, change management, a process for opening the enterprise's culture to new ways, for gaining individual employee buy-in, and for training employees to be a part of the new and better enterprise.

THE NEED FOR CHANGE

Remember that Dynamic Planning is not the catalyst for the changes already taking place around us: it is a framework for dealing with them and anticipating the next changes, responding to them, and maintaining competitiveness in the marketplace. In the 1980s, we were all astonished by the speed of change. We learned to run just to stay in place, and to push ourselves and our organizations to what we thought were intolerable limits. We put new technologies in place, downsized, merged, acquired, adopted new management techniques, and studied and planned for the new federal regulations that were being passed. And many of us waited for that day when we could sit back and look at the new world that we were helping create.

Yet in the 1990s, neither the rate of change nor global competition has slowed. Indeed, every time we turn around the world seems to change again: there are newly independent nations that may become partners in new competitive trading blocs; there are new and increasingly complex federal regulations involving diversity in the workforce, new technologies, new environmental concerns, and new business processes.

All these factors require changes in the work that people do, the way they do it, the environment they work in, the power structures that govern their enterprises, the skill sets they have, and the ways in which rewards for performance are handled. While these changes must take place to make an enterprise competitive in today's world, they are difficult to bring about because they threaten the security and comfort of employees at all levels and in all areas of the enterprise. But if the company is to succeed, even survive, resistance to change must be overcome.

Think back to the example in the last chapter. If the transportation company is to complete its evolution into a logistics company, change is going to have to take place on every level. The change is already being led by the managers who participated in the Dynamic Planning process—they have begun to serve as change agents—but that is just a beginning. The Skills and Management Development and Change Management and Communications programs are going to have to complete their work successfully to ensure implementation of the transformation. Those are critical steps to get employees to accept specific changes that are already taking place—and open them to the changes that will come tomorrow, and the day after.

In today's complex environment, there is no one method of bringing change to an organization. Dynamic Planning encourages a holistic approach, the first step of which is communications within an organization. Another part is the establishment of the external analysis task force, which we believe should remain in place (in some form) to watch the trends that will affect the organization as it moves ahead. That task force is part of, as will be seen in the next chapter, the ongoing monitoring and evaluation that must become a way of life for the organization. Another part of the new change paradigm is creating what Peter Senge calls a learning organization.[1] Yet another is a mechanism for formal change management. A combination of these will help speed acceptance of change—and teach people to deal with the fact that change is now a way of life.

THE CONTINUAL LEARNING ORGANIZATION

To start, change is much easier when workers are receptive to the notion that the world is not standing still, and aware that unless they learn new and different ways of reacting and doing, they will be among the unemployable. That is why part of the planning strategy must include finding ways to become a continual learning organization, with people reading, talking, questioning, and discussing issues that can or may affect their lives—and the lives of the enterprise.

Continual learning also means providing employees opportunities to acquire skills through internal training and incentives to take courses outside, including tuition reimbursement for pursuing degrees. In this kind of enterprise, a change management program will be little more than a method to inform people about a specific new development and arranging for the training they need. It will not have to break down mental barriers to change.

To ensure your culture is open to continual learning, everyone should be encouraged to go beyond their specific area of expertise; it is, after all, the ability to see connections across a broad spectrum, to put together "one from column A and two from column B" that marks creativity. In continual learning organizations, the buzzwords "thinking out of the box," using "both sides of the brain," or "wearing different hats" become part of the background noise of the enterprise. In continual learning organizations, managers know how to encourage, not discourage, innovative thinking. They do not routinely greet new ideas with scorn, and they accept the need for occasional failure; in other words, they foster the kind of environment that frees "people to devote time and attention to learning instead of covering their tracks and hiding errors."[2]

BREAKING THE OLD MINDSET

Opening an organization's culture to change involves a lot more than introducing a new organizational chart that was developed by senior management after months of wrangling or announcing that federal regulations mandate certain changes in the way you work or whom you hire. It requires providing people with information about new ways of doing things and convincing them of the validity of new approaches. Admittedly, the difficulties inherent in the process are enormous.

For example, the breakup of the Soviet Union is being followed by a slow and difficult process of building new governments and creating robust, modern economies in a group of newly independent and somewhat shaky nations, linked very tenuously and facing a somewhat uncertain future. Those trying to help are finding that the historical, cultural differences slow progress.

A few months after the new Polish government was in place, a young revolutionary who had been part of the leadership of the former underground Polish press was appointed to run the newly privatized major publishing group in Poland. He came to the United States seeking assistance in turning the enterprise into a profitable one. In other words, privatization was, as in the case of the African transportation company, again the issue. In this case, however, not only had the enterprise been a government entity, it was a government entity in a land where no one had witnessed profitmaking enterprises at work or even understood the nature of a free market. When the discussions turned to marketing and pricing, he listened patiently and then explained that these weren't important parts of the operation as he envisioned it. After all, he explained, people were entitled to books. And yet he was determined to establish a successful publishing company. He wanted change, but his decisionmaking was limited by his experience as well as the very deeply ingrained beliefs of his childhood.

NEW ELEMENTS IN THE CHANGE MANAGEMENT EQUATION

In the 1400s, in the city of Mainz, Germany, Johannes Gutenberg invented movable type and revolutionized the world. Typesetting, letter by letter, was done by hand from then until the 1880s, when mechanized typesetting—linotype—finally made it possible to set whole lines of type in a single operation. In the 1950s, cold type (copy produced on machines similar to typewriters thus avoiding the casting of metal) became commonplace, allowing for even faster typesetting; twenty years later, the development of affordable computers that enabled almost instantaneous typesetting began a new and continuing revolution. Today, desktop publishing means quick, easy, and less costly publication of an incredible variety of printed matter.

The times between these major changes—480 years, 70 years, 20 years, respectively—are a good indicator of the increased speed with which change now takes place. As a result, change must be managed differently: the classic change management techniques that helped organizations institutionalize change in the years when change first became revolutionary instead of evolutionary are no longer adequate to today's needs.

Classic theory says that there are three major steps in a change management program: Unfreezing, Changing, and Refreezing. (These are all thoroughly described in the writings of such gurus of change management as Kurt Lewin and Edgar Schein.)[3] You start by unfreezing the organization's existing culture, making people understand that the current way of doing things is over, that there is a new way, that the new way has senior management's support: once employees are made aware of the need to change by being made sufficiently uncomfortable, you must introduce the new way of doing things and offer enough training and education to let employees redefine what it is that they do. In other words, you create cognitive recognition to open the workforce to what is new. The final step in classic change management is to refreeze the company's culture once the change is accepted. The culture then remains the same until the next change comes along.

That may have worked when change came about every twenty years or so. In a world in which change seems to occur every twenty days (and sometimes every twenty minutes), a new framework for managing change is necessary (see Figure 13.1). In this framework, the first stage, the static stage, as in classic change management theory, calls for unfreezing the current culture by convincing employees that the organization is changing and the changes have the strong support of senior management. The second stage, the fluid stage, begins when employees start to understand that the changes will benefit them as well as the organization. They recognize the whys and wherefores of what is new and accept it. Then, breaking with the classic idea of refreezing the culture as a final stage, the culture is moved to a dynamic stage, where people work with the new machines or processes and act in the new manner but await—and even anticipate—the next changes that will be made. In other words, openness to change, anticipating change, becomes the mindset of the organization.

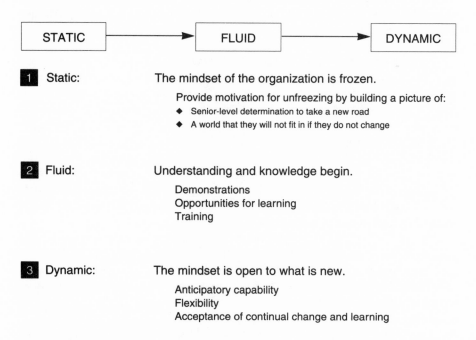

Figure 13.1. Change Communication Framework
© 1993 B. Goldberg and J. G. Sifonis

The old model of change management made sense when developments in the world proceeded at a somewhat stately pace. If you accept that the new technology you just put in place, or the new service you offer, or the new business line you have just added is likely to change again—and soon—you can see the problem with refreezing. If you know that the new health and safety requirements or federal discrimination regulation must be accepted but that new ones are likely to be put in place as further advances in medical knowledge or social changes occur—you would see the need to force acceptance of the new while anticipating the changes tomorrow will bring.

A CHANGE METHODOLOGY

Opening an organization's culture to change is a difficult process. Until Dynamic Planning is a part of the organizational mindset, problems will emerge each time a change is implemented. There are some general principles to follow to ensure that even unplanned changes are successful:

1. *Open up communications to stop the rumor mill.* What people don't know can hurt the organization. A dialogue must be opened up to forestall speculation. Knowledge prevents misinformation and disinformation; it reduces the chance that playing politics against change will succeed.

2. *Make employees aware of what is happening in the outside world.* It is important to be sure that your employees do not feel you are making change for the sake of change, but rather understand that your business cannot succeed unless you do. They must be brought to understand what is happening in the world outside and how that can impact your organization.

3. *Make employees aware of what is happening in the organization.* Letting people know what lies ahead helps them face the uncertainty brought by change and eases their adjustment to the new reality. It starts them on the road to understanding.

4. *Make clear management's commitment to taking this road to success.* Convey the fact that management is determined to move in this new direction. Present whatever is new as a constitution; it can be amended but neither overthrown nor rewritten.

5. *Assure employees that training will be available when they need it.* Promote your organization's commitment to continuous learning; let

employees know that they will be given every opportunity to learn what they need to learn (and when it comes to technology, you should emphasize the benefits in terms of personal marketability from knowing a leading-edge technology).

6. *Achieve buy-in at all levels.* Top-level acceptance is never enough; the people who manage a process and those who perform the tasks must be aware that the long-term benefits are greater than the short-term costs.

7. *Break down the barriers between employees.* Cross-functional relationships are necessary to realizing the benefits of the new technologies and processes. Most new products and technologies require business and technology and design and sales divisions working together with understanding, patience, and trust.

8. *Ensure that flexibility is built into the culture.* Do everything you can to keep people who have just woken up to the fact that they can change aware that they will need to change again and again.

These principles, implemented through a variety of techniques (ranging from new communication vehicles to training programs), inform effective change management programs. The difficult part of change management is the constant need to tailor techniques to the organization as it is and as it needs to be in the future. Thus, the first step is to gather information about the mindset of employees through interviews and observation.

THE COSTS OF IGNORING THE BASIC PRINCIPLES

It takes planning and time and sensitivity to bring about change in such a way that the only problem you have is implementing the new process. If you do not tell people what is happening early on, the discomfort caused by rumor and speculation may cause the most valuable members of your staff, exactly the ones who are most likely to learn the new system or process the easiest, to leave. Unsure of their future, they begin to look around for another position. And, of course, of all those who start looking, the most qualified find new positions first. If you communicate the news that change is taking place, explain the nature of the process, assure employees that training in the new skills will be available, and that those skills are leading edge, they are less likely to leave.

The following examples will illustrate specific techniques developed to fit specific organizational cultures.

CREATING CHANGE AGENTS

When introducing desktop publishing to a university press, we arranged for employees who would have to learn the new production skills to visit other publishers who had already moved in this direction. Although the announced goal—and a real one—was to show them the system in action, we made sure the executive who was leading the group (a strong supporter of the change) mentioned at the breakfast before the tour that this kind of change was taking place all over and that he'd noticed how many advertisements called for people skilled in desktop publishing. He reported that during the visit, some members of the group displayed a great deal of interest, asking numerous questions and even asking to try the new equipment.

The following week, those who'd shown the most interest were asked if they'd like to take a course and make the switch early. Of the four asked, three accepted the offer. They were quickly enrolled in a class, and when they returned to the office two weeks later, they were given a pilot assignment. Their new machines were set up in a central area. The pilot hit many snags, but had a few quick successes. Many co-workers who stopped by to watch became comfortable with the machines, admiring what they could do, and asking for the chance to learn the new system. As more machines came in and more books began to be produced on them, it became clear that the system offered enormous advantages.

What also became clear over the next few months was that it took far fewer people to do the work. Seeing the handwriting on the wall, those who had not bought in began to job hunt. By the time the system was fully installed, there were only a handful of people left who neither knew the system nor wanted to learn it. Many of those—but not all—were close enough to retirement (one person close to retirement was in the original threesome that went for training, and at last report, was still, at seventy-one, working in the production department) that they were happy to accept an early retirement package. Of the fifty-three people in the department, only five non-desktop-trained people remained at the end of the process, and other positions were found for them.

There were a number of factors at work to make this changeover easy. The people involved had already seen many changes in their profession over the past few years; for example, the switch in typesetting from hot metal to cold to computerized type. Moreover, many were already familiar with word processors, so they did not have to start from scratch on desktop typesetters, but simply had to enhance skills they had already acquired.

The first advantage that accrued from the way that the change was managed was that, because people knew what was happening and knew they would be given an opportunity to become part of the new way of doing things, resistance was minimal and acceptance high. The other advantage was that the best did not leave; instead, they became the change agents, learning to use the equipment first, with the least trouble. If management had not moved to tell people what was happening and provide opportunities for learning so quickly, uncertainty among employees might have left the enterprise with only the least able people by the time the new systems were brought in. That, in turn, would have meant that those doing the pilot projects would have had fewer successes—and would have taken longer to achieve them.

The other major advantage of the slow change was that those in other areas of the university press did not hear about massive downsizing. Therefore, when the next set of changes was introduced, there was less fear—and even less resistance. This was an exceptionally easy change process.

AFTER-THE-FACT CHANGE MANAGEMENT

The next example is quite different.[4] In most large companies, change is far more difficult to manage because changes are taking place in so many areas at once. A typical example of a difficult change management project is one where the change is already under way and management decides it needs a formal change management program to help pick up the pieces because the project seems doomed to failure. That was the problem in a recent engagement at a large, East Coast-based, insurance firm, where every major pitfall likely to be encountered when trying to bring about change—and a few unlikely ones—surfaced.

The goal of the technology services group of a division of the company was to gain employee acceptance of computer-aided software engineering (CASE), a leading-edge technology for developing computer programs that requires a number of changes in the way people work and the way they think about their work. CASE shifts the emphasis in developing programs from writing the programs, the job of programmers, to analyzing the business function the program will serve and then having the computer write the program.[5]

Before CASE, business groups who wanted a program that would provide information regarding the health-risks of smoking, for example, had to explain their needs to a programmer, who then wrote a program that pulled the information from the company's computers. Once the basic program was written, those who requested it would review it and ask for changes to enhance it so it finally did what they *really* wanted it to do—for example, collect information on health risks of smoking by males in a certain income bracket.

With CASE, the business people who want the program spend a great deal of time analyzing the business needs that the program will serve;

then that analysis is fed into a computer on which CASE has been installed and the program is generated automatically. The detailed, up-front business analysis prevents one of the major programming problems—miscommunication between businesspeople and programmers. Programmers, who don't understand business, are asked to develop an application by business types, who don't understand information technology. The business types assume that the programmer will inherently understand the business problem they are trying to solve and develop a program that will not only solve a particular information need, but any future information need as well.

A number of pilot projects were under way when the engagement began. Selected groups were working to develop a number of major computer applications in this new way. The use of CASE was the subject of a great deal of speculation within the technology services group because the switch to CASE technology created fears among the programmers, a cadre of skilled technologists, about the future need for their skills. At the same time, the businesspeople were concerned about the amount of time they were spending doing up-front analysis instead of concentrating on their jobs. These two groups also had trouble communicating because of their different backgrounds and special terminology—acronyms and jargon allowed for easier communication among the members of each group, but prevented communication between them—and because they had never had to work together before.

It would seem as though it would be easy to explain to the programmers that their skills would be used differently—that they could do much of the up-front analysis if they enhanced the skills they had developed over the years working with the business side to revise programs *after* they were first delivered. The businesspeople needed to see that the time they spent would eventually pay back in the form of programs that would allow them to do their jobs better. It turned out to be far from easy.

The problems of making this change were complicated by the fact that at the same time the information technology group was trying to introduce CASE technology, the company was undergoing a complete reorganization that included massive downsizing and was also introducing a new type of workstation and E-mail system. Rumors were rife. People who wanted to learn CASE were afraid that if they accepted CASE training instead of continuing to work on ongoing application projects they would be thought unnecessary if a decision were made to downsize. The situation became so bad that at one point, several weeks before a decision was due on how a level of middle management was going to be restructured, virtually all work ceased. People were too distressed and too busy chasing rumors to concentrate. A little information would have gone a long way to ease the situation.

In this case, the difficulties normally associated with bringing change were magnified by:

+ An organizational history of upheaval

+ A rumor mill that was in place because news of the pilot programs was spreading

+ A large number of other initiatives that had been or were in the processes of being launched

+ Attempts to explain what was going on that were not tailored to the specific change

+ A basic distrust of the abilities of other departments, especially communications and human resources

A FEELING OF CHAOS, NOT MANAGED CHANGE

The employees in the technology division did not trust senior management to tell them the truth because of a recent history of reorganizations accompanied by large workforce reductions and the belief, which proved well-founded, that further reorganizations were likely. Moreover, before the most recent reorganization, the company had denied rumors to the effect that reductions in workforce size were coming until hours before the announcement was made. This history made every statement issued by senior management suspect.

Senior management recognized the need to stop the negative speculation only after the pilot projects had been under way for almost a year. At that point, they became aware that, instead of greeting the introduction of CASE with enthusiasm, employees were becoming apathetic, secretive (small group discussions were taking place that would abruptly end at the sight of management), and reluctant to go off-site to attend training sessions.

The few attempts made to help employees accept the changes taking place were based on techniques taken from textbooks on change management; they ignored the company-specific problems that existed because of what was currently happening in the organization and what had happened in the past. For example, given the history of the organization, it was not enough to have middle managers tell employees that "the head of the company supports this." It wasn't enough to pass out an earlier letter from the CEO saying that "we are going to move into the future rapidly." These comments, repeated with no explanation that these leaders believed that the changes would bring certain, specified benefits to the organization, sounded like empty, and potentially threatening, words.

FAILURE TO TAP TALENT IN PLACE

The management of the technology services group was unhappy with the lack of attention its work was given in the general company newsletter or even in the communication vehicles tailored to the department. The technology group felt that the communications staff did not understand technology, neither the tools nor the language. They also believed that the human resources department was ineffective and ignored their real needs when sending them job applicants, resulting in candidates who had the wrong skills. The IT managers did not understand that the problem was their failure to explain the specific skills they needed in terms the human resources staff could understand.

In addition, the IT department managers were unaware, for example, that the human resources department had video training tapes available, discussing problems that arose whenever change took place. If they had open lines of communication with the human resources department, the need to have the change managed at an earlier point in the adoption of CASE would have been explained and the groups might have been able to keep the situation from deteriorating.

Trying to manage this change when there were so many landmines planted—and the change was already under way—required a more intensive, longer change management program than usual, one that took three to four months to establish (one to two months is usually enough to get such a program up and running). The first stumbling block was the inability to pull together the ideal team—one or two members of the group driving the change as well as members of the communications and human resources groups—because of the technology group's feelings about those two areas.

Although the client assigned a very strong individual to work on the change program, it was not the same as having a team in place. Training an in-house team is a value added for a company because the next change program can be handled internally. Moreover, since change is not going to stop, the team can be the beginning of a long-term effort to build a learning environment. If one member of a team leaves, the organization does not lose the skills. Furthermore, the mandate not to use the communications department meant that a lot of time was spent building communications vehicles from scratch. For example, the major communications vehicle, a new newsletter directed at the change to CASE, had to be designed and produced without the use of internal resources.

OPENING CHANNELS OF COMMUNICATIONS

The primary method of communicating with a group this size was the newsletter, the first edition of which contained an open letter to the IT division employees from the head of the organization. It clearly stated his determination to make the shift to CASE technology. The newsletter also provided information about other organizations that had successfully introduced this technology and information about CASE itself. Subsequent editions continued to drive the message of upper management support home and continued to provide examples of successes. There were also articles aimed at making it clear that this technology was the wave of the future and that to leave to go somewhere else instead of learning it was a delaying action, not an escape.

OPENING THE ENVIRONMENT TO CHANGE

The first step in creating such an environment was to set up an awareness program. A circulating file of relevant—and interesting—articles was built up to familiarize employees with the notion of change and with the changes being brought in the world by new technologies. When employees were asked to find additional, relevant articles, the response was immediate and the flow of information increased.

SELLING THE VISION

We believe that the first and most critical step is opening channels of communication. Working with one of the senior people, we developed a plan for cascading change throughout the group (see Figure 13.2). The idea was

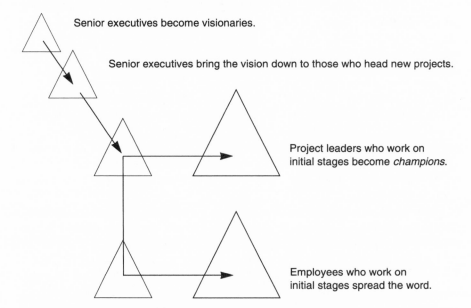

Senior executives become visionaries.

Senior executives bring the vision down to those who head new projects.

Project leaders who work on initial stages become *champions*.

Employees who work on initial stages spread the word.

Figure 13.2. Cascading Change into the Organization
© 1993 B. Goldberg and J. G. Sifonis

to drive change into the organization from two directions at once—the top and across.[6] It starts down from the top, but at the level at which the people with hands-on experience enter the scene, it is driven across the organization by change agents. This allows the vision to be reinforced by champions of the process.

This two-pronged attack ensures that senior-level commitment to change is reinforced by the visible actions of others successfully implementing the change. The message is that the new way works, and that there will be no way to get senior management to change its mind. That, in turn, suggests that those who don't buy in won't fit into the organization in the future.

This message has to be delivered publicly if it is to create a new mindset through the organization in a reasonable time frame—and it has to be reinforced at those times when the change is happening too slowly. The principal tools for delivering the message are written communications such as bulletins and newsletters. In such communications, it is important to avoid the use of the words *if, failure, might,* or *eventually.* The process or product being introduced is always talked about as if it were a fait accompli—and a successful one. The communiques are meant to make those who would resist believe that it is hopeless to do so. At the same time, opportunities to join, to become part of the future, are always held out.

The newsletter helped to drive this message home, as did a series of large meetings at which senior executives spoke about their belief in CASE and groups from the pilot project discussed the difficulties and pleasures of being part of a CASE project.

TRAINING PROGRAMS IN THE FUTURE

It is important that senior managers have enough information about the skills required to perform new functions or use new technologies to ensure that they provide the right kinds of training at the right time. Some simple changes in technology may require no more than an explanatory memo and a few people trained to answer questions. For example, a switch to a new word processing system may, in an extremely computer-literate environment, require having a good handbook available along with a few very skilled people in each department who are sufficiently trained to supplement the handbooks. When it comes to something more advanced, such as a switch to information engineering, CASE boot camps—say, a two-week program off-site—may be necessary as a first step. The range is enormous.

The development of training programs is often the responsibility of a learning center in a large enterprise. In smaller ones, individual managers may have to supervise the development of courses in conjunction with the human resources department or, in the case of many new technologies, their vendors. Whoever fills the role, we have discovered that all approaches to training are not equal. That is why, in today's difficult economic climate, when it is particularly important not to spend more training dollars than necessary, senior management has to set up training programs in such a way that employees who receive training are the ones who most want to learn. It is unproductive to spend enormous amounts of money dragging reluctant employees into the future—indeed, the education and training on a new piece of technology usually cost twice as much as the equipment itself.

Furthermore, since much technology is aimed at workforce reduction in the long term, everyone need not be trained. One way to limit costs is to set up what we call "choice" learning labs. These are rooms that are open before and after work hours to provide interested employees with the tools and teachers they need to learn new techniques or technologies. Employees decide that they want to buy in on a change and make a personal commitment to spend their own time learning. This cuts training costs and promotes teaching of the most interested, who tend to be the most able, first. This also makes it possible to select the employees who will remain once the technology or process brings the anticipated reduction in employees, the reduction that provides the company with a return on the investment it made to change the current system or approach.

THE ADVANTAGES OF AN EDUCATED WORKFORCE

The more aware your workers are of events taking place in the world, the more aware they will be of the possibility that change will one day affect them. And the less surprised they are, the less frightened they will be. In fact, if you keep employees aware of developments in various areas, you will discover that they will often ask if you are going to get that new machine or do something with a new technology they read about and see as applicable to what they are doing. If you think back to the task forces that the planning team set up as part of the Interactive Forces Model, you can see how such a program would serve, with some adjustment, as the basis for a program that produces an educated workforce.

Usually, however, such programs do not exist. One of the techniques we use to open up the workforce to new ideas is to establish various reading programs. Opening up minds, getting people to think out of the box is so critical to implementing change that we try to get clients to initiate such programs even while we are still in the process of examining the enterprise in preparation for developing a formal change plan. The programs range from having stacks of newspapers and industry newsletters available in company cafeterias and lounge areas to setting up various kinds of specialized reading "libraries." These programs not only serve to introduce fresh thinking, but spur discussion. As the change gets closer to implementation, more specific information about it can be introduced into the reading program. And the discussions can be encouraged and joined by senior management as a way of getting messages across.

This is all in keeping with our strong belief that an educated workforce is absolutely critical to an enterprise's success and that exposure to ideas is essential to building an innovative culture. Part of our work with every enterprise we deal with is a session with senior managers to get them to see the importance of such continual learning on a general level. (Most managers understand the need for training in specific skills, but have problems with the idea of learning for learning's sake until they begin to see the increase in creative thinking that accompanies such learning.) The reception of senior management to this concept has proved, engagement after engagement, a key to the degree of success the enterprise will experience in trying to change—and to keep up with the competition.

In addition, management training to increase awareness of the damages done by negative responses to new ideas is important. Pushed by time, worried by cutbacks in their ranks, all too many middle managers do not hear the ideas put forth by the people who deal directly with customers. Or if they hear those ideas, they reject them. Static organizations are very prone to cultural, managerial, and operational roadblocks to innovative thinking. Bureaucracy, office politics, unrealistic timing, procrastination, and negativism all create barriers to innovation. Unless employees at all levels, not just the highest-echelon strategic thinkers, think broadly, change will not happen. The only way to ensure corporate growth is to make sure all employees know that "they are responsible for finding new and better ways of doing things . . . that creativity is valued in their organization—and that they can make a difference."[7]

CONCLUSION

The quote from Machiavelli that opened the chapter is familiar, especially to those who have read about change and how to deal with it. The important thing to remember about it is that the very name Machiavelli has lent itself to an adjective that implies cunning, bad faith, duplicity. When embarking on planning, keep in mind that employees are likely to see any change as a Machiavellian plot, a tale of discomfort, misery, unemployment. Change management must be used to bring about the necessary change, showing employees that change can bring benefits. In fact, the goal of change management as an integral part of Dynamic Planning should be to get everyone in the organization to "learn to love change as much as [they] have hated it in the past."[8]

Keep in mind, however, that the effort must continue after the specific change has been implemented, for there is a lot of backsliding. The best example is what we saw happen in company after company after PCs were first introduced: the workforce was trained and everyone, ostensibly, knew the system, yet PCs sat on numerous desks used as little more than fancy typewriters. The difficulties inherent in making changes and making them permanent make a continual monitoring and evaluation program necessary throughout a change management program and for a number of months afterward. But keeping an eye on the implementation of a given set of changes is but a small part of the monitoring that needs to be done to ensure that the organization is in a dynamic state, as we will see in the next chapter.

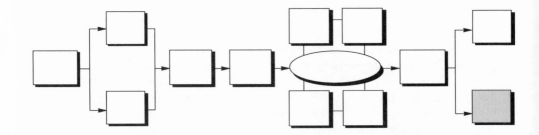

CHAPTER 14

FORMALIZING THE MONITORING AND EVALUATION PROCESS

What you measure is what you get.

Robert S. Kaplan and David P. Norton[1]

The last activity of the Dynamic Planning Framework (Activity 9.0) is formalizing the monitoring and evaluation process. It is the stage at which the planning team checks that the ongoing external review task force is tracking the right critical assumptions, and that a mechanism is in place to provide easy access to senior management when there are developments to report. It is the stage at which all the measurement processes that have been put in place are examined, and the point at which decisions are made about how often evaluations should be done in the future: in other words, how often will the business be examined in terms of the Dynamic Planning Framework in order to determine whether there are trouble spots that need measurement? Those measurements, in turn, will be used to decide when to revisit the Framework, and which activities to revisit (see Figure 14.1). This is the feedback loop: it is strategic management in action in the context of Dynamic Planning.

MANAGING DYNAMICALLY

If the results of the ongoing monitoring and evaluation are formally reviewed prior to each year's planning process, management cannot indulge in the long-term blindness that comes from planning only in terms of short-term budget numbers. By institutionalizing the monitoring process, you ensure that management notices, for example, a rise in the price of a

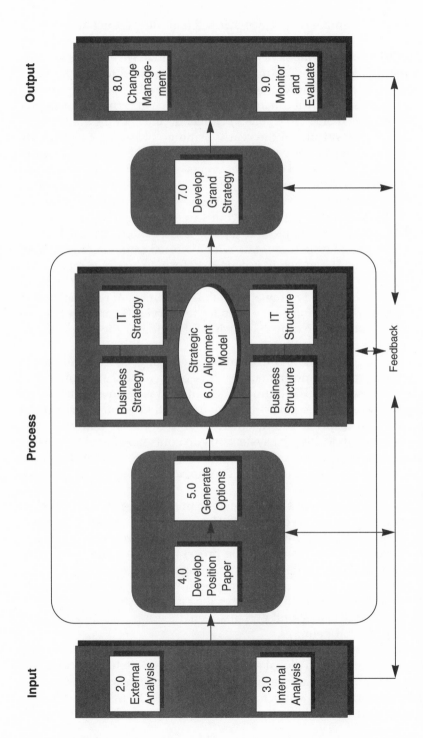

Figure 14.1. Dynamic Planning Framework:[SM] **Feedback Loop**
© 1993 B. Goldberg and J. G. Sifonis

commodity, or a similar occurrence that will make its product more expensive and therefore less profitable in the future. As a result, the company may have to redefine its mission, perhaps even change what it does for a living. Or information technology management will discover that its programmers are not using systems that were purchased to allow faster application development. As a result, it can implement a new change management program before poor short-term results force abandonment of the systems.

It is, however, critical that the yearly planning process not be the only time reevaluations take place. Continual tracking and measuring ensure that a company can respond quickly to events, particularly those that affect its competitiveness. For example, if you become aware of a development in technology that may affect the kind of product you make or service you deliver in the future, you can review your strategy and perhaps change the product or service to enhance it or replace it altogether. Federal Express developed a service called ZapMail, which offered same-day rather than next-day delivery. It planned to use an early form of facsimile machine to send the item to a Federal Express office near the recipient and then hand deliver it from there. The extremely rapid development of fax machines at an affordable price eliminated the need for the service before it got off the ground. The faster a company gets such information, the fewer resources it will invest in fruitless endeavors.

Moreover, monitoring and evaluating such things as customer satisfaction or innovation or profit margins force management and employees to focus on those areas. For example, "traditional performance measurement systems specify the particular actions that they want employees to take and then measure to see whether the employees have in fact taken those actions. In that way, the systems try to control behavior."[2] What is measured is what people pay attention to; the way to ensure that those things that you believe must happen do happen is to show your continual interest in their success.

Clearly, this activity of the Framework involves a great deal of time and energy. Not only do you have to decide what to measure, but also how to measure it; no company can afford to measure everything. The problem becomes less complex if the process is broken into two parts: tracking external factors that can have an impact on the strategic direction of the business (either creating an opportunity or recognizing a potential threat) and measuring the processes the business performs in order to deliver goods or services (and perhaps reengineering them as a result of what is or is not happening).

External factors must be tracked continually, but the factors tend to stay the same. For example, a global manufacturer may watch labor costs and political and economic indicators in all the countries in which it operates in order to determine how much production should be assigned to which plants each year.

From an internal perspective, the organization must establish performance measures to evaluate the effectiveness of its operations and its customer relations. For example, if an organization has a critical success factor that calls for reducing time to market for new products by 10 percent within twelve months, a set of reasonable metrics (time, dollars, quality) and a process for measuring and evaluating the outcome would have to track how well the action items put in place to achieve this goal were working. This would allow for corrections that would ensure the reduction was made.

Doing It Right

Management often avoids measurement as long as the bottom line is being met because the result of the measurement might mean dealing with information that mandates unpleasant action; managers may discover that employees who have been with the company for many years cannot make the grade in a retraining program, that a home office has to be moved after thirty years, that a product they developed may have to be eliminated from the line. Worse, managers may discover that an option they put in place is just not working the way they thought it would. The positive side of monitoring is that you can make these discoveries while there is time to make corrections.

The other important fact to keep in mind is that you not only must evaluate, but you must choose the right things to evaluate, the right tools with which to make the measurements, and you must set realistic goals. They must be within reach of the organization, and they must be attainable in the competitive environment. If the goals are unrealistically high and the targets are impossible to reach, morale will fall, leading many employees to just give up trying, which would place the company in a worse position than if there were no performance measures.

Similarly, if the performance measures are not in concert with the reality of the marketplace, they may be achieved, but achieving them may not be enough to make you competitive. For example, reducing product development time from two years to eighteen months is commendable when evaluated from an internal viewpoint: "We set up specific targets and they were met." However, if, during that period, your competitors introduce a new technology that reduces their product development time from two years to twelve months, you have not gained anything. By using a combination of monitoring and evaluation techniques, this kind of miscalculation can be avoided. Tracking trends in the external environment, in this case, would have let the organization know it had to try to achieve a greater reduction in development time.

THE PROCESSES FOR DOING IT

Evaluating and monitoring can be done in numerous ways, ranging from formal quantitative measurement (how many people produce how many widgets in a given number of hours) to informal surveys of opinions (the reporter who asks people on the street what they think of candidate x or company y). Each has its uses. Among the processes built into the Dynamic Planning Framework are literature searches, interviews, competitive analysis, and the tracking and analysis of demographic and regulatory trends. In addition to the processes already specified are a number that should be in every manager's arsenal: benchmarking, surveys, performance evaluation, and financial analysis, including activity-based costing.

What is measured (and how it is measured) is determined by the company's critical success factors (see Chapter 5). For example, if time to market is a critical success factor, the organization can develop a simple metric to track it. On the other hand, if a critical success factor for the IT division of an organization is user satisfaction, benchmarking may be necessary; if it is product differentiation, focus groups may be necessary. Moreover, the processes for monitoring those CSFs should span the organization: each functional area should have something to track—and the more that has to be tracked across functional areas, the better it is in terms of holistic management.

Monitoring and evaluation of the elements that go into the new enterprise plan are seen by employees as a reflection of management's determination to pursue the new mission of the organization. It reinforces your commitment to implementing the changes you have said you were making. In other words, monitoring and evaluation can serve as a driver of the Grand Strategy.

Some of the processes have been described in detail in the chapters devoted to the internal and external analysis; other methods can be added. The specifics of each tool will not be described in great detail here, because each technique must be tailored to fit the specific company doing the measuring. Generally, the following are the most valuable.

SURVEYS

Surveys can range from in-depth probing of large groups to collections of impressions from small, targeted audiences. There are numerous guides to how to construct surveys, covering subjects ranging from constructing value-free questions, assigning rates for statistical errors in results, and determining how to increase response rates. What is of particular concern here is determining the value to the company of the survey.

For example, a few years ago a major international study of quality was conducted to provide a way for organizations to determine how they compared with other organizations in terms of their approach to quality.[3] The companies that participated devoted an average of sixteen hours to filling out the survey questionnaire. The return on their investment of time was access to the findings and employees throughout the company being brought to realize how important quality was to management, who pushed employees to take the time to fill out the questionnaire.

Surveys can be done on a much smaller scale to pinpoint and eliminate specific problems. When working with a large regional bank based in the South, a critical assumption that surfaced was: "Customer service is key to increasing our core deposits and reducing the defection of customers from our bank." The related critical success factor was: "Treating customers as individuals, not transactions; going out of one's way to provide personalized service to customers even if it meant changing or waiving normal procedures to do so." A Total Quality Program was put in place to train bank employees at all levels to maintain a customer service focus. The program was announced throughout the organization, including information about the performance reward system that was being instituted and the performance measurement program that would begin two weeks after the start of training. The information gained through the measurement program, a six-question survey card developed to measure customers' perceptions of the level of service, was used to modify the training program. The survey became a tool to tailor the training, to inform customers that service was important to the bank, and to check that the program was being implemented.

ACTIVITY-BASED COSTING

Most of the old-line metrics for measurement are financial—productivity, return on investment, cost accounting. These measurements provide information about the company's financial state, but do not provide information on specific areas that could benefit from improvement. Activity-based costing (a process that serves in our experience as a useful guide and check in business process reengineering) shows the links between the activities that are performed in the course of producing a product and the resources consumed. For example, if one product produced by a company sells without any warehousing because the company is the sole provider of the product, adding a percentage of warehouse costs distorts the actual price of that product. This may not be a problem at the moment, but since some of the cost of warehousing a different product is hidden in this kind of accounting, nothing is done to address the issue of warehouse costs because of poor production schedules. Activity-based costing would assign the total cost of warehousing to the other product, making it too expensive to be competitive and revealing the need to improve the schedules for manufacturing.[4]

Trend Watching

As noted, Dynamic Planning calls for maintaining a skeleton version of the task forces that did the initial internal and external analyses. The ongoing tasks of that group have to be carefully delineated to avoid turning trend watching into a full-time occupation. In Chapter 4, when the planning team surfaced assumptions about the external environment, the industrial sector, competition, and the business that needed to be monitored because of their potential impact on the critical success factors and strategies of the organization, the assumptions were quantified. Some were labeled important and unstable—assumptions that, if they changed, would impact the strategic direction of the business. These are the factors that the ongoing task force needs to follow.

When working with the senior managers of a large Japanese bank to help them align their business and IT strategies, some of the discussions led to a decision to expand into the American market. The interviews held to gain an understanding of the business, primarily its existing strategies and culture, involved all those leaders who were part of the strategy making of the bank, including the IT leaders who were in the very top level of management. They also all became intimately involved in the external and internal analysis process for determining strengths, weaknesses, and opportunities. Among the assumptions that emerged in the course of the focus sessions was a belief that, although the bank had performed well in the post-World War II era, if they were to continue to grow in the future, they had to penetrate the American market.

Another assumption was that their core competencies would be in regional banking. After considerable discussion and investigation, we discovered that this was the equivalent of the kind of banking niche they had carved for themselves in Japan, where they were acclaimed for providing personalized service that was so superior to the competition that the loyalty of their customer base (individuals and small- to medium-sized businesses) literally spanned generations.

The next step was a careful analysis of whether and how they could transport the competencies that made them successful in Japan into the U.S. domestic market. Based upon prior experience with other banks and financial services institutions, it became clear that with careful planning, appropriate training, and factoring in the cultural differences associated with the notion of customer service, replicating the bank's core competencies was possible. The next question was how they could, once in the United States, seize opportunities for continued growth. Some of the managers who had studied the market developed a list of indicators that could be used to determine when a regional market was capable of supporting a new entrant.

One of the key measures of a region's readiness to support additional banks turned out to be growth in manufacturing. In fact, in many instances, regional banks nurtured the growth of manufacturing which, in turn, spurred additional bank growth. Consequently, establishing a program to track the number of small- to medium-sized manufacturing companies, in conjunction with a strategy to partner with and encourage Japanese manufacturers to build plants in the United States to help regions reach the critical mass necessary for putting in place an additional bank, was eventually adopted by the senior management of the bank.

BENCHMARKING

Another approach that can be used is competitive benchmarking. Competitive benchmarking is a method for comparing how a business performs one or more sets of critical processes within the company to the way that others, in other companies, perform the same processes. For example, critical processes may include order entry, distribution, or marketing. It is important to keep in mind that competitive benchmarking doesn't necessarily imply that a company must benchmark its processes against best-in-class competitors or against only those in its own industry. If you measure yourself against far larger companies, the gap could prove too great to be meaningful. And the companies need not be in the same industry but need only to be using the same processes that you are trying to benchmark. In many instances, the necessary information is easier to obtain when the companies chosen for competitive benchmarking are not direct competitors who are afraid of giving away an advantage.

The questions, in benchmarking as in the other measures discussed, are, What do you gain by going through the process? What can you learn? And about what? Depending on the techniques you use, you can learn where your weaknesses are and what processes you need to improve.[5] For example, working with a large hospital in the Northeast to help it evaluate the state of its information technology services, which were undergoing enormous changes, a decision was made to benchmark the services; that is, to determine to what degree the IT group was meeting user needs.

The design of the project incorporated new techniques for performing soft measures.[6] The choice of benchmark partners was the first step. After evaluating the hospital and the percentage of its revenues expended on information technology (about 2 percent of $500 million in revenues) and the type and governance of the institution, it was agreed that the size and scale of the benchmark partners should be similar, and that, like hospitals, none should have a bottom line to meet in the usual business sense. All were to one degree or another bound by federal and state regulations, all were providers of services to disparate populations that came to them for those services, and all were involved with federal reporting requirements.

The benchmark partners were a hospital in the Midwest, an airport, a university, and a public utility.[7] The process for unearthing the information was twofold: a questionnaire and one-on-one interviews. The survey questions were designed to elicit information about speed and timeliness of developing new programs, the accuracy of the information provided, the training offered, the quality of the system, and user-IT relations. The questions covered the importance of each of these and how well each was performed. The questions were asked of both users of the system and those responsible for it.

The analysis involved measuring the gaps. For example, did the users think that timeliness was extremely important but not performed well? And how did the user ranking of the importance of timeliness compare with the ranking given that measure by the IT group? At the same time that the survey was being filled out, a small group of individuals from both the business and IT side were interviewed; the questions covered the same issues the questionnaire did and, in addition, looked at the organizations' cultures (both user and information technology group) and processes for dealing with one another. The heads of the information technology groups were also interviewed extensively.

The final analysis revealed that the Northeast hospital was not meeting its users' expectations in many areas. The exact opposite proved true of the other hospital. Further analysis and probing showed that the problem was, in reality, one of perception: both information technology groups were doing admirable jobs. The difference was in the processes in place in the hospital in the Midwest for communicating its successes and the processes for responding to user inquiries and demands. The head of the information technology group in the Northeast subsequently used this information to design communications programs aimed at alleviating the misperceptions and put in place processes aimed at assuring users that their concerns were important to the information technology group. Within six months, there was a dramatic drop in the complaints that had led the head of the information technology group to pursue an evaluation.

Performance Measures

Performance measurement in manufacturing tends to focus on cost (that is, time and resources) and quality (for example, number of defects per batch). In the service sector, performance measurement looks more to somewhat softer issues, such as customer satisfaction (for example, the attentiveness of a cashier and willingness of a manager to rectify an error), perceived quality (that is, how many errors are there in a typed letter, how many rings before a phone is answered), efficiency (for example, do meetings start on time), and innovation (how many new products were suggested and how many came to fruition).[8]

One of the most challenging areas for performance measurement is IT. Given the enhanced role of IT, establishing the metrics for measuring IT success, especially measuring IT's ability to increase productivity, has become an issue. Several years ago when IT was used primarily as a mechanism for replacing or supporting the financial area or the company's back-office operations, the measures related to IT were fairly straightforward—some of the measures included cost per MIP (millions of instructions per second), IT budget as a percentage of the company's gross revenues (for example, normal budgets would range from 0.5 percent to 1.5 percent of gross revenues depending upon the industry sector),[9] response time, availability of the system (that is, the systems were available for users to access 98.9 percent of the time), or the number of lines printed and delivered to the customer on time. The metrics were primarily measures of efficiency related to the overall cost of computing and delivery of output to the general user community—but more important, these measure were developed, for the most part, by the IT managers. They related to the measurement of IT rather than the measurement of IT's value to the business.

These measures were relevant if IT were only viewed as being part of the administrative overhead of the company supporting all of its business functions. However, as the role of information technology changes from administrative support to being a cornerstone of the business, the conventional metrics for measuring IT success are no longer considered valid and new ones are being sought. For example, the "major costs that are hard to assess include the drain on the time of management and professionals for development (their lost productivity), business interruption costs from poor systems, lost business opportunities and loss of competitive position from overemphasis on cost reductions and control applications. Similarly, benefits that are often hard to quantify include elimination of activities and structural changes in organizations, better information quality, improved decisionmaking and communications, new business opportunities, product or service innovations, increased learning, and greater flexibility (e.g., economies of scope)."[10]

As the role of information technology—and the expenditures on it— has grown in the service sector, two new measures have begun to draw attention. One is productivity gains, the other, customer satisfaction. After years in which economists failed to find ways to measure the productivity gains from information technology, and those looking at expenditures on new technologies and the failure of those spending enormous amounts to achieve competitive advantage, methods were developed to assess service sector productivity. At first, the numbers were extremely disappointing, raising questions about the importance of technology expenditures. Finally, in early 1993 the numbers turned around; indeed, according to Stephen Roach, codirector of economics for Morgan Stanley (and one of the major analysts in this area), "the service productivity growth rate, *negative* for most of the 1987 through mid-1991 period, began to zoom at the end of 1991. It hit a healthy 3.2% [in late 1992], when it caught up with the manufacturing rate, which during the Eighties had risen at a very robust annual rate of 3.8%."[11]

The other issue in measuring IT performance, customer satisfaction, is driven to a large degree by the expectation level of the user community. Now, in addition to measures such as time to develop new applications, users who understand systems are arguing over the complexity and sophistication of those programs and their ability to interact with other systems. Should there be one set of metrics for measuring IT success in meeting the demands of power users and another set for those who know how to use the technology but aren't experts? Do you establish performance measures for the total performance of a department, or do you measure the performance of each of the individuals within the department? How do you establish the appropriate metrics for response time— for power users, anything less than instantaneous doesn't meet their needs irrespective of the fact that it may not be necessary for their job. For non-experts, subsecond response time may not be an issue because it really doesn't make a difference in how they perform their jobs. Establishing performance measures to cover all sets of users is analogous to mass customization—the measures have to apply across the user community, but each user or group of users may have to be measured uniquely if IT is to gain an understanding of what level of service they have to provide to be perceived as successful.

Another critical factor in measuring IT success is the fact that IT has become a strategic factor in many companies. What measures must be put in place to determine if a critical application, for example, blood testing for a hospital, is successful? Is it establishing metrics to measure the quality, accuracy, and consistency of the information produced? Is timeliness more of a factor than cost for measuring success, or should success be measured by the fact that the application is user friendly, and no matter what users do, they cannot corrupt the integrity of the application? If quality and consistency of information are defined by users as metrics for measuring IT performance, what defines quality and consistency? The point is that establishing performance measures is highly context specific: it depends on what the company is trying to measure and why.

The kinds of performance measures established also depend on having points of comparison. For example, when developing an information systems plan for a newly privatized British company that had as its mission refining nuclear fuels and selling them worldwide, the need for performance measures was clear. The problem was that there was no way to measure, say, increased profitability, since, as a controlled government entity, it had never had a bottom line. Baseline measures were taken for many processes so that future metrics could be established. At the same time, specific parts of each process were broken down into measures that could be compared with those for similar industries, a more difficult and less satisfying system, but at least one that conveyed the fact to employees that the company was going to have to operate differently, with a concern for profits.

KEEPING THE HOLISTIC FOCUS WHEN MONITORING AND EVALUATING

The monitoring and evaluation step is a necessary part of becoming an open, learning organization. The constant awareness it creates of change and movement makes change a normal part of life. Trend watching provides the organization with new information and insights about the dynamic, changing environment in which it competes. This, in turn, helps the organization reevaluate how it makes its living and, if necessary, generates new options that will help it remain competitive. These options are then analyzed, and the necessary changes to accommodate the options are made to the vision, mission, or enterprise plan, or potentially to all elements of the Grand Strategy. In turn, new CSFs, tactics, and action items are developed, and new metrics and performance measurement processes are put in place to move the business forward. To ensure that nothing is overlooked, the steps laid out in the Dynamic Planning Framework provide a rational process for identifying factors that may cause change and for responding to the changes before they impact the organization. The result is long-term strategic management.

But remember that monitoring and evaluation also provide a structure for evaluating the performance of the business in the near term—meeting its stated goals. This level of monitoring and evaluation is analogous to the Strategic Alignment Modeling process for aligning the business and IT strategies. Monitoring and evaluation of the processes to help a company achieve specific goals must be done concurrently and across functional areas.

Without a well-defined set of programs for monitoring and evaluation, a business will not be a successful competitor in the 1990s and beyond. Globalization, enhanced communications capabilities, rapidly evolving technologies, and the constant changes in the social, economic, and political factors that comprise the business environment make it imperative that businesses stay alert and open to growth. The notion of stability in business is dead. In the future, those businesses that focus on monitoring and evaluation and learning from the information gleaned from such measurements will not only survive, but will emerge as the best in class in the global marketplace.

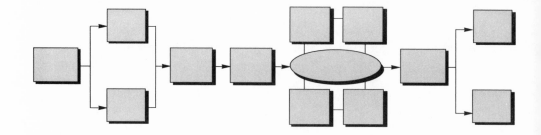

Chapter 15

Looking Beyond Tomorrow

The science of fractals (and many other areas of science) [is] pushing us to a new level of analysis, one that accounts for the system as a system, where it is impossible to know what will happen to a part without a vision of the whole.

Margaret J. Wheatley[1]

By now it should be clear that Dynamic Planning is more than a Framework—it is a way of thinking. In the world of business today, when survival has become increasingly difficult, where companies once considered invincible are collapsing, and where multiple and conflicting initiatives are bringing companies to a standstill, dynamic thinking can help you find integrated solutions that will enable your organization to survive and prosper.

As was noted at the very beginning of this book, the Dynamic Planning Framework will help you overcome the four major reasons why organizations become less competitive over time: the lack of long-term thinking (because of a focus on the next quarter's profits); management's tendency to address one problem and one solution at a time (because it does not think holistically); the lack of understanding of the new place of technology in corporations (because it is still considered an adjunct to the business); and the unwillingness to change (because cultures and mindsets tend to be frozen). If you train yourself to look at what is happening in your organization in terms of the Framework, including ideas and suggestions and events in the world around you, you will learn to think dynamically. You will integrate long-term goals, evaluate information in terms of your organization as a whole, make technology an integral part of the organization, and accept change as a basic good; your thinking will embody the four principles underlying Dynamic Planning (see Figure 15.1).

248

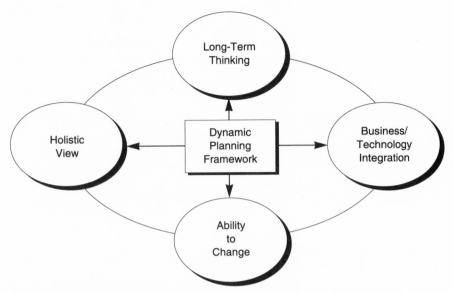

Figure 15.1. Dynamic Planning Principles
© 1993 B. Goldberg and J. G. Sifonis

The Framework forces you to think holistically: you check to see how a new process will fit into the long-term business plans of your organization before you put it in place, and if it fits you implement it formally, setting up training and change management programs. The Framework forces you to think long term: because you have ongoing teams looking at the world around you, you are aware of trends and developments that could impact your organization and your competitive environment in the years to come. The Framework forces you to think of technology as an integral part of your organization: strategies are formulated by examining the ways in which technology can help the business as well as by determining how it can help support your customers' needs. And the Framework opens the organization to change, making it impossible to play ostrich. Each of the nine activities of the Dynamic Planning Framework is aimed at these principles.

The second advantage is that going through all the activities involved in Dynamic Planning will not only help you move your organization into a more competitive position now, but it will put in place tools—monitoring and evaluation—that will warn you when the time has come to begin the ascent to the next stage (see Figure 15.2). The feedback loop not only provides a mechanism for making incremental change part of the organization's normal planning process, but also alerts the organization when it is time to move on. Alternatively, it also provides the organization the mechanism to see when an option is not working, allowing it to make changes in the way the option is being implemented or to discard it.

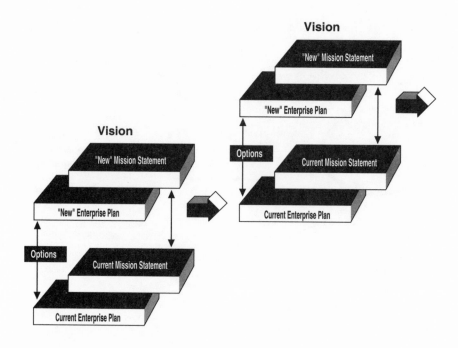

Figure 15.2. Looking Beyond Tomorrow
© 1993 B. Goldberg and J. G. Sifonis

THERE IS NO MAGIC

The Dynamic Planning Framework can be used to build an organization
that is marked by energy, is managed by people who are open to new
ideas, and has a structure that encourages innovation. By using the
Framework as a tool for thinking about and applying techniques such as
quality, reengineering, and downsizing—techniques that seem to have
merit but are reported to fail more often than not—you are forced to
explain the changes you are making and explain why you are making
them. However trendy, if they are not appropriate for your organization,
you will know it soon enough, enabling you to change or abandon something instead of ending up spending millions of dollars trying to prove
your decision was right.

Sometimes those trying to get the organization to turn to Dynamic
Planning run into enormous problems because of political infighting,
embedded beliefs, or a rigid command-and-control hierarchy. In these
cases, no matter how persuasive an argument is made for Dynamic

Planning, the individual or individuals championing it will find that their efforts to bring it into the organization are doomed to failure. This does not preclude your using the Framework as a guide to your own thinking. If you use the Framework as a tool for evaluating the way you do things, your group is more likely to be successful than others. As you become more successful, you will find many opportunities to introduce others to the principles of dynamic thinking—make the change happen by example.

It is our belief that those who adopt Dynamic Planning will be able to see and seize the moment that can dramatically alter their future, allowing them to achieve significant competitive advantage. Dynamic Planning is for those with the vision to try something new and innovative. It is for those companies that are willing to put in place the discipline of ongoing monitoring and evaluation of trends (social, political, economic, technological), markets, and customers; of constantly asking "what do we do for a living" and "what should we do for a living"; of constantly looking and thinking beyond tomorrow.

Dynamic Organizations

There are companies that have, over time, managed to remain dynamic instead of becoming dinosaurs. In order to do a reality check of the Dynamic Planning Framework, we spent some time with and thought and read extensively about companies that are long-term survivors to see if they were doing the equivalent of Dynamic Planning. If they were not, we wanted to learn their keys to survival. Since we usually apply the Framework to companies that are, as noted in the examples throughout the book, aware they need change and willing to work to make it happen, we know that opening a company's culture to the four principles underlying the Framework can bring advantages. But we wanted to see if these principles are critical to success no matter how they are brought into a company's culture.

Before looking at the two companies we chose as long-term survivors, we would like to note that the companies chosen have not been consistent stars; they have gone through bad times and in fact are fighting to improve their profitability at a time when "the only guarantee is that there are no guarantees. Companies that were the heroes yesterday are not necessarily heroes today."[2]

Two of the long-established, large companies we examined proved particularly interesting because their cultures incorporate the four principles that underlie Dynamic Planning, and they tend to do all the activities involved in Dynamic Planning, although not in a formal way.

THE ROYAL DUTCH/SHELL GROUP OF COMPANIES

Royal Dutch/Shell is more than a century old; there have been periods in its history when it faltered, but it always found a way to rebound. In the late 1970s, Royal Dutch/Shell was revitalized when Arie de Geus, then its coordinator of group planning, helped move the organization into a new way of thinking. De Geus believes that "the ability of a company's senior managers to absorb what is going on in the business environment and to act on that information with appropriate business moves," which he believes is learning, are a large part of an organization's ability to thrive.[3] The work he and his group did was aimed at changing the way the organization's leaders thought about the world around them.

The planning teams at Royal Dutch/Shell used scenario planning as part of their methodology for aiming at long-term results. One of the gurus of scenario-planning, Pierre Wack, was part of the Shell group. He believed that it was essential for managers working with scenarios to keep in mind during their discussions the fact that the process involves the way that perceptions are dealt with "inside the heads of decisionmakers. Their purpose is to gather and transform information of strategic significance into fresh perceptions."[4] This process is very similar to the option generation process in Dynamic Planning. Shell believes that scenarios "promote a discussion of possibilities other than the 'most likely' one and encourage the consideration of 'what if' questions. They also help us recognize more of what is going on around us, including the early weak signals of change, and illuminate the uncertainties and issues that are critical for the future."[5]

In addition, like most oil companies, Royal Dutch/Shell turned to technology early for its use in exploration. The group was a leader in the "application of three-dimensional seismic modeling . . . [which] involves analyzing rock formations for oil deposits and requires extensive use of supercomputers."[6] It was also pushed along this road by the fact that it is a multinational organization, in governance, in structure, and in its mindset. Former Shell executive Peter Schwartz reports that when he was a member of its planning group, they "had a tough time sharing ideas among the scenario-planners who were scattered over 120 countries. So we decided to open up the community. . . . We acquired the services of a computer conferencing system, equipped around fifty of our planners with computer terminals and taught them to use them. . . . [K]nowledge is the only kind of wealth that multiplies when you give it away, and computer conferencing can be used as an engine for generating and multiplying that kind of wealth. Shell continues to experiment with computer networking."[7]

Domestically, the Shell Oil Company is very aware of the need to watch developments in the area of technology. Senior management on the business side recognizes the need to give its information division advance warning when it is contemplating changes in corporate governance that might affect the way technology is used and the kinds of technology it needs. The notion of careful planning is such an integral part of Shell Oil Company thinking that the members of the information technology group are quite used to serving on planning teams and have an unusual knowledge of the business side, even at the programmer level. (At Shell Oil Company, however, levels are an interesting phenomenon; it currently has in place a management tool that most American companies are just beginning to use. People with special skills who do not like administration can choose a technical career path and receive adequate compensation, rising in stature and salary as specialists; the result is that Shell's technologists are very skilled and experienced individuals who have been with the company long enough to understand the business needs of their users.)

Finally, benchmarking, measurement, and change management are a very normal part of life. The Shell Oil Company has employees in human resources knowledgeable about change management and responsible for helping the technology department create buy-in for new technologies on both the business and the information technology sides of the organization. The company also conducts numerous internal surveys and does performance and quality measurements.

The Shell Oil Company is planning dynamically; it does not do it according to the Framework, but it certainly does it. It looks at things holistically, it integrates technology, it is open to change, and it plans for the long term. Shell has evolved over a century into the kind of organization that knows how to plan and survive. Perhaps some of its success lies in the fact that early in its corporate life it merged and remerged, adding different core competencies and products—learning to change what it did for a living to make a living.

THE WEYERHAEUSER COMPANY

One of the most interesting visits we made to explore the reasons for organizational longevity was to the Weyerhaeuser Company in Tacoma, Washington. We became more and more interested in the company in the course of arranging our visit because everyone we spoke with, from the receptionist to senior management, told us about some aspect of the company that would be particularly interesting for us to look at; at all levels, there was a clear awareness of what the company was doing. This impression was borne out during our visit by the enormous amount of information we were able to gather from everyone we met, from guards and sales people in the Weyerhaeuser store to the executive vice president.

Weyerhaeuser has been shaped by a clear vision: "This is not for us, nor for our children—but for our grandchildren." These are the words of Frederick Weyerhaeuser in 1900, when signing the papers that marked the start of the company. That vision is respected by everyone in the company and is at the root of much of the work it does in reforestation, which has had an additional benefit in the form of many successful new techniques and products.

At the same time, the company is not afraid of change, performing frequent internal reviews. John W. Creighton, Jr., president of Weyerhaeuser, explained in the 1991 *Annual Report,* that "back in 1989, when we undertook our refocusing reviews and the establishment of our business improvement plans, we determined that our performance was hampered by complexity in our organization, confusion and duplication in accountabilities, and deficiencies in manufacturing competitiveness. In addition, lack of standardization in processes and barriers to communication within and among our businesses were widespread. Sorting out and remedying these problems has been, and continues to be, a primary focus."

These are not idle words. In our meetings, we learned that these problems were being systematically and carefully addressed. For example, Cliff Hall, who had recently joined the company as the vice president, information technology, explained that although the company's business strategy calls for highly decentralized operations, he was trying to find ways to align and integrate information technology along functional lines across the company's locations. "We do a lot of cross-functional teaming. These teams are essential when you have to make critical decisions that must be viewed in the context of what is best for the company." One of his major objectives was balancing "empowerment, coordination, standards, and infrastructure needs." To accomplish this, he spent five months traveling around the business and the user community to determine where the company could "take advantage of technology, not just IT, to transform the business." His confidence in the future is in part based on the access he has to senior management: "The ability to use technology to help transform the business depends on where IT reports." However, the higher up you report, the more you need good communication and presentation skills— "you have to demystify the IT message to senior management; you can't speak bits and bytes"—in order to get your message across. Moreover, he said that he is a firm believer in building "implementation and change management into the process of planning."

The discussion indicated a combination of long-term, holistic thinking that would end up furthering the integration of IT and business strategies at Weyerhaeuser. The dedication to long-term thinking also came through in a discussion of Weyerhaeuser's future with Charles W. Bingham, executive vice president. He noted that "while benchmarking data revealed that our [Weyerhaeuser] forestry practices are world-class, all too frequently being the best is not good enough. If we are going to provide our shareholders with superior returns into the twenty-first century, our current management practices and forestry research focus must continue to evolve." Our meeting with Bingham also highlighted the continuing belief

of everyone at Weyerhaeuser that they had to always work toward refor-
esting, preserving the lands for "our grandchildren."

He pointed out that when you know it takes some thirty-five to eighty
years to grow a new timber crop, you have a culture that thinks long term.
Moreover, because of a history of family ownership, Bingham noted, they
have a "feeling of responsibility to their employees and the people of the
community." The result is an early and continuing emphasis on environmental concerns. They are such strong believers in the values of the original culture that, when they acquire new forest lands in other regions, they
set up programs to educate new employees at all levels into the value of
the land and its preservation. Indeed, their dedication to environmental
and community concerns has put them on the *Fortune* magazine annual list
of "Most Admired Companies," every year since 1983.[8]

THE ISSUES FOR TOMORROW

If Dynamic Planning works as we believe it does, will it solve tomorrow's
problems and those beyond tomorrow? We believe that if used correctly it
will. That is, if it is used as an approach rather than as a methodology; a
methodology is a rigid set of procedures, the Dynamic Planning Framework is an adjustable tool that can be made to fit the corporate context in
which it is employed.

More and more, corporate America is beginning to focus on issues of
leadership and governance. Given that downsizing and rightsizing and
becoming lean and mean have been adopted by almost every corporation
(including the ones who always believed they would never layoff their
employees) in the struggle to increase productivity and remain competitive, the need for new ways of governing and leading becomes clear. The
Framework works as well when applied to these structural issues as it
does with actual operations.

GOVERNANCE

By governance we do not mean corporate governance—that body of contracts, regulations, and stockholder and board relationships that governs
the legal existence of the corporation—but rather the governance structures
that prevail within the operation of the organization. (Governance on this
level is discussed in Chapter 8.) The way the company is structured—from
decentralized to centralized or anything in between—affects the information technology strategy. The business and information technology governance structures have to work together, each enabling the organization
to interact across all lines and strata. For the first time, however, there
seems to be strong recognition from the business side that their decisions

have enormous, often costly, effects on the technology side. The result is a drive to ask the IT side to develop alternate strategies to accommodate possible future business governance changes. The Dynamic Planning Framework and the Strategic Alignment Model are proving strong tools for dealing with these issues.

LEADERSHIP

The corporate changes brought about by the move to a less hierarchical structure include teams and far less middle management, both of which call for empowering employees who once took direction and were expected to follow it blindly. The so-called flattened and empowered organization is becoming the new norm. In addition, such employees as salespeople, administrative assistants, and telephone customer representatives are being asked to take on additional responsibility by responding directly to customers in such a way that a sale is never lost, a customer never dissatisfied. What are the boundaries of this kind of empowerment; what rules have to be put in place? These are questions about leadership that cannot be handled within a rule-based structure, yet to avoid costly mistakes, there have to be boundaries. The Framework can help address this issue through the change management and training it puts in place. But that is not a complete answer.

The answer lies in the ability to think holistically and long term, to take into consideration the benefits of integrating business and technology, and to accept change. The Framework is the key to that kind of thinking—it is the key to building leadership at all levels of the organization. And leadership is what business is all about.

NOTES

CHAPTER 1

1. Carol J. Loomis, "Dinosaurs?" *Fortune*, May 3, 1993, p. 37.
2. Keith H. Hammonds, "Why Big Companies Are So Tough to Change," *Business Week*, June 17, 1991, p. 28.
3. "The Fall of Big Business," *The Economist*, April 17, 1993, p. 13.
4. J. E. Garten, *A Cold Peace: America, Japan, Germany, and the Struggle for Supremacy*, A Twentieth Century Fund Book (New York: Times Books/Random House, 1992).
5. Alexander King and Harlan Cleveland, eds., *Bioresources for Development: The Renewable Way of Life* (New York: Pergamon Press, 1980), p. xix.
6. Harlan Cleveland, *The Knowledge Executive: Leadership in an Information Society* (New York: Truman Talley Books/Dutton, 1989), p. 197.
7. "Stars of the 1980s Cast Their Light," *Fortune*, July 3, 1989, p. 66.
8. Although many of our clients would have no objection to citation, some would. If we listed those who had no problem, we were concerned that general knowledge of our client lists could then be used to narrow down the field, resulting in the identification of those who sought anonymity.

CHAPTER 2

The Dynamic Planning Framework was not developed overnight. It is an outgrowth of years of practical experience, countless hours of discussion with a variety of other consultants and academics, reading and research into documents far too numerous to include in the Select Bibliography, and our process for setting up client engagements—challenge sessions that are both contentious and exhilarating.

1. John C. Henderson and N. Venkatraman, "Understanding Strategic Alignment," *Strategic Alignment: Managing for Synergy*, supplement to *Business Quarterly* 55, no. 3 (Winter 1991): 14.
2. A business's mission statement is its credo, the statement of what it is and what it does. It is assumed that businesses embarking on Dynamic Planning have a mission statement and enterprise plan in place, whether formal or informal. Part of the object of Dynamic Planning is to help refine, elaborate, or change the mission statement as well as the enterprise plan and its associated elements. This critical element of the business will be further discussed and examples of mission statement formulation will be set forth in Chapter 11, the discussion of the business's Grand Strategy.

Appendix to Chapter 2

1. James Gleick, *Chaos: Making a New Science* (New York: Viking, 1987), p. 8.

Chapter 3

Most of the material in this chapter is a result of experience. There are good basic books that cover parts of these subjects, but a total of more than four decades of collective experience in holding and facilitating meetings in the business and in the nonprofit sector are the basis of our current thinking about planning sessions.

For specific information on the role of the facilitator, the literature on negotiating is invaluable, particularly the work of Max Bazerman. Also see Robert H. Waterman, Jr., *Adhocracy: The Power to Change* (New York: Norton, 1992), for a good account of another, looser, approach to meetings and teams. There are also lessons to be learned from articles in such journals as *Human Resource Management, Journal of Organizational Behavior, Organizational Dynamics,* and *Human Relations.* For a good dictionary of key technological terms and concepts, see Peter G. W. Keen, *Every Manager's Guide to Information Technology* (Boston: Harvard Business School Press, 1991).

1. Geoffrey M. Bellman, *The Consultant's Calling* (San Francisco: Jossey-Bass, 1990), p. 73.

2. In our experience as consultants, we have found that without clear word from above that the company's survival is in doubt, senior management simply does not tend to proclaim its support for planning with the necessary vigor. There are countless cases in the literature of leaders who do—or don't—work hard enough at communicating this kind of message. One of the best examples of one who does is in Rosabeth Moss Kanter, "Championing Change: An Interview with Bell Atlantic's CEO Raymond Smith," *Harvard Business Review,* January–February 1991.

3. Frank K. Sonnenberg, *Marketing to Win* (New York: Harper & Row, 1990), p. 190.

4. Harlan Cleveland, *The Knowledge Executive: Leadership in an Information Society* (New York: Truman Talley Books/Dutton, 1989), p. 11.

5. Understanding individual terms is less difficult than understanding how they fit together and their relevance to an organization's operations.

6. See Max H. Bazerman and Margaret A. Neale, *Negotiating Rationally* (New York: Free Press, 1992), and D. Lax and J. Sebenius, *The Manager as Negotiator* (New York: Free Press, 1986).

Chapter 4

On the back of the dust jacket of Michael E. Porter's *Competitive Strategy: Techniques for Analyzing Industries and Competitors* (New York: Free Press, 1980), Fred Gluck, a director of McKinsey & Company, said: *"Competitive Strategy* provides managers with the raw material for thinking about how to change the rules of the marketplace in their favor." Indeed, that has been the case for us and a generation of managers and consultants. Much of the thinking that shaped our approach as practitioners, particularly in this and the next chapter, is based on the insights Porter put forward over a decade ago.

Analyzing the external environment takes relentlessly tracking events of numerous kinds. There is a wealth of information on the kinds of material to track, much of which is spelled out in Peter Schwartz, *The Art of the Long View: Planning for the Future in an Uncertain World* (New York: Doubleday, 1991). More than twenty years in a think tank (the Twentieth Century Fund) has convinced one of the authors of this volume that it is pointless to follow a formal process for studying the external world. The best solution in this age of endless information is to "follow your head." Among the most useful journals and magazines to try to keep up with are: *The Economist, Survey of Current Business, Business Week,* publications of the World Bank, *Fortune, Forbes, New Republic, Foreign Affairs, Technology Review, Datamation,* the publications of the American Management Association (especially *Management Review), Science, Nature, Information Week, Industry Week, Harvard Business Review, Sloan Management Review, Technology Forecasting and Social Change, Issues in Science and Technology,* and publications of the Brookings Institution, the Twentieth Century Fund, the Hudson Institute, and the American Enterprise Institute.

When it comes to future planning, the works of Herman Kahn and Alvin Toffler are unsurpassed; see also Spyros G. Makridakis, *Forecasting, Planning, and Strategy for the 21st Century* (New York: Free Press, 1990), and John Naisbitt, *Megatrends* (New York: Warner Books, 1982).

1. Max Dublin, *Futurehype: The Tyranny of Prophecy* (New York: Dutton, 1991), p. 265.

2. Edward A. Filene, *The Way Out: A Forecast of Coming Changes in American Business and Industry* (New York: Doubleday, Page & Company, 1926), p. 16.

3. Michael E. Porter, *Competitive Advantage: Creating and Sustaining Superior Performance* (New York: Free Press, 1985), p. 479.

4. James Gleick, *Chaos: Making a New Science* (New York: Viking, 1987), p. 8.

5. Peter M. Senge, *The Fifth Discipline: The Art & Practice of the Learning Organization* (New York: Doubleday, 1990), p. 139.

6. John Holusha, "Pushing the Envelope at Boeing," *The New York Times,* November 10, 1991, Sect. 3, p. 1.

7. "Plane Geometry: Boeing Uses CAD to Design 130,000 Parts for Its New 777," *Scientific American,* March 1991.

8. Much of the material in this section is drawn from Beverly Goldberg, "Finding Profit in Not-for-Profits," *Management Review,* June 1991.

9. Filene, *The Way Out,* p. 16.

10. There are many specialists in this area. Michael Sloan, founder of the Concorde Group, is among the leaders in this field. He has developed proprietary software, with which he generates multiple scenarios for very large organizations. See Michael P. Sloan, "Strategic Planning by Multiple Political Futures," *Executives Forum,* 1983.

11. Drucker, quoted in Pierre Wack, "Scenarios: Shooting the Rapids," *Harvard Business Review,* November–December 1985, p. 150. See also Wack, "Scenarios: Unchartered Waters Ahead," *Harvard Business Review,* September–October 1985.

CHAPTER 5

Again, much of the material in this chapter is based on years of experience. There are many textbooks that provide invaluable information about how to develop questionnaires and conduct interviews, but questionnaires are worse than useless if not tailored to the specific organization and a specific issue. Common sense, an understanding of how to write questions that do not color the answer (either by implying the answer wanted ["Do you prefer technology A over technology B" instead of "Circle the technology you prefer: A or B"] or by implying a value judgment), and a clear picture of the kinds of information that are necessary should allow readers to construct their own tools based on the broad examples presented here (which are meant for use when doing organization-wide Dynamic Planning).

1. Stephen W. Hawking, *A Brief History of Time* (New York: Bantam Books, 1988), p. 8.

2. Much of the material in this section was developed by John Sifonis in the course of consulting engagements while at Ernst & Young and Siberg Associates, Inc. The assistance of the members of his teams during those engagements was invaluable; the early field work was incorporated in Arthur Young & Co., *Strategic Information Systems Planning* (New York, 1983).

3. The major work in this area includes John F. Rockart, "Chief Executives Define Their Own Data Needs," *Harvard Business Review*, March–April 1979; Christine Bullen and John F. Rockart, "A Primer on Critical Success Factors," *CISR Working Paper no. 69*, Center for Information Systems Research, Sloan School of Management, MIT, Cambridge, Mass., June 1981; and Andrew C. Boynton and Robert W. Zmud, "Critical Success Factors: A Case-Based Assessment," *Sloan Management Review* 25, no. 1 (Summer 1984).

4. Rockart, "Chief Executives Define Their Own Data Needs," p. 80.

5. Joel K. Leidecker and Albert V. Bruno, "Identifying and Using Critical Success Factors," *Long Range Planning*, February 1984, p. 24.

6. The classic work in this area was done by Richard O. Mason and Ian I. Mitroff, *Challenging Strategic Planning Assumptions: Theory, Cases, and Techniques* (New York: Wiley, 1981). In 1984, John F. Rockart, John C. Henderson, and John G. Sifonis co-authored a paper for the Center for Information Systems Research entitled: "A Planning Methodology for Integrating Management Support Systems." The paper, which addressed the definition and development of critical assumptions and their relevance in the planning process, later appeared in a very useful volume: *The Rise of Managerial Computing: The Best of the Center for Information Systems Research, Sloan School of Management*, ed. John F. Rockart and Christine V. Bullen (Homewood, Ill.: Dow-Jones Irwin, 1986), pp. 257–82.

CHAPTER 6

1. We are describing here a very simple form of structural linguistics, an art developed by Noam Chomsky and his followers. (See Chomsky, esp. *Aspects of the Theory of Syntax* [Boston: MIT. Press, 1965]; *Syntactic Structures* [Mouton, 1978, orig., 1957], *Rules & Representations* [New York: Columbia University Press, 1982]; and for a brief explanation of current thinking on the use and force of language, Beth Horning, "Language Busters," *Technology Review*, October 1991.) The analytical techniques put forth by Chomsky are used on a very sophisticated level by scenario planners such as Michael Sloan of the Concorde Group.

We had not thought about suggesting any form of this to clients until a visit to the Exploratorium in San Francisco, an interactive museum that provides a superb introduction to science. In its section on language, it has a display that offers a box of plain wooden rectangular blocks with words written on four sides. There is a color code that describes the parts of speech on a given block. At the most basic level, you are instructed to take at least three blocks, representing at a minimum a noun, a verb, and an object. You then put them together so that at least on one surface you have a possible sentence. You then rotate the three blocks to reveal another surface. It is rare that the sentence that emerges makes any sense in the real world. The other two sentences displayed as you rotate will also tend to be impossible. They are "legal" sentences grammatically; they just make no sense. Watching children playing with the blocks led us to develop the organization-specific vocabulary idea as a means of introducing clients to a new way of thinking.

2. Peter Schwartz, *The Art of the Long View: Planning for the Future in an Uncertain World* (New York: Doubleday, 1991), p. 64. Schwartz, like most scenario planners, has favorite magazines and journals and other sources of information. He details his readings and his experiences doing scenario planning through analysis of perceptions that are pulled out of the thinking inspired by broad observation and study.

3. For a full detailed account of how to analyze competitive forces and do a value-chain analysis, see the seminal works by Michael E. Porter, *Competitive Strategy: Techniques for Analyzing Industries and Competitors* (New York: Free Press, 1980), and *Competitive Advantage: Creating and Sustaining Superior Performance* (New York: Free Press, 1985).

4. For a description of the techniques used for mapping assumptions on Porter's framework, see John C. Henderson and John G. Sifonis, "The Value-Added of Strategic IS Planning: Understanding Consistency, Validity, and IS Markets," *MIS Quarterly* 12, no. 2 (June 1988).

CHAPTER 7

1. This tendency to focus on the short term is a reflection of current investment policies by institutional investors. See *The Report of the Twentieth Century Fund Task Force on Market Speculation and Corporate Governance*, background paper by Robert Shiller, "Who's Minding the Store?" (New York: Twentieth Century Fund Press, 1992), and Michael T. Jacobs, *Short-Term America: The Causes and Cures of Our Business Myopia* (Boston: Harvard Business School Press, 1991).

CHAPTER 8

The issue of governance is complex and difficult: there is considerable confusion between corporate governance, which tends to refer to the host of legal and contractual and shareholder issues surrounding the actual structure of the organization, and business policy or governance, which refers to the internal administrative structure.

One of the leading scholars examining corporate governance issues is Oliver Williamson; see especially *The Economic Institutions of Capitalism* (New York: Free Press, 1985), and *The Nature of the Firm: Origins, Evolution, and Development* (New York: Oxford University Press, 1993), a collection of essays edited by Williamson and S.G. Winter. In addition, see Ronald Coase, *The Firm, the Market, and the Law* (Chicago: University of Chicago Press, 1988), and Edward S. Herman, *Corporate Control, Corporate Power*, A Twentieth Century Fund Study (New York: Cambridge University Press, 1981).

For more information on internal structural issues, see, for example, P. Nystrom and W. Starbuck, eds., *Handbook of Organizational Design* (New York: Oxford University Press, 1981); S. Ranson, B. Hinings, and R. Greenwood, "The Structuring of Organization Structures," *Administrative Science Quarterly* 25 (1980); Sumantra Ghoshal and Nitin Nohria, "Horses for Courses: Organizational Forms for Multinational Corporations," *Sloan Management Review* 34, no. 2 (Winter 1993); Geary A. Rummler and Alan P. Brache, "Managing the White Space on the Organization Chart," *Supervision*, May 1991; and Margaret J. Wheatley, *Leadership and the New Science* (San Francisco: Berrett-Koehler, 1992).

1. Alfred D. Chandler, Jr., *Strategy and Structure: Chapters in the History of the American Industrial Enterprise* (Cambridge, Mass.: MIT Press, 1962), p. 16.

2. Commodity Products, Inc., and Leading-Edge Technologies, Inc., are composites of companies we have been involved with over the years.

3. Michael Treacy and Fred Wiersema, "Customer Intimacy and Other Value Disciplines," *Harvard Business Review*, January–February 1993.

CHAPTER 9

The cases in this chapter are based on consulting assignments with specific clients, except for the RTC example, which was developed from three projects involving regional telecommunications companies over a five-year period.

1. Rosabeth Moss Kanter, "Thinking Across Boundaries," *Harvard Business Review*, November–December 1990, p. 9.

CHAPTER 10

1. See Raanan Weitz, *New Roads to Development*, A Twentieth Century Fund Essay (Westport, Conn.: Greenwood Press, 1986).

CHAPTER 11

There are hundreds of books on leadership and visionaries. We make no pretense to having read them all, but of those we have, our favorites are James Brian Quinn, *Intelligent Enterprise* (New York: Free Press, 1992); John Diebold, *The Innovators* (New York: Dutton, 1990); John P. Kotter, *A Force for Change: How Leadership Differs From Management* (New York: Free Press, 1990 (also Kotter's *The Leadership Factor* [New York: Free Press, 1988]); Tom Peters and Nancy Austin, *A Passion for Excellence: The Leadership Difference* (New York: Random House, 1985); Tom Peters and R. H. Waterman, *In Search of Excellence: Lessons From Americas's Best Run Companies* (New York: Harper & Row, 1982); Robert Heller, *The Decision Makers* (New York: Truman Talley Books, 1991); Warren Bennis and Burt Nanus, *Leaders: The Strategies for Taking Charge* (New York: Harper & Row, 1985); Michael Beer, Russell A. Eisenstat, and Bert Spector, *The Critical Path to Corporate Renewal* (Boston: Harvard Business School Press, 1990).

1. Edward N. Luttwak, *Strategy: The Logic of War and Peace* (Cambridge, Mass.: Harvard University Press, 1987), p. xii. Luttwak's work on military strategy, like Sun Tzu's and Harry G. Summers, Jr.'s, provides interesting insights for business managers.

2. The discussion of mission statements is a reflection of our observation and a study, over many years, of the views of mission statements by those who have made this part of the planning process their particular area of expertise. Anyone desiring to discover more about mission statements would be well advised to obtain annual reports of organizations they admire as well as to review the following: R. Ackoff, "Mission Statements," *Planning Review* 15, no. 4 (1985); Joyce Anderson, "Mission Statements Bond Corporate Culture," *Personnel Journal*, October 1987; Fred R. David, "How Companies Define Their Mission," *Long Range Planning*, February 1989 (David is the author or co-author of a number of important examinations of mission statements); Mark P. Frohman and Perry Pascarella, "How to Write a Purpose Statement," *Industry Week*, March 23, 1987; John A. Pearce and Kendall Roth, "Multinationalization of the Mission Statement," *Advanced Management Journal*, Summer 1988; J. H. Want, "Corporate Mission," *Management Review*, August 1986; R. Duane Ireland and Michael A. Hitt, "Mission Statements: Importance, Challenge, and Recommendations for Development," *Business Horizons* 35, no. 3 (May–June 1992).

3. Peter F. Drucker, *Management: Tasks, Responsibilities, and Practices* (New York: Harper & Row, 1973), p. 88.

CHAPTER 12

1. Although all of the steps need to be taken and the activities performed, the way they are done must be adapted to the organization. In this example, as you will see, the external task force draws on the skills of an already established group and adds the work of outside experts for a specific analysis, the focus sessions are in a somewhat different format than usual, and the option generation process is done in two steps.

2. The meeting involved some of the key people who had worked on the MIT "Management in the 1990s Project," especially N. Venkatraman, who later became a critical member of the team on the assignment and whose insights helped make the project so successful.

3. The Dynamic Planning Framework was developed by the authors subsequent to their work on SAM.

4. Michael S. Scott Morton, ed., *The Corporation of the 1990s: Information Technology and Organizational Transformation* (New York: Oxford University Press, 1991), and numerous working papers prepared by the members of the group and others involved in the "Management in the 1990s Project" at MIT were used to explain SAM.

CHAPTER 13

There is an extensive literature on change management that has informed our thinking and our approach to the work we do in this area. Among the most valuable sources are the work of Kurt Lewin, a noted psychologist of the 1940s and 1950s; Edgar Schein, esp. *Organizational Culture and Leadership* (San Francisco: Jossey-Bass, 1985); and Rosabeth Moss Kanter, esp. *The Change Masters* (New York: Simon & Schuster, 1983). In addition, see John Lawrie, "The ABCs of Change Management," *Training & Development Journal*, March 1990, which discusses the role of human resources in helping managers develop change programs; Terrence E. Deal and Allan A. Kennedy, *Corporate Cultures: The Rites and Rituals of Corporate Life* (Reading, Mass.: Addison-Wesley, 1982), esp. Chapter 9; Carol A. Beatty and Gloria L. Lee, "Leadership Among Middle Managers—An Exploration in the Context of Technological Change," *Human Relations* 45, no. 9 (1992); Joanne Martin, *Cultures in Organizations* (New York: Oxford University Press, 1992); L. R. Sayles, *Leadership: What Effective Managers Really Do and How They Do It* (New York: McGraw-Hill, 1976); A. M. Pettigrew, "Is Corporate Culture Manageable?" in *Managing Organization*, ed. D. C. Wilson and R. H. Rosenfeld (London: McGraw-Hill, 1990); L. Pondy et al., eds., *Organizational Symbolism* (Greenwich, Conn.: JAI Press, 1983); and Elmer H. Burack, "Changing the Company Culture—The Role of Human Resource Development," *Long Range Planning* 24, no. 1 (February 1991).

In addition to the usual journals and magazines, such as *Harvard Business Review*, change management issues are addressed in major journals on management such as the *Journal of Management, Administrative Science Quarterly, Organization Studies, Journal of Management Studies*, and the *Academy of Management Review*; journals covering psychological and sociological issues such as the *Journal of Social Issues, American Sociology Review, Journal of Applied Behavioral Science*; and journals addressing issues of training and human resources such as *Training & Development, Training, Human Resources Planning*, and *Personnel Journal*.

1. Peter M. Senge, *The Fifth Discipline: The Art & Practice of the Learning Organization* (New York: Doubleday, 1990). See also the work of Peter F. Drucker (esp. *The New Realities: In Government and Politics, in Economics and Business, in Society and World View* [New York: Harper & Row, 1989]); Tom Peters and Robert H. Waterman, Jr. (esp. *In Search of Excellence: Lessons from America's Best Run Companies* [New York: Harper & Row, 1982]): Edward de Bono (esp. *Six Thinking Hats* [Boston: Little, Brown, 1985]); and Peter B. Vaill, *Managing as a Performing Art: New Ideas for a World of Chaotic Change* (San Francisco: Jossey-Bass, 1989).

2. Frank Sonnenberg and Beverly Goldberg, "Encouraging Employee-Led Change Through Constructive Learning Processes," *Journal of Business Strategy* 13, no. 6 (November–December 1992): 54.

3. See the general note to this chapter.

4. This case study, and much of the material presented in this chapter, is drawn from Beverly Goldberg, "Manage Change—Not the Chaos Caused by Change," *Management Review*, November 1992.

5. John A. Stone, *Inside ADW and IEF: The Promise and Reality of CASE* (New York: McGraw-Hill, 1992).

6. There are a number of arguments about whether change should be driven across an organization or should be top-down. In our experience, the combination, while somewhat more difficult to manage, brings faster results. For an example of contrasts, see Michael Beer, Russell A. Eisenstat, and Bert Spector, "Why Change Programs Don't Produce Change," *Harvard Business Review*, November–December 1990; the sentence "Effective corporate renewal starts at the bottom, through informal efforts to solve business problems" appears above the title of the article (p. 158). For an emphasis on the top-down approach, see Rosabeth Moss Kanter, "Championing Change: An Interview with Bell Atlantic's CEO Raymond Smith," *Harvard Business Review*, January–February 1991; here the sentence above the title (p. 119) is "Infusing bureaucracy with entrepreneurial energy starts at the top."

7. Frank Sonnenberg and Beverly Goldberg, "It's a Great Idea, But. . . ," *Training and Development*, March 1992, p. 68.

8. Tom Peters, *Thriving on Chaos: Handbook for a Management Revolution* (New York: Knopf, 1987), p. 9.

CHAPTER 14

The literature on measuring manufacturing productivity goes back to the work of efficiency experts of the 1920s, esp. Frederick W. Taylor and Frank and Lillian Gilbreth (see esp. C. D. Wrege and R. G. Greenwood, *Frederick W. Taylor the Father of Scientific Management: Myth and Reality* [Homewood, Ill.: Business One Irwin, 1991]). Among the most useful books covering these areas that lend themselves to so-called hard measures are, for manufacturing, Paul Kleindorfer, ed., *The Management of Productivity and Technology in Manufacturing* (New York: Plenum, 1985), and for the service sector, H. David Sherman, *Service Organization Productivity Management* (Hamilton, Ont.: Society of Management Accountants of Canada, 1988), and Paul A. Strassmann, *Information Payoff: The Transformation of Work in the Electronic Age* (New York: Free Press, 1985).

There is also considerable literature on financial measurements of which the development of activity-based costing is among the most useful for measuring the value of information technology (which is complicated by the fact that future value of the capital investment in hardware is dependent on application development), esp. Robin Cooper and Robert S. Kaplan, "Profit Priorities from Activity-Based Costing," *Harvard Business Review*, May–June 1991.

Among the most useful journals in this area are *Performance Improvement Quarterly*, *Training and Development*, *Management Review*, and *Organizational Behavior and Human Decision Processes*.

1. Robert S. Kaplan and David P. Norton, "The Balanced Scorecard—Measures That Drive Performance," *Harvard Business Review*, January–February 1992, p. 71.

2. Ibid., p. 79.

3. The study was a joint effort by the American Quality Foundation and Ernst & Young. Over five hundred companies in four nations took part.

4. The literature on activity-based costing, as noted in the general note to this chapter, is growing, including texts produced by accounting firms and commercial publishers.

5. For the most useful accounts of benchmarking, see Robert C. Camp, *Benchmarking: The Search for Industry Best Practices That Lead to Superior Performance* (Milwaukee: ASQC Quality Press, 1989), and Michael Spendolini, *The Benchmarking Book* (New York: AMACOM, 1992). Also see Beverly Geber, "Benchmarking: Measuring Yourself Against the Best," *Training*, November 1990; Rob Walker, "Rank Xerox—Management Revolution, *Long Range Planning* 25 (Fall 1992); and Alexandra Biesada, "Benchmarking," *Financial World*, September 17, 1991.

6. The process used grows out of involvement with Professor Jonathan Miller of the Graduate School of Business at the University of Cape Town in South Africa and one of his graduate students, Pamela Innes, who were pursuing a technique for measuring perceptions of the relative importance and performance of IT. See Jonathan Miller, "I/S—How Effective Is Information Technology in Principal and Practice?" in *Management's Measurement of Information Services*, ed. Robert Medvedeff (Carrollton, Texas: Chantico, 1992), pp. 106–22.

7. Arranging for benchmarking partners can sometimes be difficult. In this case, contacts at high levels in the organization helped persuade their CIOs to cooperate, reassuring them that we would not reveal the results to anyone in the cooperating organization except the CIO (and that each CIO would learn only the identity of the hospital that asked for the benchmarking). Our initial contacts in each organization faithfully adhered to that promise,

never asking about the results. Our ability to do this was a result of networks created over decades; for most groups that choose to benchmark, there are organizations such as the International Benchmarking Clearinghouse, the Council on Benchmarking, and the Benchmarking Competency Center that are very helpful. For details on these groups and other useful information, see Barbara Ettorre, "Benchmarking: The Next Generation," *Management Review*, June 1993.

8. Useful discussions of general business performance measurement can be found in H. James Harrington, *Business Process Improvement: The Breakthrough Strategy for Total Quality, Productivity, and Competiveness* (New York: McGraw-Hill, 1991), esp. chap. 7; Dorsey J. Talley, *Total Quality Management—Cost and Performance Measures* (Milwaukee: ASQC Quality Press, 1991); and Harry V. Roberts and Bernard F. Sergesketter, *Quality Is Personal* (New York: Free Press, 1993).

9. This number is significantly lower than that for, say, airlines, which run 6 to 8 percent because of their intense reliance on information technology. The organizations involved in the benchmarking project also ran above average.

10. Charles Kriebel, "Understanding the Strategic Investment in Information Technology," in *Information Technology & Management Strategy*, ed. Kenneth C. Laudon and Jon Turner (Englewood Cliffs, N.J.: Prentice Hall, 1989), p. 113.

11. Myron Magnet, "Good News for the Service Economy," *Fortune*, May 3, 1993, p. 47.

CHAPTER 15

1. Margaret J. Wheatley, "Comprehending Chaos," *Brigham Young Magazine*, February 1993, p. 25.

2. Oren Harari, "The Danger of Success," *Management Review*, July 1993, p. 29.

3. Arie de Geus, "Planning as Learning," *Harvard Business Review*, March–April 1988, p. 70.

4. Pierre Wack, "Scenarios: Shooting the Rapids," *Harvard Business Review*, November–December 1985, p. 140.

5. A. Kahane, *Global Scenarios for the Energy Industry: Challenge and Response* (England: Shell International Petroleum Company, 1991), p. x.

6. Philip Hunter, "Tanking Up on Technology," *InformationWeek*, February 18, 1991, p. 20.

7. Peter Schwartz, *The Art of the Long View: Planning for the Future in an Uncertain World* (New York: Doubleday, 1991), p. 95.

8. Bruce Smart, ed., *Beyond Compliance: A New Industry View of the Environment* (Washington, D.C.: World Resources Institute, 1991), p. 275.

Select Bibliography

Ackoff, R. "Mission Statements." *Planning Review* 15, no. 4 (1985).

Alexander, C. *Notes on the Synthesis of Form*. Cambridge, Mass.: Harvard University Press, 1964.

Altany, D. "Copycats." *Industry Week,* November 5, 1990.

Anderson, J. "Mission Statements Bond Corporate Culture." *Personnel Journal,* October 1987.

Baily, M. N., and Chakrabarti, A. K. *Innovation and the Productivity Crisis*. Washington, D.C.: Brookings Institution, 1988.

Barone, M. *Our Country: The Shaping of America from Roosevelt to Reagan*. New York: Free Press, 1990.

Barriff, M. L., and Galbraith, J. R. "Intraorganizational Power Considerations for Designing Information Systems." *Accounting, Organizations and Society* 3, no. 1 (August 1978).

Bazerman, M. H., and Neale, M. A. *Negotiating Rationally*. New York: Free Press, 1992.

Beatty, C. A., and Lee, G. L. "Leadership Among Middle Managers—An Exploration in the Context of Technological Change." *Human Relations* 45, no. 9 (1992).

Beer, M., Eisenstat, R. A., and Spector, B. *The Critical Path to Corporate Renewal*. Boston: Harvard Business School Press, 1990.

Beer, M., Eisenstat, R. A., and Spector, B. "Why Change Programs Don't Produce Change." *Harvard Business Review*, November–December 1990.

Bellman, G. M. *The Consultant's Calling*. San Francisco: Jossey-Bass, 1990.

Benjamin, R. I., Rockart, J.F., Scott Morton, M. S., and Wyman, J. "Information Technology: A Strategic Opportunity." *Sloan Management Review* 255, no. 3 (1984).

Bennis, W., and Nanus, B. *Leaders: The Strategies for Taking Charge*. New York: Harper & Row, 1985.

Berle, A. A., and Means, G. C. *The Modern Corporation and Private Property*. New York: Macmillan, 1932.

Bidgood, T., and Jelley, B. "Modelling Corporate Information Needs: Fresh Approaches to the Information Architecture." *The Journal of Strategic Information Systems* 1, no. 1 (December 1991).

Biesada, A. "Benchmarking." *Financial World,* September 17, 1991.

Bleeke, J., and Ernst, D., eds. *Collaborating to Compete: Using Strategic Alliances and Acquisitions in the Global Marketplace*. New York: Wiley, 1993.

Boland, R. J., Jr. "The Process and Product of System Design." *Management Science* 24, no. 9 (May 1978).

Bostrom, R. P., and Heinen, J. S. "MIS Problems and Failures: A Socio-Technical Perspective, Parts I and II." *MIS Quarterly* 1, no. 3 (September 1977).

Bostrom, R. P., and Heinen, J. S. "MIS Problems and Failures: A Socio-Technical Perspective, Parts III and IV." *MIS Quarterly* 1, no. 4 (December 1977).

Boynton, A. C., and Zmud, R. W. "An Assessment of Critical Success Factors." *Sloan Management Review* 25, no. 4 (Summer 1984).

Boynton, A. C., and Zmud, R. W. "A Critical Assessment of Information Technology Planning Literature." Working paper, University of North Carolina, Chapel Hill, 1985.

Boynton, A. C., and Zmud, R. W. "Information Technology Planning in the 1990s: Directions for Practice and Research." *MIS Quarterly* 11 (1987).

Brown, L. R., Flavin, C., and Kane, H. *Vital Signs: 1992: The Trends That Are Shaping Our Future.* New York: Norton/Worldwatch Books, 1992. This is the ninth annual edition in this valuable series.

Brown, T. "Larry Miller: The Cover on a Jigsaw-Puzzle Box." *Industry Week*, May 20, 1991.

Bulkeley, W. "Information Age: Computers Start to Lift U.S. Productivity." *The Wall Street Journal*, March 1, 1993: B8.

Bullen, C., and Rockart, J. F. "A Primer on Critical Success Factors." CISR Working Paper no. 69. Center for Information Systems Research, Sloan School of Management, MIT, Cambridge, Mass., June 1981.

Burack, E. H. " Changing the Company—The Role of Human Resource Development." *Long Range Planning* 24, no. 1 (February 1991).

Business Week editors. "Who's Excellent Now? Some of the Best-Seller's Picks Haven't Been Doing So Well Lately." *BusinessWeek*, November 5, 1984.

Camp, R. C. *Benchmarking: The Search for Industry Best Practices That Lead to Superior Performance.* Milwaukee: ASQC Quality Press, 1989.

Caracas Report on Alternative Development Indicators. *Redefining Wealth and Progress.* New York: Bootstrap Press/TOES, 1989.

Carroll, J., Thomas, J., and Miller, L. "Aspects of Solution Structure in Design Problem Solving." IBM Research Report, RC–7078, 1978.

Cash, J. J., and Konsynski, B. "I/S Redraws Competitive Boundaries." *Harvard Business Review*, March–April 1985.

Cascio, W. F. "Downsizing: What Do We Know? What Have We Learned?" *Academy of Management Executive* 7, no. 1 (1993).

Cetron, M., and Davies, O. *American Renaissance: Our Life at the Turn of the 21st Century.* New York: St. Martin's Press, 1989.

Chandler, A. D., Jr. *Strategy and Structure: Chapters in the History of the American Enterprise.* Cambridge, Mass.: MIT Press, 1962.

Chandler, A. D., Jr. "Corporate Strategy and Structure: Some Current Considerations." *Society*, March–April 1991.

Chomsky, N. *Aspects of the Theory of Syntax.* Boston: MIT Press, 1965.

Chomsky, N. *Language and Mind.* New York: Harcourt Brace Jovanovich, 1972.

Chomsky, N. *Syntactic Structures.* Mouton, 1978 (orig. 1957).

Chomsky, N. *Rules & Representations.* New York: Columbia University Press, 1982.

Churchman, C. W. *The Design of Inquiring Systems: Basic Concepts of Systems and Organization.* New York: Basic Books, 1971.

Clement, R. W. "The Changing Face of Organization Development: Views of a Manager-Turned-Academic." *Business Horizons* 35, no. 3 (May–June 1992).

Cleveland, H. *The Knowledge Executive: Leadership in an Information Society.* New York: Truman Talley Books/Dutton, 1989.

Coase, R. *The Firm, the Market, and the Law.* Chicago: University of Chicago Press, 1988.

Cohen, J. "Benchmarking for Competitive Advantage." *Management Review* September 1990.

Cohen, J. "Rediscovering the Market Drive." *Management Review*, September 1990.

Cohn, J. *The Conscience of the Corporations: Business and Urban Affairs 1967–1970.* Baltimore: Johns Hopkins University Press, 1971.

Cooper, R., and Kaplan, R. S. "Profit Priorities from Activity-Based Costing." *Harvard Business Review*, May–June 1991.

Corcoran, E. "Racing Light: Can Computer Networks Handle the Traffic?" *Scientific American*, December 1992.

Corcoran, E. "Thinking Green: Can Environmentalism Be a Strategic Advantage?" *Scientific American*, December 1992.

Cunningham, J. B., Farquharson, J., and Hull, D. "A Profile of the Human Fears of Technological Change." *Technological Forecasting & Social Change* 40, no. 4 (December 1991).

Daft, R. L., and Weick, K. E. "Toward a Model of Organizations as Interpretation Systems." *The Academy of Management Review* 9, no. 2 (April 1984).

Davenport, T. *Process Innovation: Reengineering Work Through Information Technology*. Boston: Harvard Business School Press, 1992.

David, F. R. "How Companies Define Their Mission." *Long Range Planning*, February 1989.

Davis, G. B. "Comments on the Critical Success Factors Method for Obtaining Management Information Requirements in Article by John F. Rockart." *MIS Quarterly* 3, no. 3 (September 1979).

Davis, G. B. "Letter to the Editor." *MIS Quarterly* 4, no. 2 (June 1980).

Davis, S., and Davidson, W. *Twenty-Twenty Vision: Turbocharge Your Business Today to Thrive in Tomorrow's Environment*. New York: Simon & Schuster, 1991.

Deal, T. E., and Kennedy, A. A. *Corporate Cultures: The Rites and Rituals of Corporate Life*. Reading, Mass.: Addison-Wesley, 1982.

de Bono, E. *Six Thinking Hats*. Boston: Little, Brown, 1985.

De Greene, K. B. *Sociotechnical Systems: Factors in Analysis, Design and Management*. Englewood Cliffs, N.J.: Prentice Hall, 1979.

DeLong, D. W., and Rockart, J. W. *Executive Support Systems: The Emergence of Top Management Computer Use*. Homewood, Ill.: Business One Irwin, 1988.

Dennis, A. R., Nunamaker, J. F., Jr., Paranka, D., and Vogel, D. R. "A New Role for Computers in Strategic Management." *The Journal of Business Strategy*, September–October 1990.

Dertouzos, M. L., Lester, R. K., and Solow, R. M. *Made in America: Regaining the Productive Edge*. Cambridge, Mass.: MIT Press, 1989.

Diebold, J. *The Innovators*. New York: Dutton, 1990.

Drucker, P. F. *Management: Tasks, Responsibilities, and Practices*. New York: Harper & Row, 1973.

Drucker, P. F. "The Coming of the New Organization." *Harvard Business Review*, January–February 1988.

Drucker, P. F. *The New Realities: In Government and Politics, in Economics and Business, in Society and World View*. New York: Harper & Row, 1989.

Dublin, M. *Futurehype: The Tyranny of Prophecy*. New York: Dutton, 1991.

Duffy, N. M., and Assad, M. G. *Information Management: Strategy Formulation and Implementation*. Cape Town, South Africa: Oxford University Press, 1989.

Edwards, M. R. "Symbiotic Leadership: A Creative Partnership for Managing Organizational Effectiveness." *Business Horizons* 35, no. 3 (May–June 1992).

Eigerman, M. R. "Who Should Be Responsible for Business Strategy?" *The Journal of Business Strategy*, November–December 1988.

Ettorre, B. "Benchmarking: The Next Generation." *Management Review*, June 1993.

Filene, E. A. *The Way Out: A Forecast of Coming Changes in American Business and Industry*. New York: Doubleday, Page & Company, 1926.

Finkelstein, J., ed. *Windows on a New World: The Third Industrial Revolution*. New York: Greenwood Press, 1989.

Fisher, R., and Ury, W. *Getting to Yes: Negotiating Agreement Without Giving In*. New York: Penguin Books, 1983.

Fligstein, N., and Brantley, P. "Bank Control, Owner Control, or Organizational Dynamics: Who Controls the Modern Corporation?" *American Journal of Sociology* 98, no. 2 (September 1992).

Foster, R. *Innovation: The Attacker's Advantage*. New York: Summit Books, 1986.

Frohman, M. P., and Pascarella, P. "How to Write a Purpose Statement." *Industry Week*, March 23, 1987.

Gane, C., and Sarson, T. *Structured Systems Analysis: Tools and Techniques*. Englewood Cliffs, N.J.: Prentice Hall, 1979.

Garten, J. E. *A Cold Peace: America, Japan, Germany, and the Struggle for Supremacy*, A Twentieth Century Fund Book. New York: Times Books/Random House, 1992.

Geber, B. "Benchmarking: Measuring Yourself Against the Best." *Training*, November 1990.

Geisler, E., ed. *Strategic Management of Information and Telecommunication Technology*. Special issue of the *International Journal of Technology Management*. Geneva: Intersciences Enterprises, 1992.

Ghoshal, S., and Nohria, N. "Horses for Courses: Organizational Forms for Multinational Corporations." *Sloan Management Review* 34, no. 2 (Winter 1993).

Gleick, J. *Chaos: Making a New Science*. New York: Viking, 1987.

Goldberg, B. "Finding Profit in Not-for-Profits." *Management Review*, June 1991.

Goldberg, B. "Manage Change—Not the Chaos Caused by Change." *Management Review*, November 1992.

Grumball, K. "Change Management—Vital Role for 'User Champions.'" *Financial Times*, June 14, 1991.

Gunn, T. G. *21st Century Manufacturing: Creating Winning Business Performance*. New York: Harper Business, 1992.

Hammer, M. "Reengineering Work: Don't Automate, Obliterate." *Harvard Business Review*, July–August 1990.

Harmon, R. L. *Reinventing the Factory II: Managing the World Class Factory*. New York: Free Press, 1992.

Harrington, H. J. *Business Process Improvement: The Breakthrough Strategy for Total Quality, Productivity, and Competitiveness*. New York: McGraw-Hill, 1991.

Harris, G. T. "The Post-Capitalist Executive: An Interview With Peter F. Drucker." *Harvard Business Review*, May–June 1993.

Hawking, S. W. *A Brief History of Time*. New York: Bantam Books, 1988.

Hax, A. C., and Majluf, N. S. *Strategic Management: An Integrative Perspective*, Englewood Cliffs, N.J.: Prentice Hall, 1984.

Heckscher, C. *The New Unionism: Employee Involvement in the Changing Corporation*, A Twentieth Century Fund Book. New York: Basic Books, 1988.

Heckscher, C. "State of the Debate: Can Business Beat Bureaucracy?" *The American Prospect*, Spring 1991.

Heller, R. *The Decision Makers*. New York: Truman Talley Books, 1991.

Henderson, J. C. "Managing the Design Environment." Working paper, Massachusetts Institute of Technology, Cambridge, 1986.

Henderson, J. C. "Plugging into Strategic Partnerships: The Critical I/S Connection." *Sloan Management Review* 31, no. 3 (1990).

Henderson, J. C., and Nutt, P. C. "On the Design of Planning Information Systems." *The Academy of Management Review* 3, no. 4 (October 1978).

Henderson, J. C., Rockart, J. F., and Sifonis, J. G. "A Planning Methodology for Integrating Management Support Systems." In *The Rise of Managerial Computing: The Best of the Center for Information Systems Research, Sloan School of Management*, edited by J. F. Rockart and C. V. Bullen. Homewood, Ill.: Dow Jones-Irwin, 1986.

Henderson, J. C., Rockart J. F., and Sifonis, J. G. "A Planning Methodology for Integrating Management Support Systems into Strategic Information Systems Planning." *Journal of Management Information Systems* 4, no. 1 (Summer 1987).

Henderson, J. C., and Sifonis, J. G. "The Value-Added of Strategic IS Planning: Understanding Consistency, Validity, and IS Markets." *MIS Quarterly* 12, no. 2 (June 1988).

Henderson, J. C., and Sifonis, J. G. "Middle Out Strategic Planning: The Value of IS Planning to Business Planning." In *Information Technology & Management Strategy*, edited by K. C. Laudon and J. Turner. Englewood Cliffs, N.J.: Prentice Hall, 1989.

Henderson, J. C., and Sifonis, J. G. "A Model Predicts Future Use of CASE Technology." *Chief Information Officer Journal* 2, no. 2 (Fall 1989).

Henderson, J. C., and Venkatraman, N. "Understanding Strategic Alignment." *Strategic Alignment: Managing for Synergy*, supplement to *Business Quarterly* 55, no. 3 (Winter 1991).

Herman, E. S. *Corporate Control, Corporate Power*, A Twentieth Century Fund Study. New York: Cambridge University Press, 1981.

Hirsch, F. *Social Limits to Growth*, A Twentieth Century Fund Study. Cambridge, Mass.: Harvard University Press, 1976.

Hofer, C. W., and Schendel, D. *Strategy Formulation: Analytical Concepts*. St. Paul: West, 1978.

Hofer, C. W., and Schendel, D., eds. *Strategic Management: A New View of Business Policy and Planning*. Boston: Little, Brown, 1979.

Holusha, J. "Pushing the Envelope at Boeing." *The New York Times*, November 10, 1991, Sect. 3, p. 1.

Horning, B. "Language Busters." *Technology Review*, October 1991.

Horton, F. W., Jr., and Marchand, D. A. *Infotrends: Profiting From Your Information Resources*. New York: Wiley, 1986.

Howard, G. S., and Rai, A. "Making It Work: Tips for Implementing IS Innovations." *Information Strategy: The Executive's Journal* (Winter 1993).

Howard, W. G., and Guile, B. R., eds. *Profiting from Innovation*. New York: Free Press, 1992.

Huge, E. C., and Vasily, G. "Leading Cultural Change: Developing Vision and Change Strategy." In *Total Quality: An Executive's Guide for the 1990s*, edited by C. Huge. Homewood, Ill.: Dow Jones-Irwin, 1990.

IBM Corporation. *Business Systems Planning: Information Systems Planning Guide*. Application Manual GE20–0527–4, White Plains, N.Y., July 1984.

Ireland, R. D., and Hitt, M. A. "Mission Statements: Importance, Challenge, and Recommendations for Development." *Business Horizons* 35, no. 3 (May–June 1992).

Ives, B., and Learmonth, G. P. "The Information System as a Competitive Weapon." *Communications of the ACM* 27, no. 12 (December 1984).

Jacobs, M. T. *Short-Term America: The Causes and Cures of Our Business Myopia*. Boston: Harvard Business School Press, 1991.

Janeway, E. *The Economics of Chaos on Revitalizing the American Economy*. New York: Dutton, 1989.

Johnston, W. B., and Packer, A. H. "Work and Workers in the Year 2000." In *Workforce 2000: Work and Workers for the 21st Century*. Indianapolis: Hudson Institute, 1987.

Kanter, R. M. *The Change Masters*. New York: Simon & Schuster, 1983.

Kanter, R. M. "Thinking Across Boundaries." *Harvard Business Review*, November–December 1990.

Kanter, R. M. "Championing Change: An Interview with Bell Atlantic's CEO Raymond Smith." *Harvard Business Review*, January–February 1991.

Kanter, R. M. *Dancing with Elephants*.

Kaplan, R. S., and Norton, D. P. "The Balanced Scorecard—Measures That Drive Performance." *Harvard Business Review*, January–February 1992.

Kaufmann, J., ed. *Effective Negotiation: Case Studies in Conference Diplomacy*. The Netherlands: Martinus Nijhoff, 1989.

Kearns, R. L. *Zaibatsu America: How Japanese Firms Are Colonizing Vital U.S. Industries*. New York: Free Press, 1992.

Keen, P. G. W. *Every Manager's Guide to Information Technology*. Boston: Harvard Business School Press, 1991.

Keen, P. G. W. *Shaping the Future*. Boston: Harvard Business School Press, 1991.

Keen, P. G. W., and Gerson, E. M. "The Politics of Software Systems Design." *Datamation* 23, no. 11 (November 1977).

Keen, P. G. W., and Scott Morton, M. S. *Decision Support Systems: An Organizational Perspective.* Reading, Mass.: Addison-Wesley, 1978.

Kemerer, C. F., and Sosa, G. L. "Systems Development Risks in Strategic Information Systems." *Information and Software Technology* 33, no. 3 (April 1991).

Kidder, R. M. *An Agenda for the 21st Century.* Cambridge, Mass.: MIT Press, 1989.

Kiechel, W. III. "Corporate Strategists Under Fire." *Fortune*, December 27, 1982.

King, W. R. "Strategic Planning for Management Information Systems." *MIS Quarterly* 2, no. 1 (March 1978).

King, W. R. "Evaluating Strategic Planning Systems." *Strategic Management Journal* 4, no. 3 (July–September 1983).

King, W. R., and Zmud, R. W. "Managing Information Systems: Policy Planning, Strategic Planning and Operational Planning." In *Proceedings of the Second International Conference on Information Systems*, pp. 299–308, Cambridge, Mass., December 7–9, 1981.

Kleindorfer, P., ed. *The Management of Productivity and Technology in Manufacturing.* New York: Plenum, 1985.

Konsynski, B. B., Kottemann, J. E., Nunamaker, J. F., and Stott, J. W. "PLEXSYS–84: An Integrated Development Environment for Information Systems." *Journal of Management Information Systems* 1, no. 3 (Winter 1984–85).

Kotlikoff, L. J. *Generational Accounting: Knowing Who Pays, and When, for What We Spend.* New York: Free Press, 1992.

Kottemann, J. E., and Konsynski, B. R. "Metasystems in Information Systems Development." In *Proceedings of the Fifth International Conference on Information Systems*, pp. 187–204, Tucson, November 28–30, 1984.

Kotter, J. P. *The Leadership Factor.* New York: Free Press, 1988.

Kotter, J. P. *A Force for Change: How Leadership Differs From Management.* New York: Free Press, 1990.

Kotter, J. P., and Heskett, J. L. *Corporate Culture and Performance.* New York: Free Press, 1992.

Kriebel, C. "Understanding the Strategic Investment in Information Technology." In *Information Technology & Management Strategy*, edited by K. C. Laudon and J. Turner. Englewood Cliffs, N.J.: Prentice Hall, 1989.

Lawrie, J. "The ABCs of Change Management." *Training & Development Journal*, March 1990.

Lax, D., and Sebenius, J. *The Manager as Negotiator.* New York: Free Press, 1986.

Leicht, K. T., Parcel, T. L, and Kaufman, R. L. "Measuring the Same Concepts Across Diverse Organizations." *Social Science Research* 21 (1992).

Leidecker, J. K., and Bruno, A. V. "Identifying and Using Critical Success Factors." *Long Range Planning*, February 1984.

Leonard-Barton, D. "Introducing Production Innovation into an Organization: Structured Methods for Producing Computer Software." Center for Information Systems Research Working Paper no. 103, Sloan School of Management, Massachusetts Institute of Technology, Cambridge, Mass., June 1983.

Linden, L. H. "The Business of Technology." *Issues in Science and Technology*, Summer 1992.

Lorange, P., and Vancil, R. F. *Strategic Planning Systems.* Englewood Cliffs, N.J.: Prentice Hall, 1977.

Lozano, B. *The Invisible Workforce: Transforming American Business with Outside and Home-Based Workers.* New York: Free Press, 1989.

Luttwak, E. N. *Strategy: The Logic of War and Peace.* Cambridge, Mass.: Harvard University Press, 1987.

McFarlan, F. W. "Information Technology Changes the Way You Compete." *Harvard Business Review*, May–June 1984.

McGee, J., and Prusak, L. *Managing Information Strategically.* New York: Wiley, 1993.

McLean, E. R., and Soden, J. V. *Strategic Planning for MIS.* New York: Wiley, 1977.

Magnet, M. "Good News for the Service Economy." *Fortune*, May 3, 1993.

Makridakis, S. G. *Forecasting, Planning, and Strategy for the 21st Century*. New York: Free Press, 1990.

Markus, M. L., and Pfeffer, J. "Power and the Design and Implementation of Accounting and Control Systems." *Accounting, Organizations and Society* 8, nos. 2/3 (July 1983).

Martin, J. *Cultures in Organizations*. New York: Oxford University Press, 1992.

Mason, J. H. "Innovation in Professional Services: Potential Productivity and Trade Improvement." *Technological Forecasting & Social Change* 42, no. 1 (August 1992).

Mason, R. O., and Mitroff, I. I. "A Program for Research on Management Information Systems." *Management Science* 19, no. 5 (January 1973).

Mason, R. O., and Mitroff, I. I. *Challenging Strategic Planning Assumptions: Theory, Cases, and Techniques*. New York: Wiley, 1981.

Michman, R. D. "Why Forecast for the Long Term?" *The Journal of Business Strategy*, September–October 1989.

Miller, J. "I/S—How Effective Is Information Technology in Principal and Practice?" In *Management's Measurement of Information Services*, edited by R. Medvedeff. Carrollton, Tex.: Chantico, 1992.

Minsky, H. P. *Stabilizing an Unstable Economy*, A Twentieth Century Fund Report. New Haven, Conn.: Yale University Press, 1986.

Mintzberg, H. *Mintzberg on Management: Inside Our Strange World of Organizations*. New York: Free Press, 1989.

Mitroff, I. I., and Featheringham, T. R. "On Systematic Problem Solving and the Error of the Third Kind." *Behavioral Science*, December 1974.

Monks, R. A. G., and Minow, N. *Power and Accountability*. New York: Harper Business, 1991.

Moore, B., and Rader, E. "A Blueprint for the Change Process." *Hospitals*, July 5, 1991.

Moore, J. M. *Writers on Strategy and Strategic Management*. New York: Penguin Books, 1992.

Morgan, G. *Images of Organizations*. Newbury Park, Calif.: Sage, 1986.

Morton, Michael S. ed. *The Corporation of the 1990s: Information Technology and Organizational Transformation*. New York: Oxford University Press, 1991.

Mostow, J. "Toward Better Models of the Design Process." *The AI Magazine* 6, no. 1 (Spring 1985).

Munro, M. C., and Wheeler, B. R. "Planning, Critical Success Factors, and Management's Information Requirements." *MIS Quarterly* 4, no. 4 (December 1980).

Myerson P., and Hamilton, R. D. IV. "Matching Corporate Culture and Technology." *SAM Advanced Management Journal*, Winter 1986.

Naisbitt, J. *Megatrends*. New York: Warner Books, 1982.

Naumann, J. D., and Jenkins, A. M. "Prototyping: The New Paradigm for Systems Development." *MIS Quarterly* 6, no. 3 (September 1982).

Nystrom, P., and Starbuck, W., eds. *Handbook of Organizational Design*. New York: Oxford University Press, 1981.

Ohmae, K. *Beyond National Borders: Reflections on Japan and the World*. Homewood, Ill.: Dow Jones-Irwin, 1987.

Parsons, G. L. "Information Technology: A New Competitive Weapon." *Sloan Management Review* 25, no. 1 (1983).

Pearce, J. A., and Roth, K. "Multinationalization of the Mission Statement." *Advanced Management Journal*, Summer 1988.

Pearson, C. M., and Mitroff, I. I. "From Crisis Prone to Crisis Prepared: A Framework for Crisis Management." *Academy of Management Executive* 7, no. 1 (1993).

Perrow, C. *Complex Organizations: A Critical Essay*. New York: Random House, 1986.

Perry, L. T., Stott, R. G., and Smallwood, W. N. *Real-Time Strategy: Improvising Team-Based Planning for a Fast-Changing World*. New York: Wiley, 1993.

Peters, T. *Thriving on Chaos: Handbook for a Management Revolution*. New York: Knopf, 1987.

Peters, T., and Austin, N. *A Passion for Excellence: The Leadership Difference*. New York: Random House, 1985.

Peters, T., and Waterman, R. H. *In Search of Excellence: Lessons from America's Best Run Companies*. New York: Harper & Row, 1982.

Pettigrew, A. M. "Is Corporate Culture Manageable?" In *Managing Organization*, edited by D. C. Wilson and R. H. Rosenfeld. London: McGraw-Hill, 1990.

Phillips, T. L., and Quinn, J. "The Effects of Alternative Flowcharting Techniques on Performance on Procedural Tasks." *Performance Improvement Quarterly* 6, no. 1 (1993).

Pirow, P. C. *Excellence in Information Systems*. Rough Lea, Eng.: Woodacres, 1988.

Pondy, L., et al., eds. *Organizational Symbolism*. Greenwich, Conn.: JAI Press, 1983.

Porter, M. E. "How Competitive Forces Shape Strategy." *Harvard Business Review*, March–April 1979.

Porter, M. E. *Competitive Strategy: Techniques for Analyzing Industries and Competitors*. New York: Free Press, 1980.

Porter, M. E. *Competitive Advantage: Creating and Sustaining Superior Performance*. New York: Free Press, 1985.

Porter, M. E., and Millar, V. E. "How Information Technology Gives You Competitive Advantage" *Harvard Business Review*, July–August 1984.

Pyburn, P. J. "Linking the MIS Plan with Corporate Strategy: An Exploratory Study." *MIS Quarterly* 7, no. 2 (June 1983).

Quinn, J. B. *Intelligent Enterprise*. New York: Free Press, 1992.

Ranson, S., Hinings, B., and Greenwood, R. "The Structuring of Organization Structures." *Administrative Science Quarterly* 25 (1980).

Roach, S. S. "Services under Siege—The Restructuring Imperative." *Harvard Business Review*, September–October 1991.

Roberts, H. V., and Sergesketter, B. F. *Quality Is Personal*. New York: Free Press, 1993.

Rock, M. L., and Rock, R. H., eds. *Corporate Restructuring: A Guide to Creating the Premium-Valued Company*. New York: McGraw-Hill, 1990.

Rockart, J. F. "Chief Executives Define Their Own Data Needs." *Harvard Business Review*, March–April 1979.

Rockart, J. F., and Bullen, C. V., eds. *The Rise of Managerial Computing*. Homewood, Ill.: Dow Jones-Irwin, 1986.

Rockart, J. F., and Scott Morton, M. S. "Implications of Changes in Information Technology for Corporate Strategy." *Interfaces* 14, no. 1 (1984).

Rockart, J. F., and Short, J. E. "I/T in the 1990s: Managing Organizational Interdependence." *Sloan Management Review* 30, no. 2 (1989).

Rummler, G. A., and Brache, A. P. "Managing the White Space on the Organization Chart." *Supervision*, May 1991.

Sabherwal, R., and King, W. R. "Towards a Theory of Strategic Use of Information Resources." *Information & Management* 20 (1991).

Salk, G. "Time—The Next Source of Competitive Advantage." *Harvard Business Review*, July–August 1988.

Sayles, L. R. *Leadership: What Effective Managers Really Do and How They Do It*. New York: McGraw-Hill, 1976.

Schein, E. H. *Organizational Culture and Leadership*. San Francisco: Jossey-Bass, 1985.

Schendel, D. E., and Hofer, C. W., eds. *Strategic Management: A New View of Business Policy and Planning*. Boston: Little, Brown, 1979.

Schnaars, S. P. *Megamistake: Forecasting and the Myth of Rapid Technological Change*. New York: Free Press, 1989.

Schonberger, R. J. "Is Strategy Strategic? Impact of Total Quality Management on Strategy." *Academy of Management Executive* 6, no. 3 (1992).

Schwartz, P. *The Art of the Long View: Planning for the Future in an Uncertain World*. New York: Doubleday, 1991.

Senge, P. M. *The Fifth Discipline: The Art & Practice of the Learning Organization*. New York: Doubleday, 1990.

Serlin, O. "Measuring OLTP With a Better Yardstick." *Datamation*, July, 15, 1990.

Sherman, H. D. *Service Organization Productivity Management*. Hamilton, Ont.: Society of Management Accountants of Canada, 1988.

Shiller, R. "Who's Minding the Store?" Background paper, in *The Report of the Twentieth Century Fund Task Force on Market Speculation and Corporate Governance*. New York: Twentieth Century Fund Press, 1992.

Sifonis, J. G. "Four Trends in Applying Information Technology." *The President* 24, no. 5 (May 1988).

Sifonis, J. G. "Using Information Systems to Achieve a Competitive Edge." *Chief Information Officer Journal* 1, no. 1 (Summer 1988).

Sifonis, J. G. "The Impact of Technology on Restructuring." In *Corporate Restructuring: A Guide to Creating the Premium-Valued Company*, edited by Milton L. Rock and Robert H. Rock. New York: McGraw-Hill, 1990.

Sivula, C. "The Benchmark War in Transaction Processing." *Datamation*, September 1, 1990.

Sloan, M. P. "Strategic Planning by Multiple Political Futures." *Executives Forum* (1983).

Smart, B., ed. *Beyond Compliance: A New Industry View of the Environment*. Washington, D.C.: World Resources Institute, 1992.

Sonnenberg. F. K. *Managing with a Conscience*. New York: McGraw-Hill, 1993.

Sonnenberg, F. K. *Marketing to Win*. New York: Harper & Row, 1990.

Sonnenberg, F. K., and Goldberg, B. "It's a Great Idea, But. . ." *Training and Development*, March 1992.

Sonnenberg, F. K., and Goldberg, B. "Encouraging Employee-Led Change Through Constructive Learning Processes." *Journal of Business Strategy* 13, no. 6 (November–December 1992).

Spendolini, M. *The Benchmarking Book*. New York: AMACOM, 1992.

Stone, J. A. *Inside ADW and IEF: The Promise and Reality of CASE*. New York: McGraw-Hill, 1992.

Strassmann, P. A. "What Executives Should Know About Information Payoff." *The Consultant* (1985).

Strassmann, P. A. *Information Payoff: The Transformation of Work in the Electronic Age*. New York: Free Press, 1985.

Strassmann, P. A. *The Business Value of Computers: An Executive Guide*. New Canaan, Conn.: Economic Information Press, 1990.

Talley, D. J. *Total Quality Management—Cost and Performance Measures*. Milwaukee: ASQC Quality Press, 1991.

Taravella, S. "Managing Change Successfully: Helping Hospitals Manage a Process Called Change." *Modern Health Care*, July 22, 1991.

Tarr, S. C. "Multiple Perspectives Analysis for Integrating Technology into a Business: A Knowledge Systems Case Study." *Technological Forecasting & Social Change* 40, no. 2 (September 1991).

Thomas, J. C., and Carroll, J. M. "Psychological Study of Design." *Design Studies* 1 (1979).

Tolchin M., and Tolchin, S. *Buying into America: How Foreign Money Is Changing the Face of Our Nation*. New York: Times Books, 1988.

Treacy, M., and Wiersema, F. "Customer Intimacy and Other Value Disciplines." *Harvard Business Review*, January–February 1993.

Ulm, D., and Hickel, J. K. "What Happens After Restructuring?" *The Journal of Business Strategy* 11, no. 4 (July–August 1990).

Ulrich, D., Brockbank, W., and Yeung, A. "Beyond Belief: A Benchmark for Human Resources." *Human Resources Management* 28, no. 3 (Fall 1989).

Vaill, P. B. *Managing as a Performing Art: New Ideas for a World of Chaotic Change*. San Francisco: Jossey-Bass, 1989.

Venkatraman, N. "Research on MIS Planning: Some Guidelines from Strategic Planning Research." *Journal of Management Information Systems* 2, no. 3 (Winter 1985–86).

Venkatraman, N. "Information Technology-Induced Business Reconfiguration: The New Strategic Management Challenge." In *The Corporation of the 1990s: Information Technology and Organizational Transformation*, edited by M. S. Scott Morton. New York: Oxford University Press, 1991.

Wack, P. "Scenarios: Uncharted Waters Ahead." *Harvard Business Review*, September–October 1985.

Wack, P. "Scenarios: Shooting the Rapids." *Harvard Business Review*, November–December 1985.

Walker, R. "Rank Xerox—Management Revolution." *Long Range Planning* 25 (Fall 1992).

Wall, J. "What the Competition Is Doing: Your Need to Know." *Harvard Business Review*, November–December 1974.

Walers, J. "The Cult of Total Quality." *Governing*, May 1992.

Want, J. H. "Corporate Mission." *Management Review*, August 1986.

Waterman, R. H., Jr. *Adhocracy: The Power to Change*. New York: Norton, 1992.

Weitz, R. *New Roads to Development*, A Twentieth Century Fund Essay. Westport, Conn.: Greenwood Press, 1986.

Wheatley, M. J. *Leadership and the New Science: Learning about Organization from an Orderly Universe*. San Francisco: Berrett-Koehler, 1992.

Wheatley, M. J. "Comprehending Chaos." *Brigham Young Magazine*, February 1993.

Whiting, R. "Benchmarking: Lessons from the Best-in-Class." *Electronic Business*, October 7, 1991.

Wilkes, R. B. "Draining the Swamp: Defining Strategic Use of the Information Systems Resource." *Information & Management* 20 (1991).

Williamson, O. *The Economic Institutions of Capitalism*. New York: Free Press, 1985.

Williamson, O., and Winter, S. G., eds. *The Nature of the Firm: Origins, Evolution, and Development*. New York: Oxford University Press, 1993.

Woolfe, R. "The Path to Strategic Alignment." *Information Strategy: The Executive's Journal*, Winter 1993.

Wrege, C. D., and Greenwood, R. G. *Frederick W. Taylor, the Father of Scientific Management: Myth and Reality*. Homewood, Ill.: Business One Irwin, 1991.

Zuboff, S. *In the Age of the Smart Machine*. New York: Basic Books, 1988.

INDEX

Absenteeism, 55
Academic experts, 59, 202
Accountability, 45, 167, 215, 254
Acquisition of companies, 111, 114, 151, 253
Action items for critical success factors, 181, 183–84, 196; developing, 217–18, 247; monitoring, 184–85, 239
Activity-based costing, 240, 241
Activity 1.0. *See* Resource organization
Activity 2.0. *See* External analysis
Activity 3.0. *See* Internal analysis
Activity 4.0. *See* Position paper
Activity 5.0. *See* Options generation
Activity 6.0. *See* Strategic Alignment Model
Activity 7.0. *See* Grand Strategy
Activity 8.0. *See* Change management
Activity 9.0. *See* Monitoring process; Evaluation of planning
Administration, 99, 114–15. *See also* Governance
Administrative infrastructure, 41, 126–27, 128, 143, 144, 155; of information technology, 134–35, 149, 166, 245
Advertising, 52, 63, 137, 145, 226
Aeronautics, 51–52
Agenda-setting, 105, 107
Airlines, 51, 62, 130, 198, 199, 200, 207, 265n. 9
Airports, 51, 62, 96, 243
Alliances: business, 62, 63, 100, 125, 127, 133, 161–63, 166, 168, 243
American Telephone & Telegraph Co. (AT&T), 55, 150, 151
Analyses, 19, 244; evaluation of, 17, 39–41, 42. *See also* Concurrent analyses; External analysis; Integrated strategy; Internal analysis
Analytical process, 121–22

Annual reports, 58
Apple Computer Inc., 175
Assets, 66, 67, 80, 130–31, 134, 155–57, 161–62, 169. *See also* Resources of companies
Assumptions. *See* Critical assumptions
AT&T. *See* American Telephone & Telegraph Co.
Authority, 126, 127, 134, 135, 156, 211–12, 216
Automobile manufacturers, 3–4, 61, 74, 76, 96, 147
Automobile rental companies, 51, 62, 93–94, 95, 96–97, 147–49
Autonomy, 213, 214, 215, 216

Banks, 91, 144–46, 241, 242–43
Baseball, 55, 61
Bellman, Geoffrey M., 35
Bellsouth Company, 57
Benchmarking, 29, 43, 92, 240, 243–44, 253, 254, 265n. 7
Big firms. *See* Large companies
Bingham, Charles W., 254–55
Board members, 56, 199
Boeing Co., 51–52
Book reviews, 59
Bottom line, 40, 138, 197, 239, 246; responsibility for, 145
BPR. *See* Business process redesign
Branch offices, 127
Budget, 72, 181, 198, 199, 200, 201, 245
Budgeting, 41, 236
Bureaucracy, 99, 199, 218, 234, 250
Business. *See* Companies
Business environment, 15, 20, 64, 71, 96–97, 210, 247, 252; competitive, 13, 51, 150, 167, 200, 205, 206, 209, 239, 249. *See also*

Global business environment;
Organizational environment
Business process redesign (BPR), 18, 102–3,
154, 164–65, 167, 168, 183, 241
Business processes, 127–29, 144, 155, 218,
220, 243
Business scope, 24, 65–67, 123–24, 138, 154,
156, 169, 201, 206
Business sector. *See* Industrial sector
Business strategy, 8, 15, 22, 123–26, 203,
218; changing, 18, 101, 175–76, 199,
201–2, 211–13, 254; control over, 124–26,
156–57, 186–87, 215; developing, 188,
198, 201; goals, 64, 165, 254; impact of,
132, 138–39, 143, 144–49, 163, 164–68;
impact on, 23–24, 143, 154–57, 168–69,
208, 242; options for, 114–15, 116, 122,
214–17; support for, 126, 128–29, 166;
understanding, 17, 22, 90–92, 205, 207,
227–29, 242
Business structure, 8, 123, 126–30, 198–99,
201, 205, 218, 250; analyzing, 101–3;
changing, 14, 18; impact of, 208; impact
on, 23–24, 138–39, 143, 144–46, 150–57,
163, 164–65, 167–68, 169–70, 220; options
for, 122, 208–9, 211–17; questions about,
126, 129, 138–39, 144–57; support for,
165; understanding, 17, 125, 206. *See also*
Functional areas of business;
Operational areas of business
Business transformation, 139, 143, 154–57,
168–69, 213–14, 220, 254

Carnegie Endowment, 58
Car rental companies. *See* Automobile
rental companies
CASE. *See* Computer-aided software engineering
Centralization, 115, 116, 127, 135, 145,
147–48, 149, 161, 212
CEO. *See* Chief Executive Officer
Chandler, Alfred D., Jr., 121
Change, 4, 50, 53–55; adapting to, 3, 5, 42,
158; anticipating, 19, 50, 57, 193; forces
of, 6–7, 22, 247; impact of, 4, 5–6, 42, 46,
49, 50, 54, 83, 94, 104; resistance to, 219,
234; speed of, 7, 49, 54, 212, 220, 222. *See
also* Organizational change; Trends
Change agents, 9, 25, 214, 220, 226–27,
231–32
Change managers, 31, 99
Change management (Activity 8.0), 35, 41,
116, 185, 218, 219, 234–35, 253; classic

theory of, 222–24; examples, 226–29, 238;
goals, 12, 19, 46, 234; importance of, 27,
29, 219–20; methods in, 224–25, 230–34
Chaos theory, 50
Chemical industry, 66
Chief Executive Officer (CEO), 37, 38, 70,
78, 99, 114–15. *See also* Managing
Director
Chief Financial Officer (CFO), 37, 70, 112,
126
Chief Information Officer (CIO), 37, 38, 63,
70, 71–72, 126
Choice. *See* Decisionmaking
CIO. *See* Chief Information Officer
Clendenin, John, 57
Cleveland, Harlan, 6, 36
Client server systems, 39–40, 115, 132, 134
Communication: in companies, 57, 208, 218,
224–25, 228–32; with customers, 241, 244;
in management, 20, 35, 38–39, 42, 92,
116, 117, 236, 254; in planning, 36, 38–39,
41–44, 116–17, 136, 148, 214, 217, 218,
220. *See also* Telecommunications;
Vocabulary, and communication
Communications department, 229, 230
Communications management, 41, 230
Communications sector, 52, 54, 150–54,
155–57
Communications technology, 131, 132, 133,
134, 149, 196, 174–75
Companies, 7, 55, 68–69, 90, 123; alignment
of, 142, 158, 169, 182–83, 202, 242, 247;
effectiveness of, 143, 154, 197, 210, 239;
responsibilities, 149, 156–57, 189, 195–96;
threats to, 22, 94, 100, 101; uniqueness of,
26, 89, 90, 124, 145, 199, 205, 246. *See also*
Large companies; Small companies;
companies in specific industries, e.g., Oil
companies
Companion programs, 62
Company goals, 71, 76, 176, 188, 239, 247;
changing, 38, 78, 181; and competition,
103; consistency in, 90, 91; defining, 150;
identifying, 72–73, 189–90, 196; support
for, 73, 74; understanding, 116; view of,
70. *See also* Mission statement
Company growth, 91, 146, 161, 187, 188–89,
194, 196; constraints on, 80; opportunities for, 62, 66, 67, 99, 109, 110, 175,
242–43, 247
Competencies, 99, 123, 147, 156, 193; acquiring, 218; assessing, 124, 143; assumptions about, 242; of information

technology, 131, 132–33, 134, 200; support for, 149, 154; understanding, 206
Competition, 206, 212, 218; analysis of, 17, 42, 51–52, 54, 62–63, 76, 99, 101, 192, 209; assumptions about, 71, 92, 78, 84, 147; competencies of, 147, 192; creating, 56, 110, 150, 200
Competitive advantage, 71, 80, *81*, 110; effect of change on, 6, 55, 63, 197, 251; gaining, 54, 64, 74, 79, 83–84, 245
Competitive Advantage (Porter), 50
Competitiveness, 42, 124, 167, 190, 208; ability, 4, 22, 94, 238; loss of, 4, 248, 254; maintaining, 5, 12, 127, 151–54, 197, 210, 219–20
Competitive strategy, 258
Complaints, 46–47, 91, 108, 180, 201, 207–8, 244
Computer-aided software engineering (CASE), 227–28, 229, 230–32
Computer applications, 130, 134, 166, 167, 200
Computer architecture, 31, 134, 151, 152, 156
Computer companies, 3–4, 55, 175; case histories, 161–63, 164–69; examples using, 101, 123, 124, 125, 127, 128, 129, 132, 133, 135, 136
Computer experts, 63, 135–36, 166, 228
Computer hardware, 63, 130; and IT strategy, 39–40, 115, 116, 131, 132, 134, 135; and IT structure, 146, 150, 165, 166
Computer software, 130, 133, 134, 135, 165, 187
Computer systems, 130, 134, 148–49, 166
Computer technology, 51–52, 54, 150, 151–54, 163, 165, 166
Conceptual Planning Model, 15–19. *See also* specific activities, e.g., Internal analysis (Activity 3.0)
Concurrent analyses, 138, 167, 196, 203, 213–14; of external and internal analyses, 15, 20, 47, 64, 65; of strategies, 18, 123, 143, 213–14
Conferences, 56, 59
Conflict management, 39–40
Consensus building, 107, 108, 115, 180, 182
Consultants. *See* External experts
Container shipping, 201, 205
Contingency plans, 50
Continuous learning. *See* Learning organization
Contracting out. *See* Outsourcing

Control, 94, 193. *See also* Empowerment; Control under subjects, e.g., Business strategy, control over
Convenience store sector, 94, 100, 109–12
Cooperation, 98, 115, 185, 205, 208, 212–13, 214, 216, 217, 218
Coordination, 36, 212–13, 216, 217–18. *See also* Information, coordination
Core competencies, 124, 147, 149, 193, 242
Core technologies, 176
Corporate behavior, 45–46, 50, 199, 208, 218, 234, 238
Corporate culture, 3, 23, 103, 126, 176, 198, 244; adapting to change in, 25, 203, 219, 221–29, 251; changing, 19, 35, 37, 46, 210, 234; conflict in, 134, 161, 180, 227–30; flexibility in, 14, 50, 175, 208, 212, 225, 255; understanding, 206
Corporate image, 56, 145, 147–48, 176, 181, 183, 189, 190, 193
Corporations. *See* Companies
Costs, 55, 56, 80, 190, 195, 225; of employees, 136, 154, 183, 233, 238; of operations, 73, 101–3, 127, 183, 244; of options, 105, 111, 113, 115, 133, 170; of planning, 6, 58, 59–60; of products, 66, 241; of services, 95, 96, 97, 147, 150, 151, 153, 154, 187; sharing, 133; of technology, 52, 136, 153, 154, 166, 207, 208, 245
Creativity, 5, 8, 53, 63, 155, 221, 234
Credit checks, 128, 129, 151, 164–65
Creighton, John W., Jr., 254
Crime and business, 109, 110
Critical assumptions (CAs), 71, 93, 98, 181, 209–10, 242; changing, 101; definition, 77; developing, 72, 115, 150–51, 190, 217–18, 241; identifying, 115; importance of, 78–80, 113; inconsistency in, 90–91; monitoring, 79–84, 236; number of, 80
Critical processes, 132, 133, 167, 220, 243
Critical success factors (CSFs), 43–47, 71, 93, 98, 181, 209, 216, 234, 246; achievability of, 75, 181–85, 239; changing, 101; of competition, 62; consistency in, 90, 103; control over, 76, 79, 184–85, 238; developing, 72, 74–77, 79, 150, 240, 241, 247; identifying, 73–74, 78–79, 80, 92, 147, 153, 190, 207, 209; impact on, 242, 251; questions about, 77
Cross-functional integration, 128, 254
CSFs. *See* Critical success factors
Culture: American, 5; differences in, 242. *See also* Corporate culture

Customers, 101, 123, 124, 153, 169, 176, 186,
191; changes in, 62, 64, 189, 195; expectations of, 54, 147, 210; information about,
79, 96, 110, 111, 137–38, 149, 155, 156,
162, 194; relations with, 37, 66, 100, 201,
209, 239
Customer satisfaction, 46–47, 54, 132, 164,
190, 238, 244, 245, 246, 256
Customer service, 128, 129, 164–65, 180,
188, 195, 200–201, 206, 211, 241, 242; level
of, 110, 124, 147–48, 150, 200
Cutting edge technology. See Leading edge
technology

Databases, 51–52, 58, 60, 62, 63–64, 83, 101,
155, 162, 166, 175
Decentralization, 115, 116, 126, 135, 145–46,
148–49, 208, 209, 213, 254
Decisionmaking, 8–9, 17, 24, 36, 84, 114,
151, 217, 236, 242; flexibility in, 212, 216;
impact of, 123, 125, 144, 146, 156–57, 175,
199, 200, 255–56; implementing, 14,
128–29; importance of, 57; information
for, 71, 94, 222; about information technology, 131, 132, 133, 135, 164, 211–12,
214–17; responsibility for, 127, 130, 145,
211–12, 214–17
de Geus, Arie, 197, 252
Demographics, 110, 111, 186; changes in,
56, 62, 64, 80, 94, 95, 97, 240
Deregulation of business, 200
Distribution companies, 66, 101, 102,
161–63, 184
Distribution processing, 132, 164–65, 189,
194, 206
Diversification, 56, 64, 78, 114–15
Downsizing companies, 4, 7, 69, 113, 116,
228
Drivers, 61, 62, 94–97, 101, 137, 143, 146,
153, 232, 240, 256
Driving force analysis, 62, 101, 138–39
Drucker, Peter, 60–61, 188
Dublin, Max, 48
Dynamic Planning, 49, 98–99, 108, 138,
202–3; benefits of, 4, 19; case histories,
11–12, 144–46, 147–49, 150–54, 155–57,
174; definition, 14, 26; goals, 14–15, 68,
105, 218, 219–20
Dynamic Planning Framework, 5–6, 8, 148,
203; benefits of, 103, 132, 175, 218,
248–49; case histories, 185–96; design,
9–12, 15–19, 20–25, 71, 240; goals, 8–9, 14,
50–51; implementing, 57; modifying, 26,

205; as a tool, 12, 13–14, 27–31, 68, 89,
108, 197, 218, 250–51

Early mover advantage, 64
Eastern Europe, 56
Economies of scale, 199
Economist, The (magazine), 4
Economy, 51, 55, 95, 97, 108, 187, 194, 198,
217, 221; interrelatedness of, 6–7, 49, 55–56.
See also Global business environment
Education, 7, 56, 58, 136, 198, 255
Electronic companies, 92
Employees, 154, 169, 188, 189, 200, 255;
acceptance of change by, 197, 218, 219,
220, 223, 226–27; and change, 9, 60, 105,
116, 168, 185, 224–25, 230–32, 235; effect
of change on, 113, 129–30, 136–37, 210,
220, 221, 222–24; and planning, 25, 37,
58–59, 108; recruiting, 128, 137, 145, 151,
166, 168, 181, 186, 190, 201, 230; resistance to change by, 4, 117, 129, 227–30;
responsibilities of, 56, 66, 256; sharing,
201, 208, 212; turnover, 110, 168, 225,
233. See also Human resources; Skill sets
of employees; Training of employees
Employment, 51, 63, 94, 184, 194
Empowerment, 23, 146, 168, 199, 211–12,
214–17, 218, 254
Energy companies, 38, 39–40, 54, 66–67,
80–84, 114–16, 246–47, 252– 53
Energy sector, 54, 55, 66, 80–83
Enterprise plan, 19, 38, 43, 80, 174, 181–85,
191, 217, 219, 240; definition, 181
Enterprises. See Companies
Entertainment sector, 55, 61
Environmental Analysis, 20, 22, 48, 51, 93
Environmentalism, 7, 49, 55, 196, 220,
254–55
Evaluation, 18, 46, 93, 190; questions in,
234, 244, 246. See also Evaluation under
subjects, e.g., Industrial sector, evaluation of
Evaluation of planning (Activity 9.0), 14,
19, 203, 220, 235, 236, 238–39; importance
of, 12, 25, 27, 29; methods for, 43, 58–59,
240–47
Exclusive products, 123
Executive management. See Senior management
Executives. See Management
Experts, 36, 63, 104; utilizing, 29, 31, 56,
58–59, 60, 201. See also Computer
experts; External experts

External analysis (Activity 2.0), 17, 19, 47, 48, 71, 93, 94, 190, 203; efficiency in, 56–57; evaluation in, 27, 93, 111, 132, 148; examples, 192, 206; formal summary of, 64; goals, 10, 20, 42, 50, 89; information from, 85; methods used in, 51, 56–60, 71; questions in, 57
External experts, 29, 31, 56, 58–59, 64, 148, 150, 203, 205, 253
External facilitator, 29, 39, 40, 41, 99, 210
External factors, 6, 41, 52–55, 220; control over, 61, 76, 79, 105, 106; and critical success factors, 71, 100; importance of, 175; monitoring, 114, 116, 238, 242, 258; problems from, 94, 109, 110, 217, 218; turbulence of, 4–5, 15, 53, 60–61, 73. *See also* Business environment; Political environment; Social environment

Facilitator, 29; importance of, 180; qualities, 39, 41, 108; responsibilities, 41, 42, 64, 70, 76, 85, 176; role of, 23, 27, 39, 40, 99–100, 107–8, 192
Family-owned companies, 185–96, 253–55
Fast follower in technology, 132, 175
Fast food companies, 61, 80, 93; case histories, 109–10, 185–96
Federal Express Corp., 238
Fifth Discipline, The (Senge), 50
Filene, Edward A., 49, 56
Finance, 8, 66, 109, 110, 111, 135, 136, 187; analysis of, 240, 241; impact of, 45, 80, *81, 82, 83*, 108; impact on, 76, 78–79, 80; reporting, 146; *See also* Budget; Costs; Credit checks; Profit; Revenue
Financial services, 109, 110, 111–12
Firms. *See* Companies
Fleet management, 95, 96, 97, 147, 149
Flexibility, 127, 168, 197, 218; in responses, 212, 216; understanding, 180
Focus sessions, 27, 240, 262n.1; goals, 109, 122; issues in, 91–92, 97, 103, 104, 105–6, 108–9, 111, 180; preparation for, 84–85; running, 99–100, 107–8
Food industry, 56, 61, 78, 79, 80, 93, 109–10, 185–87, 192, 193, 195–96
Forecasting, 50, 56, 59–60, 71, 94–97, 103
Foreign policy, 51, 56
Fortune (magazine), 3–4, 255
Foundations, 56
Framework, 167–68, 219–20. *See also* Dynamic Planning Framework
Franchises, 147, 149, 161, 185, 186–87, 192, 193

Functional areas of business, 8, 14, 114, 127–29, 136, 155, 220; analyzing, 68–69, 102, 240; control over, 215; efficiency of, 138, 183, 210, 244; goals, 73, 74–75; redesigning, 164–65. *See also* specific areas, e.g., Marketing
Functional personnel, 37, 70, 165, 181, 184

Gap analysis, 17, 18, 22, 64, 148, 243, 244; definition, 48, 72; examples, 93–94, 207–8
Gas stations, 94, 100, 109, 110
General Motors Corp. (GM), 3–4
Generating options. *See* Options generation (Activity 5.0)
Gerber Products Company, 56, 177
Germany, 51
Giorgio Armani SpA, 123
Global business environment, 5, 6–7, 98, 156, 198; competitive, 13, 206, 238, 247; interrelatedness of, 6–7, 49, 55–56
Global environment, 51, 53–54
Gluck, Fred, 258
GM. *See* General Motors Corp.
Goals, 50, 168, 173, 184; definition, 72. *See also* Goals under subjects, e.g., Business, goals
Governance, 31, 143, 148–49, 210, 252–53, 255–56, 261; and business strategy, 123, 124–26; changing, 4, 29; and information technology strategy, 131, 133–34, 154
Government, 221–22; responsibility of, 55
Government-run companies, 198–200. *See also* Privatized companies
Grand Strategy (Activity 7.0), 18–19, 72, 158, 170, 173, 203, 217–18, 219, 240; changing, 79, 217; definition, 24–25; elements of, 173–74, 247; goals, 11; importance of, 27. *See also* Enterprise plan; Mission statement; Vision
Grievances: employee, 91, 108, 198–99, 217
Ground transportation, 51, 198, 200
Group vice president (GVP), 198–99, 217
Grove, Andrew S., 4
GVP. *See* Group vice president

Hall, Cliff, 254
Heavy equipment companies, 183
Help-wanted ads, 63, 226
Henderson, John C., 13
Hierarchy of business, 126, 134, 183, 198–99, 217, 220, 250–51, 256
Hierarchy of Enterprise Plan Elements, 191
Holistic planning, 37–38, 43, 149, 220, 240

Holistic thinking, 5, 6, 13, 44, 142, 161, 213, 247, 248–49, 253, 256
Home Depot, Inc., 124
Hospitals, 134, 243–44
Human resources, 20, 128, 129; as a critical success factor, 77, 80, 81, 82, 83, 181, 183, 184. See also Employees
Human resources management, 36, 41, 99, 184, 253
Human services division, 229, 230, 232

IBM. See International Business Machines Corp.
IFM. See Interactive Forces Model
Image. See Corporate image
Imagination. See Creativity; Innovative thinking
Imaging systems, 130–31
Immigration laws, 55–56, 94
Implementation, 14, 44, 113, 203, 220; of change, 222–25, 232, 233, 235, 238, 240; consistency in, 182–83; of information technology, 134, 169, 201, 218; of options, 19, 23, 116, 144–46, 147–48, 152–54, 161, 211–13, 214, 217, 249; responsibility for, 37, 45, 57, 168; time frame for, 40, 45. See also Strategy execution
Implementation processes, 4, 90, 185
Incremental change, 6, 152–53, 203, 210–11, 249
Industrial development, 5, 159
Industrial sector, 51, 55, 61, 67, 71, 93, 136, 245; changes in, 63, 64, 94; evaluation of, 17, 42, 54, 61–62, 103. See also specific sectors, e.g., Transportation sector
Industry-specific vocabulary. See Organization-specific vocabulary
Information, 17, 93, 173; access to, 51–52,73–74, 115, 130, 148, 149, 169; analysis of, 39, 42, 50–51, 63–64, 89, 209; collecting, 20, 22, 56, 57, 58–63, 65–71, 79; content, 200–201, 211; coordination, 84–85, 103–4, 149; evaluation of, 93–94; growth of, 3; inconsistency in, 43,67, 72, 90–92; need for, 57, 61, 71, 77, 83, 104; sharing, 202, 212, 224, 231, 252–53; sources of, 58–59, 61–62, 63, 83
Information Age, 5, 25, 175
Information base, 85
Information provider, 162–63
Information services, 60, 101, 155–57, 161–63, 243–44; developing, 102, 111, 137–38, 169, 194, 195

Information technology (IT), 61–62, 265n. 9; control over, 133–34, 211–12; effectiveness of, 168, 199; efficiency of, 136, 151, 187, 199, 207, 213, 245; evaluation of, 98, 244–46; impact of, 96, 97; importance of, 209–10; perception of, 200, 207–8, 244; role of, 63, 162, 245, 248, 249
Information technology (IT) division, 176, 180, 205, 228, 229, 230, 252–53
Information technology (IT) infrastructure, 134–35, 151–52, 166, 199, 207–8, 209, 212, 252
Information technology (IT) management, 37, 134, 165–67, 242; decisionmaking by, 31, 64, 166–67; information from, 71–72, 244; questions for, 69, 165; responsibilities, 126, 168, 217; role of 8, 29, 31, 201, 206, 217; understanding by, 202, 230
Information technology (IT) personnel, 146, 153–54, 229, 230–31, 238, 244. See also Computer experts; Skill sets of IT personnel
Information technology (IT) processes, 134, 135–36, 149, 166
Information technology (IT) scope, 131–32, 134, 199
Information Technology Steering Committee (ITSC), 202, 205, 209
Information technology (IT) strategy, 8, 15, 24, 36, 130–34, 163, 198, 199; changing, 38; developing, 126, 202–3, 210–11, 218; impact of, 18, 139, 143, 149, 150–57, 168–69, 208; impact on, 146–49, 165–67, 256; information about, 71–72; options for, 19, 39–40, 108, 111–12, 114–15, 116, 122, 209, 211–13; understanding, 205, 214, 248
Information Technology Strategy (ITS) Manager, 202
Information technology (IT) structure, 8, 18, 24, 134–37, 199–200, 207; changing, 38, 168, 238; impact on, 14, 31, 138–39, 143, 144–54, 163, 165, 166–68, 252–53; options for, 110, 111–12, 114–16, 122, 212, 213
Information technology (IT) task force, 114, 115
Infrastructure, 58, 156, 198, 254. See also Administrative infrastructure; Information technology infrastructure
Innovative thinking, 8, 14, 52–53, 57, 63, 110, 168, 169; promoting, 23, 40, 97, 107–8, 181–82, 221, 234
Insurance industry, 56, 227–32

Integrated logistics, 164, 165, 168
Integrated strategy, 132, 157, 198, 203, 210–11, 212–13, 252–53; as a goal, 10, 15; process for, 18, 128, 218; understanding, 201–2, 205
Integrated thinking, 5–6, 142, 205
Interaction of organizational blocks, 24, 68, 114, 122, 137, 138–41, 163, 211–13, 216, 218
Interactive Forces Model (IFM), 52–55, 233
Interest rates, 76, 78–79, 95, 97, 129
Internal analysis (Activity 3.0), 6, 19, 27, 47, 150; evaluation of, 22, 116–17, 132, 181; examples, 188–91; goals, 10, 20, 22, 65, 89, 124; information from, 48, 65–72, 90, 98, 102, 116, 148, 203, 205–8; methods for, 43, 70, 72, 205; questions in, 70–71, 206, 207
Internal facilitator, 29, 39, 40, 41, 99
Internal factors, 38; monitoring of, 239, 254
Internalizing, 22, 38, 90, 106, 121, 122, 218, 220, 252
Internal market, 130, 199
International Business Machines Corp. (IBM), 3–4, 55
International companies. *See* Multinational companies
Interviews, 22, 42, 148, 203, 205, 206–8, 244; goals, 90, 206, 242; preparation for, 67–69; techniques in, 43, 70–71, 72, 206
Inventory, 200, 201, 211, 241
Investment in business, 187, 188, 190, 233
IT. *See* Information technology
ITSC. *See* Information Technology Steering Committee

Japan, 242–43
Jobs, Steve, 175
Job supply, 7
Johnson & Johnson, 179
Joint ventures, 125, 127, 133
Journals, 52; as information sources, 58, 61–62, 63; mailing lists for, 137–38

Kanter, Rosabeth, 142
Kaplan, Robert S., 236
Key indicators, 74, 190
King, Alexander, 6
Knowledge base, 57, 58–59, 60, 93, 95, 104, 112, 132
Knowledge Executive, The (Cleveland), 36

L. L. Bean, Inc., 123
Labor. *See* Workforce

Language barriers, 10, 36, 49, 228, 230
Large companies, 4, 66, 198, 227–29, 232; and Dynamic Planning Framework, 14, 24–25, 197, 205–18, 251, 252–55; problems with, 35, 67. *See also* Multinational corporations
Law firms, 60
Leadership, 4, 39, 99, 106, 126, 161, 214, 222, 256 *See also* Market position
Leading edge technology, 63, 123, 132–33, 155–56, 157, 166, 225, 227–28
Learning organization, 25, 50, 220, 247; creating, 42, 221, 224–25, 230, 233–34; importance of, 197, 221, 252
Legal area of business, 7, 8, 49, 55–56, 187, 200
Leisure sector, 62, 94, 97
Level of service. *See* Service level
Lewin, Kurt, 222
Librarians, 56, 60
Life cycle, 64, 75, 76, 98
Line managers, 143, 146
Linkage of analyses. *See* Analyses, linkage of
Lobbying, 51
Location: information about, 166; of meetings, 41–42
Location of companies, 109, 114–16, 186, 188; importance of, 96, 111–12, 145, 193; need for, 127, 191, 242–43; new, 189, 190, 192, 195
Logistics, 164, 165, 168, 205
Logistics companies, 200–201, 206, 211, 212, 213, 218, 220
Long-term planning, 5, 70, 75, 99, 154, 158, 188, 249; implementing, 252, 253–55; need for, 107; problems in, 106, 236, 248
Loyalty, 195; of customers, 54, 55, 96, 242; of employees, 106, 168, 183
Luttwak, Edward N., 173

Machiavelli, Niccolò, 219, 234
Magazines. *See* Journals
Mailing lists, 59, 137–38, 194
Maintenance, 135, 136
Management, 4, 13, 92; information from, 67–70, 71; interviews with, 22, 42, 70–71, 74, 90; responsibilities, 31, 127, 144, 149, 168, 184; *See also* Information technology (IT) management; Middle management; Senior management
Management Board, 199, 202, 210, 213, 217
Managing Director, 199, 200–202, 206, 207, 210, 214–15, 217, 218

Manufacturing, 8, 57, 125, 128, 132, 135, 183, 242–43; evaluation of, 241, 244–47; goals of, 73, 74–75, 92

Market creation, 162, 163

Market entry, 62, 78, 94, 100, 101, 186, 242–43

Marketing, 8, 66, 67, 79, 98, 137, 138, 151, 175, 222; regional, 145, 189; responsibility for, 127

Market organizer, 162, 163

Market position, 4, 71, 109, 132, 147, 152, 156, 157, 162–63, 169

Markets, 66, 79, 101, 123, 176; changing, 3–4, 55, 62, 78, 106, 162, 169, 191; control over, 161–63, 169; local, 115, 147, 148–49, 186–87, 190; response to, 212

Market share, 54, 74, 92, 96, 97, 110, 124, 132, 151, 161, 175

Mass market products, 110, 123

Measurement, 31, 46–47, 74. *See also* Evaluation of planning; Monitoring process

Meetings, 27, 39–41, 42, 57, 63, 64; goals of, 107–8, 109. *See also* Conferences; Focus sessions; Working sessions

Methodology, 167, 168, 197, 224–25, 240–47, 252

Middle management, 7, 69, 228, 229, 256

Military sector, 51

Mining companies, 4

Minnesota Mining & Mfg. Co. (3M), 175

Mission statement, 73; achieving, 181; changing, 18–19, 101, 176, 180, 217, 238, 240; creating, 19, 188, 190, 195–96, 219; definition, 173–74, 257n. 2; review of, 72, 174, 176

Money order business, 109, 110, 111

Monitoring, 108–9. *See also* Trend watching

Monitoring process (Activity 9.0), 14, 19, 203, 220, 235, 236–40; importance of, 12, 25, 27, 29; methods for, 43, 58–59, 240–47

Multinational companies, 29, 57, 60, 78, 176, 180, 184, 252

Name recognition, 98, 109, 194

National environment, 51, 53–54, 55, 56, 187, 194, 198, 217. *See also* External factors

Natural gas companies, 54, 66–67, 80, 83

Netherlands, 92

Networking, 62, 63, 169

Networks, 111–12, 133, 146, 149, 151–52, 166, 194

New ideas, 23, 68, 91, 108, 193, 194–95, 233–34

New products, 109–10, 136, 175, 192, 244; developing, 62, 99, 190; development cycle time for, 75, 76, 98, 239, 240

Newsletters, 60, 194, 195, 230–31, 232

New York City, 58

Nordstrom, 124

Norton, David P., 236

Objectives. *See* Goals

Objectivity, 39–40, 99

Oil companies, 38, 54, 80, 83, 208, 252–53

Operational areas of business, 8, 45, 126, 134–35, 198–99, 255; analyzing, 38, 101–2, 207, 239, 246–47; changing, 14, 115; efficiency of, 96, 110, 111; understanding, 38–39, 205

Operational personnel, 62, 67, 70, 203, 205; responsibilities of, 127, 217

Options, 104, 173–74, 187–88; analysis of, 10–11, 14, 18, 108, 121, 122, 143, 213–14; changing, 249; evaluation of, 17, 105, 108, 112–17, 161, 211–13, 214–17, 239; impact of, 122, 137, 138–39, 155, 158, 161, 169–70, 181, 213; implementing, 99, 213; questions about, 112–13, 144, 157, 215

Options generation (Activity 5.0), 10–11, 65, 72, 85, 99, 105–6, 142–43, 203, 208–9, 211, 213; examples, 144–45, 193–94; goals, 23; number of, 105; problems in, 39–40; time frame for, 109–12, 210

Order processing, 128, 129, 132, 133, 164–65. *See also* Purchasing

Organizational change, 200, 207, 217; adapting to, 14, 25, 42, 50, 219, 223, 230–32, 234, 256; commitment to, 68, 108, 180, 214, 253; impact of, 7, 24, 138–39, 143, 149; implementing, 211–14; methods for, 13–19, 107, 122, 137–38, 218, 221–22, 224–25; need for, 4, 156–57, 165, 219–20, 222, 225; problems in, 60, 250–51; resistance to, 35, 91, 106, 107, 205–6, 209, 220, 248. *See also* Business transformation; Employees, and change; Restructuring companies

Organizational culture. *See* Corporate culture

Organizational environment, 46, 90, 134, 198–200, 220, 221, 234; perception of, 66, 154, 200, 207–8

Organizations. *See* Companies

Organization-specific vocabulary, 61, 62, 64, 94, 95, 96, 97, 102–3, 192, 193

Organizing resources. *See* Resource organization (Activity 1.0)
Outside experts. *See* External experts
Outsourcing, 115, 116, 125, 133–34, 206
Ownership, 125, 133, 134, 147–49, 161, 168, 189

Partnerships, 100, 127, 166, 168, 243
Performance level, 4, 81, *83*, 148, 163, 198; evaluating, 19, 75, 181
Performance measures, 46–47, 76, 184, 189–90, 238–39, 240, 241, 244–47, 253. *See also* Evaluation of planning; Monitoring process
Personnel. *See* Employees; Management
Plan: achievability of, 45; agreement on, 45–46, 74; success of, 45–46, 98–99, 218, 226, 232, 251. *See also* Grand Strategy (Activity 7.0)
Planning, 92, 110–12, 153–54, 181, 201, 206, 207, 208, 221; goals, 14, 37–39, 43, 68, 202. *See also* Dynamic Planning; Long-term planning; Short-term planning
Planning process, 17–18, 41, 80, 198, 214, 216–17, 240; agreement on, 37–39, 45–46; benefits of, 6, 14, 221, 225; commitment to, 43–44, 67–68, 168, 222–25, 226–27, 231, 232; effectiveness of, 20, 25, 38–39, 219; problems with, 15, 50, 78, 159, 205–7. *See also* Dynamic Planning Framework
Planning team, 25, 42, 43, 95, 104; agreement between, 37–38, 44, 45–46, 84–85, 91–92, 103, 114, 180, 209; beliefs of, 106, 230; cooperation between, 98–100, 115; creating, 15, 37, 39, 214, 230; disagreement between, 39–40, 91, 103, 180, 182, 210; information from, 124, 206; qualities of, 45, 89; responsibilities, 20, 27, 57, 89–90, 105, 107–9, 110–16, 169–70, 176, 181–83, 208; understanding by, 38–39, 124, 176, 180, 206. *See also* Task forces
Poland, 222
Political change, 49, 56, 198, 206, 221–22, 238
Political environment, 6, 7, 198, 199, 200, 217, 218
Port operations, 198–99
Porter, Michael, 50, 101–2, 258
Position paper (Activity 4.0), 48, 65, 72, 89, 103–4, 203; baseline for, 93; definition, 10; goals, 22–23, 85, 103, 105; possibilities analysis in, 94–97, 193–94; preparing, 209–11; review of, 17, 106, 108–9

Possibilities analysis, 94–97, 192. *See also* Scenario planning
Prices, 80, *81*, *82*, 83, 97, 128, 154, 186, 241; and competitiveness, 74, 124, 151, 190, 195, 222; importance of, 92, 96, 236, 238
Privatized companies, 197–98, 200, 201, 214, 222, 246
Problems, 90, 116, 167–68, 228–29, 241, 248; analyzing, 93–94, 103–4, 200; anticipating, 121; avoiding, 43, 146, 152, 239; identifying, 4, 15, 35, 48, 65, 84; resolving, 4, 13, 43, 91–92, 162; technical, 146, 162
Procedures, 145, 146, 153, 184, 199, 208
Processes, 181. *See also* Business processes; Critical processes; Implementation processes; Information technology (IT) processes; Monitoring process; Planning process
Product differentiation, 124, 132–33, 240
Productivity, 151, 154, 245–46
Product managers, 127, 128
Products, 98, 109, 137, 186, 188, 189, 192, 239, 241. *See also* New products
Professors. *See* Academic experts
Profit, 66, 76, 147, 187, 188, 254
Profitability, 200, 246, 247, 251; impacts on, 6, 145
Project management, 167, 168
Project managers, 27, 29
Proprietary systems, 63
Publication catalogs, 59
Public utility companies, 39–40, 114–16, 200, 243
Publishing companies, 52, 137–38, 175, 222, 226–27
Purchasing, 102–3, 187, 190, 194–95, 196, 201
Purpose. *See* Goals

Quality: of employees, 77, 181; improvement, 46–47, 164–65, 183, 241; measurement of, 240–41, 244, 253
Questionnaires, 42, 67–69, 70, 206, 241, 244

R&D. *See* Research and development
Railroads, 51, 198
Raw materials, 56
Real estate development, 111, 112
Regional managers, 127, 145
Regional offices, 127, 145–46, 148–49, 242–43
Regulation of business, 7, 49, 200, 220, 221, 224, 243

Reputation of companies, 183
Research and development (R&D), 8, 80, 99, 132, 133, 166; examples of, 51–52, 63, responsibility for, 135–36. *See also* New products
Resource organization (Activity 1.0), 10, 15, 20, 25, 35, 48, 187–88, 203, 205
Resources of companies, 23, 80, *82*, 103, 108, 113; allocation of, 135, 181, 182, 184, 211–12, 216; sharing, 115, 199, 201, 208, 212. *See also* Assets; Human resources
Responsiveness, 176, 180, 208
Restaurants, 55, 61, 186, 187, 192
Restructuring companies, 4, 66–67, 102–3, 145–46, 147–49, 228
Retail trade companies, 3–4, 94, 100, 109–12, 127, 161
Retraining of employees, 146, 149, 181, 183, 233, 239
Revenue, 52, 66, 74–75, 76, 111, 187, 189, 195, 243
Risk evaluation, 105, 112–16, 125, 152
Roach, Stephen, 245–46
Royal Dutch/Shell Group, 252–53

Safety factors, 199, 110, 224
Sales, 8, 79, 123, 128, 137, 138, 151, 162–63; changes in, 5, 52, 66; responsibility for, 156–57. *See also* Customers; Marketing
SAM. *See* Strategic Alignment Model
Scenario planning, 50, 59–60, 252. *See also* Possibilities analysis
Schein, Edgar, 222
Schwartz, Peter, 97
Scope, 143. *See also* Business scope; Information technology (IT) scope
Sears, Roebuck & Co., 3–4
Seminars, 58, 63
Senge, Peter, 50, 220
Senior management, 37, 59, 62, 116, 117, 165–66, 233, 236, 252–53, 254; adapting to change by, 107, 150, 175, 234; attitudes of, 200, 207–8; attitudes toward, 229; beliefs of, 66, 67, 68–69, 109, 210, 218, 222; commitment by, 43, 68, 108, 202, 214, 222–25, 231–32; and critical success factors, 75, 78, 92, 151; inconsistency by, 78, 90–91, 92, 93–94; information from, 42, 43, 57, 66–72, 90, 98, 148, 203, 205–7, 221; questions for, *68*; resistance by, 4, 91, 106, 107, 205–6, 209, 232; responsibilities, 22, 44, 45, 126, 127, 135–36, 145, 215–16, 217; role of, 41, 45, 72, 73, 126,
184, 214, 220, 226, 231–32; understanding by, 89, 154, 167, 201–2
Service companies, 60, 101, 102, 111–12, 123, 124, 145, 238. *See also* Information services
Service level, 139, 143, 148, 150–54, 167–68, 200, 213, 245–46. *See also* Customer service; User services
Service sector, 55, 61, 96, 97, 109–12, 242–43
Sessions. *See* Meetings
Shareholders, 37, 254
Shell Oil Company. *See* Royal Dutch/Shell Group
Short-term impacts, 143, 238
Short-term planning, 5, 106, 154, 236, 248
Size: of companies, 90; of teams, 37, 205. *See also* Large companies; Small companies
Skilled workers, 7, 58, 60, 81, 152, 198, 212, 233–34
Skill sets of employees, 20, 99, 144, 155, 156, 169, 206, 253; availability of, 58, 183, 218; changes in, 129–30, 210, 211, 219, 226, 232–33; evaluation of, 117; need for, 112, 129, 135, 203
Skill sets of IT personnel, 58, 72, 134; availability of, 58, 152, 168, 201; changes in, 136–37, 149, 167; need for, 135, 153–54, 166, 226, 230
Skill sets of management, 98, 149
Sloan, Michael, 259n. 10
Small companies, 4, 66, 67, 151, 185–87, 194, 232–33, 243; and Dynamic Planning Framework, 174, 187–95
Social change, 49, 55–56, 62, 80, 94, 206, 224
Social environment, 6, 7, 198, 199, 200
Soft drink companies, 78, 79
Solutions, 14, 248; analyzing, 17, 108, 116–17, 158, 213–14; implementing, 217–18, 219; search for, 10, 47, 48, 85, 89, 208–9. *See also* Options generation (Activity 5.0)
South Africa, 155–57, 198
Specialties, 36, 60, 149, 169
Sports sector, 55, 61
Staff. *See* Employees; Management
Staged development, 159, 161, 173
Stakeholders, 37, 45, 100, 102, 176
Standards, 145, 146, 254; competition as, 135; for information technology, 135, 153, 199, 200, 211, 212, 213
State-of-the-art technology, 63, 133, 166, 199, 200, 212

Strategic Alignment Model (SAM, Activity 6.0), 8, 14, 29, 49, 112, 116, 143, 174, 202–3, 247; applying, 122, 169–70, 214, 217; benefits of, 161; effect of time on, 158, 159, 213; examples, 144–46, 147–49, 150–54, 155–57, 161–69, 194–95; goals, 11, 18, 121, 137–38, 141, 142; importance of, 23–24, 27, 108, 114; questions in, 24
Strategic alliances, 125, 127, 133
Strategic decisions, 138, 153, 166, 167, 168. *See also* Decisionmaking
Strategic direction, 45–46, 62, 163, 167, 202
Stategic management. *See* Dynamic planning.
Strategic options, 17, 18, 24. *See also* Options generation (Activity 5.0)
Strategic planning, 110–12, 206, 207, 208, 221
Strategic thinking, 45, 201
Strategy, 258; questions about, 125, 131–32, 134–35, 138–39, 146–49, 165, 189. *See also* Grand Strategy (Activity 7.0)
Strategy blocks. *See* Business strategy; Information technology (IT) strategy
Strategy execution, 138, 143, 163, 167, 213–14; examples of, 144–46, 164–65; implementing, 25, 101, 166, 169; monitoring, 19; responsibility for, 45
Strengths and weaknesses of companies, 156–57, 193; assessing, 17, 22, 98–103, 109–12, 124; information about, 71, 85, 89, 242; understanding, 90, 93. *See also* Competencies
Stretch goals, 73
Study groups, 62, 154
Substitute products, 62, 101, 110
Success, 219, 238; of companies, 74, 89, 104, 106, 150, 186–87, 188, 192, 244, 247, 253; of goals, 25; of information technology, 245, 246; of vision, 174. *See also* Critical success factors
Summers, Harry, 256n. 1
Sun Tzu, 158, 262n. 1
Suppliers, 130, 161, 196, 201, 233; changes in, 75, 209; information about, 63, 101, 187; relations with, 37, 100, 190, 194–95
Support system, 79, 84; by information technology, 131–32, 153, 163, 165, 199, 210, 213–14; for information technology, 245
Surveys, 46, 70, 240–41, 244, 253
Survival of companies, 35, 151, 200, 247, 251, 253
SWOT (strengths, weaknesses, opportunities, threats) analysis, 98–103

Systems development, 168
Tactics for critical success factors, 181–84, 190–91, 196, 247
Task forces, 22, 89, 93, 107, 168, 262n. 1; creating, 20, 114, 184; problems for, 70, 76, 77; responsibilities, 31, 42, 48, 57–59, 64, 67, 85, 90, 114, 236, 242; role of, 48, 49, 220
Taxation, 55–56, 80, 136
Team work, 135–36, 256
Technological change, 6, 7, 49, 51–52, 63, 198, 211, 220, 222, 224, 238
Technology, 81, 129–30, 176, 189, 254; effect on competition, 51–52, 63, 64; relevance of, 6, 7, 8, 36, 108. *See also* Communications technology; Information technology
Technology transformation, 64, 139, 143, 146–49, 163, 165–67, 213–14
Telecommunications, 57, 150–54, 205
Television networks, 55
Texaco, 178
Thinking, 45, 68–69, 96; flexibility in, 109. *See also* Holistic thinking; Innovative thinking
Think tanks, 56, 58–59
3M Company. *See* Minnesota Mining & Mfg. Co.
Timber companies, 254–55
Time, 57; to adjust, 180; cost of, 105, 152; and customer service, 110, 164, 165, 244; and Dynamic Planning Framework, 159, 161; to grow, 187; and product development, 239, 240; value of, 41, 106, 202, 206, 238; and vision, 174, 232
Time frame, 20, 41, 43, 44, 76, 112, 184, 217; problems with, 40, 45, 90, 208
Tracking. *See* Monitoring
Trade, 56. *See also* Sales
Trading blocs, 7, 56, 220
Training of employees, 129, 152, 190, 219, 233, 241, 249; need for, 136, 153–54, 210; opportunities for, 221, 222–23, 224–25, 226–27, 232, 233–34; responsibility for, 153, 232–33. *See also* Retraining of employees
Transportation companies, 58, 190–201, 203, 206, 213, 220; case histories, 205–18
Transportation sector, 51–52, 61, 62, 83, 93–94, 95, 96–97, 147–48, 198, 200–201, 206
Transportation services, 200–201, 211
Travel sector, 62, 94, 96, 97
Trends, 6–7, 42, 57, 104. *See also* Economy; Political environment; Social environment; Technology

Trend watching, 57, 61–63, 162, 163, 169,
    206, 239, 242–43, 247, 251; determining
    what to watch, 83, 238; responsibility for,
    58, 60, 114
Triggers. *See* Drivers
Trucking companies, 58
Turbulence. *See* External factors.
Turkey, 51
Twentieth Century Fund, 56, 58

Uncertainty, 4, 50, 224
Understanding in companies, 132, 148, 174,
    181, 206–7; importance of, 125–26;
    process of, 121–22, 203, 205. *See also*
    Communication; Internal analysis
    (Activity 3.0)
Unemployment, 51, 198
United States, 51, 187, 194
Unskilled workers, 7, 221
User friendly technology, 133
User services, 130, 133, 199, 209, 240, 245,
    246; problems with, 200, 201, 207–8,
    227–28

Value-added: to business, 105, 106, 188,
    207, 230; to customers, 200–201; informa-
    tion products, 156, 162; in planning, 103
Value chain analysis, 101–3

Vendors. *See* Suppliers
Venkatraman, N., 13, 262n. 2
Vertical integration, 74, 198–99
Vice presidents, 135, 181, 184, 198–99, 217
Video rental companies, 109, 110
Vision, 25, 173, 174–75, 219, 231–32; exam-
    ples of, 200–201, 206, 207, 208, 210, 211,
    212; long term, 161–63, 173, 253–55; of
    mission statement, 188, 190, 195–96;
    qualifiers for, 174
Vocabulary, 192, 193; and communication,
    10, 36, 49, 61, 201, 207, 228, 230, 232, 254;
    meaning of, 176, 180, 207. *See also*
    Organization-specific vocabulary

Weaknesses of companies. *See* Strengths
    and weaknesses of companies
Weyerhaeuser, Frederick, 253
Weyerhaeuser Company, 253–55
Wheatley, Margaret J., 248
Work environment. *See* Organizational
    environment
Workforce, 51, 55, 56, 58, 63, 77, 81, 198;
    diversity of, 7, 220. *See also* Employees
Working sessions, 23, 40–41, 84, 91
Workshops, 214
Wozniak, Steve, 175
Wriston, Walter, 6

DATE DUE

MAR 1 6 1995			

Demco, Inc. 38-293